Jeffrey Frank is a senior editor at the *New Yorker* and was formerly an editor and writer at the *Washington Post* and the *Washington Star*. He is the author of the novel *The Columnist*.

Diana Crone Frank has a PhD in linguistics and works at ABC News.

Praise for *The Stories of Hans Christian Andersen*

'Diana Crone Frank and Jeffrey Frank restore the vitality of Andersen's original language' *Daily Telegraph*

'An exhilarating new translation of Andersen's best loved stories' *Daily Mail*

'A superb book of Andersen tales, lively to read and true to the originals' *Star Tribune*

'Andersen has a subtle and immediately recognisable tone of voice which the current translators have been very apt in catching' *Weekly Standard*

'Timeless tales continue to thrill' *Publishers Weekly*

The Stories of
Hans Christian
Andersen

The Stories of
Hans Christian Andersen

SELECTED AND TRANSLATED BY

Diana Crone Frank *and* Jeffrey Frank

Including the Original Illustrations of

Vilhelm Pedersen *and* Lorenz Frølich

Granta Books
London

Granta Publications, 2/3 Hanover Yard, Noel Road, London N1 8BE

First published in Great Britain by Granta Books 2004
This edition published in Great Britain by Granta Books 2005
Published by special arrangement with Houghton Mifflin Company

Parts of the introduction first appeared, in slightly different form,
in the *New Yorker.*

Illustration credits: Frontispiece: Painting by C. A. Jensen. © Odense City
Museums/The Hans Christian Andersen Museum. Page 4: Engraving by J. W. Tegner,
after an 1845 painting by J. Roed. © Odense City Museums/The Hans Christian
Andersen Museum. Page 7: Painting by Wilhelm Marstrand, 1842. © Odense City
Museums/The Hans Christian Andersen Museum. Page 11 left: Painting by Adam
Müller, 1827. Reproduced courtesy of a private collection. Page 11 right: Lithograph
by R. J. Lane, 1847. © Odense City Museums/The Hans Christian Andersen
Museum. Page 16: Courtesy of Dr Allene M. Parker. Page 29: Photograph by
Budtz Müller and Company. © Odense City Museums/
The Hans Christian Andersen Museum.

Frontispiece: Hans Christian Andersen in 1836,
about the time that his first tales
'for children' were published.

A CIP catalogue record for this book is available from the British Library.

1 3 5 7 9 10 8 6 4 2

ISBN-13: 978-1-86207-793-5
ISBN-10: 1-86207-793-2

Typeset by M Rules
Printed and bound in Great Britain by
Mackays of Chatham plc

CONTENTS

Contents

ABOUT THE TRANSLATION

The stories that we chose are meant to give modern readers an essential Andersen: his finest canonical works as well as lesser-known tales. The twenty-two stories cover the five decades in which he published, although there is a heavy emphasis on the 1830s and 1840s, when his most celebrated work appeared. Together, they reveal an original and important literary legacy.

In translating Andersen, we aimed to be faithful to the Danish text and his distinctly colloquial voice, which was often lost in the Victorian language of earlier versions. The freshness of his writing shines through his autobiographical obsessions – his awkward encounters with class and privilege, his awareness of Aladdin-like good fortune. By the time of his last published story, 'Auntie Toothache', it was almost as if Andersen had decided, finally, to shed the storyteller's disguise and let the melancholy, first-person modernist leap into the present.

ABOUT THE ARTISTS

Andersen's earliest and most famous tales and stories were published without illustrations, but that changed when his popularity began to grow. In 1849 a new collection of tales was accompanied by drawings by Vilhelm Pedersen, a young naval officer whose informal style and light pencil seemed to catch the spirit of Andersen's work. Woodcuts from Pedersen's drawings were first done for the German edition published by Carl B. Lorck in Leipzig; Andersen's publisher, Reitzel, then had to pay Lorck for the rights.

Andersen loved Pedersen's witty detailed work, which now seems almost inseparable from the stories. After Pedersen, who was thirty-nine, died in 1859, the commission went to Lorenz Frølich, a popular artist in his own right. Frølich, who lived into the early twentieth century, illustrated the remainder of Andersen's tales. The works of both Pedersen and Frølich appear again in this volume.

Diana and Jeffrey Frank
New York City

INTRODUCTION

The Real H. C. Andersen

I

In the summer of 1874, a year before he died, Hans Christian Andersen got a fan letter from an American schoolgirl. Attached were a dollar bill and a newspaper clipping that detailed his bad health and supposed poverty. Soon, other children began sending small sums to pay off what a Philadelphia newspaper, the *Evening Bulletin,* had called the 'children's debt' to the Danish writer. The newspaper's editor, Gibson Peacock, wrote to Andersen to explain that he knew 'how little you had received in money from America, where your works have given so much delight', and that 'various readers have sent me sums of money, none of them large, but all given cheerfully to be remitted to you'. A week later Peacock wrote again to tell Andersen that 'the largest part of the sums contributed to this little fund were given or collected by a widow and her children, who have taken great delight in your works'. When the American ambassador personally gave Andersen two hundred Danish *rix*-dollars raised in the United States, Andersen, who was not at all impoverished, tried to put a stop to it. He wrote to Peacock to say that, although he was pleased that 'my stories have found readers so far from my homeland and from the narrow confines of language', and of course deeply moved that so many American children were 'breaking their little banks open to share what they have saved with their old author', he was not truly in need and could not accept the gifts. Rather than pride or gratitude, he wrote, he felt humiliation.

(Although he did not say it, he was also annoyed at the smallness of the gift.) Andersen's embarrassment may, however, have been offset by a certain satisfaction.

All his life Andersen had wanted to be famous, to be recognized as an artist, sometimes to the point that this longing overshadowed everything else. 'My name is gradually beginning to shine, and that is the only thing for which I live,' he had written to his friend Henriette Hanck on September 20, 1837, when he was in his early thirties. 'I covet honour and glory in the same way as the miser covets gold.' He was now sixty-nine, and the American newspaper campaigns (another was started, then halted, by Whitelaw Reid's *New-York Tribune*) were evidence of the breadth of his fame. By 1874 Hans Christian Andersen was perhaps better known than any other living writer, an international celebrity often found in the company of other celebrities, and his work had been widely read since the 1840s, although not always in the manner that he had intended. Stories such as 'The Ugly Duckling', 'The Emperor's New Clothes', 'Thumbelisa', and 'The Little Match Girl' had already gone through so many interpretations and shoddy translations that the originals had been virtually obliterated. Mary Howitt, for instance, was an Englishwoman who didn't speak Danish and based her translations on the German texts; Caroline Peachey, an alarmingly improvisational British translator, expurgated whole passages that offended her. Far better versions eventually came along (the most accurate, in the mid-twentieth century, by the Andersen scholar R. P. Keigwin), but two hundred years after Andersen's birth a sort of literary entropy persists. The Moira Shearer film *The Red Shoes* is better known than the Andersen story on which it was based. Film and cartoon versions of his tales are available on video, and Disney has insisted on rewriting – complete with happy endings for young audiences – some of Andersen's best material, such as 'The Little Mermaid', In short, beyond Scandinavia, Andersen has generally been regarded not as a literary genius but as a quaint nineteenth-century writer of charming children's stories.

Nothing contributed more to this view than *Hans Christian Andersen*, the 1952 Danny Kaye film. Although it had almost nothing to do with the real Andersen – and, to be fair, never claimed to – the film helped to make an idealized version of the writer's life as familiar as his fairy tales, almost an extension of them. In the film a young man from the provinces makes his way to Copenhagen, where he triumphs over adversity, falls in love with a ballerina who rejects him, and ultimately finds success. That was to some extent the spirit of Andersen's autobiography, which he called, without intended irony, *The Fairy Tale of My Life.* It was also the way, to Andersen's great annoyance, he was regarded in America; two years before he died, he wrote to an American editor that he was furious about a newspaper article that said he was called 'Little Hans' in Copenhagen and that 'when I walk on the street, I'm soon followed by a flock of children who pull at my coat and beg me for a fairy tale', (No one ever called him Hans, just Andersen, and he had no particular fondness for children, although he liked some as individuals.) Elias Bredsdorff, one of his best biographers, made a lifetime campaign, as he put it, of getting Andersen out of the nursery.

In Denmark, however, the Danny Kaye movie, with its melodic Frank Loesser score ('Wonderful Copenhagen'), is regarded as a giddy, slightly embarrassing, ally to tourism; there, H. C. Andersen, as he is known, is taken very seriously, and he is studied in much the way that students examine the life and work of Andersen's contemporary, Søren Kierkegaard. Almost since the day of Andersen's death, critics, researchers, and doctoral candidates have been excavating his family history and devouring his private journals and papers, as well as a raw early memoir that was found and published in the 1920s. Much of this research has been extraordinarily detailed and painstaking; writing about Andersen today has been made far easier by people like Erik Dal, Erling Nielsen, and Flemming Hovmann, the heroic annotators of his complete fairy tales, and Johan de Mylius, the director of the Hans Christian Andersen Center in Odense (Andersen's birthplace), who in 1993 published an exhaustive year-by-year chronology of Andersen's life. This ongoing project (and the journal *Anderseniana*) has given Danes an intimate knowledge of Andersen – down to the frequency with which he masturbated – and a portrait that is very much at odds with the cheerful souvenirs one finds in shop windows along Strøget, Copenhagen's main shopping street. Not that interest in the real Andersen is confined to Scandinavia. In 2000, for instance, Jackie Wullschlager, a writer for the (London) *Financial Times,* published a fine new biography, the first serious study by an English speaker since R. Nisbet Bain's excellent 1895 life.

By now most scholars know that neither Andersen's own memoir nor the relics in his somewhat reimagined childhood home in Odense come close to depicting reality. Both frame as a sort of romantic poverty what was in fact a demeaning family history – one that includes a grandfather who went mad, a grandmother who was jailed as a young woman for repeatedly having illegitimate children, and an aunt who apparently ran a brothel in Copenhagen. (Writing on March 9, 1838, Andersen told his friend Frederik Læssøe, 'You don't know what a battle I have fought! My childhood passed without my learning anything . . . nobody guided me, nobody gave my mental powers any direction . . . it is a miracle that I didn't perish.' Scholars know too that his literary career was deeply affected by the snobbery, rivalries, and intrigues of nineteenth-century Copenhagen, as well as by his appearance: with his huge feet, long arms, and tiny eyes, he was strikingly unattractive. All his life – even when his international celebrity was equal to, or surpassed, that of Charles Dickens – Andersen was hypersensitive to slights, real and imagined. Those, like almost everything in his life, found their way into his work.

II

Andersen was born in Fyn on April 2, 1805, an odd, solitary child who liked to play with puppets. He went to school in Odense, where he learned to read. His father, a cobbler and an autodidact, died at thirty-four, when Andersen was eleven; his mother, an alcoholic washerwoman, was superstitious and barely literate. She died in an almshouse in 1833 when Andersen was twenty-eight. (Andersen regarded her with love and regret

The influential Jonas Collins became the young Andersen's rescuer.

until the day she died; he portrayed her in a bitter, late story, 'She Was Good for Nothing',) In 1819 the fourteen-year-old Andersen travelled alone to the Danish capital, a two-day trip by coach and ship; it was certainly the bravest and most important step of his life, and he arrived in Copenhagen with little more than the conviction that he was a genius. (By chance he arrived on the day of Denmark's last pogrom, an experience that made its way into *Only a Fiddler*, an early novel: 'The Jew's entire house was in flames; a shower of sparks rained down on the neighbour's yard. The sky shone red; flames leaped up in strange tongues.') Andersen knew no one in Copenhagen, but he immediately began knocking on the doors of its prominent citizens. One, J. M. Thiele, a writer and editor quoted in most Andersen biographies, later recalled:

I was surprised to see a lanky boy, of a most extraordinary appearance, standing in the doorway, making a deep theatrical bow down to the floor. He had already thrown his cap down by the door and when he raised his long figure in a shabby grey coat, the sleeves of which did not reach as far as his emaciated wrists, my glance met a couple of tiny Chinese eyes, badly in need of a surgical operation to give them a free view, behind a large protruding nose ... He began his high-flown speech with these words: 'May I have the honour of expressing my feelings for the stage in a poem written by myself?'

Despite his demeanour – one imagines a young, awkward, semiliterate Roberto Benigni – Andersen managed to get a tenuous attachment to the Royal Theatre's singing school, and, after his voice began to change, as a supernumerary in a Royal Theatre ballet. At the same time (and something has always been a little mysterious about this), during the next three years he was helped by several distinguished Danes – among them H. C. Ørsted, who discovered electromagnetism, and a circle of literary lions that included the poet and dramatist Adam Oehlenschläger and the popular novelist and poet B. S. Ingemann. ('Counting on your goodness,' he wrote to Ingemann, 'I dare to ask you to read the enclosed sheets – I feel that I need to ask this of strangers and see that there is no other way for me to reach the goal that I see as my greatest happiness.') Most important for the destitute Andersen, who came close to starving, he was noticed by Jonas Collin, the new director of the Royal Theatre and the secretary of a trust fund administered by the king. Collin, whether he was acting out of philanthropy or social duty or sheer kindness, saw to it that Andersen, at the advanced age of seventeen, could attend a 'Latin school' in Slagelse, about fifty miles away (his fellow pupils were eleven and twelve), that could lead to admission to the university. One Danish writer, Jens Jørgensen, trying to understand Andersen's unlikely and relatively rapid ascent in Copenhagen's social life – Andersen called himself a 'swamp plant' – has written two books that make the improbable but entertaining argument that Andersen was the illegitimate son of a Danish king.

In a painting made when Andersen was twenty-nine, he looks like a dandy, with a high collar and a moustache. But the many photographs of the older Andersen – awkward, uncomfortable, distant, and sad – seem to get closer to the real thing. 'I would describe Andersen's general mood as sorrowful,' Jonas Collin's son, Edvard, wrote in a memoir, and Andersen's writings give repeated fragmentary glimpses of social snubs, sexual frustration, and a fear that his past would some day catch up with him. Throughout his life he had nightmares about the four years that he spent at the Slagelse school, where he was terrified of failing, tormented by a merciless headmaster named Simon Meisling, and ordered to stop what had become an almost compulsive tendency to write verse. In 1827, when he sent a self-pitying letter to the wife of Admiral P. F. Wulff, another of his Copenhagen benefactors, she replied, 'You certainly do your utmost to tire your friends, and I can't believe that it amuses you – all in consequence of your constant concern with YOURSELF – YOUR OWN SELF – THE GREAT POET [*digter*] YOU THINK YOU'LL BE – my dear Andersen! Don't you realize that you are not going to succeed in all these ideas and that you are on the wrong track?'

Andersen could not help himself. He was determined to be a great writer – as great as Oehlenschläger! – and in 1826, as a pupil of twenty-one, he wrote a treacly poem called 'The Dying Child', which had lines like 'Mother, I am tired, I want to sleep,/let me rest beside your heart.' A Danish newspaper printed it the following year, and it became hugely popular. So, three years later, did Andersen's prose fantasy, *Journey on Foot to Amager . . .* , after parts of it appeared in a literary magazine produced by Copenhagen's cultural tyrant, J. L. Heiberg. This gave Andersen his first taste of public attention, and it thrilled him so much that Ingemann scolded him for courting the 'thousand-tongued, fickle audience',

Andersen and Edvard Collin (here with his wife, Henriette) had a complicated relationship

Andersen by then was eager to court another kind of audience: his eminent contemporaries. During his first trip to Paris in 1833, when he was twenty-eight and barely known outside Denmark, he surprised Victor Hugo by turning up at his house. This almost feverish pursuit of celebrity continued, and during his life Andersen made contact with, among others, Franz Liszt, Dumas père et fils, Honoré de Balzac, Felix Mendelssohn, the Brothers Grimm (with whom he was frequently confused), Heinrich Heine (who liked him but also saw him as a social climber), Robert Schumann, Antonio Rossini, Richard Wagner, the Brownings, and Charles Dickens.

At the same time Andersen wrote incessantly; during his fifty-year career he produced thirty-six theatrical works, half a dozen travel books, six novels, hundreds of poems, and about 170 fairy tales and stories. (In Danish he always made a distinction between the fairy tales – *eventyr* – and the *historier*). He also wrote as many as fourteen letters a day. 'Here, read this, I've just written it,' he seemed always to be saying. His critics in Denmark complained of a lack of discipline, and particularly when he was in his twenties and thirties, he was like a literary spigot that could not be shut off. Through most of his publishing career, Andersen was viewed with mild contempt by many in the Copenhagen literary establishment – and even by those closest to him, including the family of Jonas Collin, his Royal Theatre benefactor, whose house he came to consider his 'home of homes', One particularly hurtful letter, written on December 18, 1833, came from Edvard Collin, to whom Andersen had just sent a prized recent manuscript (Edvard was often the first to read Andersen's writing, and Andersen regarded him almost as a brother):

> You write too much! While one work is being printed, you have half completed the manuscript of another; due to this mad, this deplorable productivity, you depreciate the value of your works to such an extent that in the end no bookseller wants them, even to give away as presents . . . It is really extraordinarily selfish of you to assume such an interest in you among people, and the fault is undoubtedly yours, for the reading public has certainly not given you any reason to think so and the critics least of all.

In his diary Andersen reacted to this letter with almost suicidal gloom, writing on January 6, 1834, 'It shocked my soul deeply, I was so utterly overwhelmed that I lost all feeling, my faith in God and man, the letter brought me to despair.'

To his contemporaries Andersen could seem absurdly sensitive, vulnerable to far less aggressive assaults than this. Edvard Collin recalled Andersen's fleeing the room in mid-conversation in tears. 'Occasionally,' Collin wrote in his memoir, 'you could point to the possibility of a reason, for example, a misunderstood word, special attention paid to a guest, and, above all, the interruption of one of his innumerable recitations when the maid ran out of the room to answer the door.'

Andersen craved attention, yet he lived alone in a series of rented rooms in the centre of Copenhagen. He had crushes but never married. He was unnerved by anything having to do with sex and flustered by the sexuality of women. On January 6, 1834, when he was in Rome, he wrote in his diary of visiting the studio of the painter Albert Küchler: 'And while I sat, a young model of about sixteen arrived with her mother. Küchler said that he wanted to see her breasts. The girl was a little embarrassed at my being there, but her mother said, "Tsk, Tsk!" and unbuttoned her dress, pulled it all the way down to her waist, and there she stood, half-naked, quite dark skinned, her arms a little too thin but with beautiful, round breasts . . . I felt my whole body tremble.'

His journals are surprisingly frank on the subject of his own body. 'Penis sore' or similar notes are often accompanied by a mark resembling a cross to indicate that he had masturbated. During a trip to Italy when he was in his late twenties, he wrote in his diary, on February 28, 1834: 'My blood is hot. Headache; the blood rose into my eyes, and a passion I've never known drove me outside – I didn't know myself where I went, but I . . . sat on a rock by the sea where the water rose up. The red fire streamed down Vesuvius, and the air didn't cool me – I burned. When I headed back, two men came along and suggested women. No, no! I cried, and went home, where I soaked my head.'

When Andersen was sixty-one and in Paris, he visited a brothel for the first time – something, he confessed in his diary on August 30, 1866, that he had always been eager to do. 'Four girls came up to me; the youngest was no more than eighteen. I asked her to stay – she wore a simple dress. I felt very sorry for her.' He paid the madame five francs 'but didn't do anything; just looked at the poor child, who was totally ashamed, and was surprised that I only looked at her.'

Since 1901, when a Danish writer using the pseudonym Albert Hansen broached the subject in a German magazine, researchers have conducted a somewhat tedious debate about whether Andersen was gay. But the only evidence for that comes from a literal reading of the often overheated language of the nineteenth century. As an older man, he was occasionally infatuated with men as well as with women, most notably with the dancer Harald Scharff, but Andersen's virginity almost certainly remained intact. His novels and plays, though intended for adults, rarely touched on desire in any form other than the standard literary tropes of the era – sighs, tears, and polite embraces.

Andersen's writing more often reflected his anxiety about his origins and his persistent terror of not being recognized as an important artist. His debut novel, *The Improvisatore*, published in 1835, followed the life of an Italian singer who succeeds despite his lower-class background, and it became a mild international success; its admirers later included the Brownings. ('The writer seems to feel, just as I do, the good of the outward life; and he is a poet in his soul,' Elizabeth Barrett wrote in April 1845 to Robert Browning.)

When he was thirty-one, Andersen published *O.T.*, a novel whose proletarian protagonist attempts to conceal his past; he followed with *Only a Fiddler* (1837), which had much the same plot as *The Improvisatore* but an unhappy ending: a talented young violinist fails to overcome his low birth. The novels (three more were to follow) have their moments. But all are dated, and two were out of print for a long time, even in Denmark. They would probably be unknown today were it not for Andersen's other, immense achievement.

III

It is an understatement to say that Andersen frequently felt misunderstood, even abused, by Danish critics. When his first novels were published, the reviews tended to be mixed, filled with praise or pointing out (as one did in the case of *The Improvisatore*), a 'sickly sentimentality'. But when Andersen learned that a twenty-five-year-old student and sometime journalist named Søren Kierkegaard was going to write about him, he was unusually apprehensive. 'Suffered torments of the soul at Kierkegaard's not-yet-published criticism,' the thirty-three-year-old Andersen noted in his *Almanak* on August 30, 1838, and a curiosity of literary history is that Kierkegaard's debut, *From the Papers of One Still Living*, published the same year, was in large part an attack on Andersen. Kierkegaard had not yet developed his subtle epigrammatic style, and he wrote this slight book – closer to a pamphlet – in the sort of prose that only Hegel's mother could love. (The critique was not translated into English until 1990.) But Kierkegaard had a sure instinct for a writer's soft spots. 'Like La Fontaine, Andersen sits and weeps over his unlucky hero, who must fail, and why?' he wrote. 'Because Andersen is the same person. Andersen's own miserable struggle is repeated in his writing.' He went on, 'If the novels are in a physical relationship to Andersen himself, their existence should not be regarded so much as a production as an amputation of himself.' Kierkegaard was annoyed by Andersen's seeming lack of a coherent philosophical viewpoint and by his apparent misunderstanding of the nature of genius. ('Genius is not a wick that's blown out by a wind, but a firestorm that the wind only challenges,' he lectured.) He was especially cruel about the protagonist of *Only a Fiddler*, an obvious stand-in for the author. 'Andersen doesn't show a genius in its struggle,' Kierkegaard said, 'but is rather a *flæb*' – a sniveller – 'who's certain that he's a genius, although all he has in common with a genius is that he suffers a few setbacks.'

When Kierkegaard wrote *From the Papers of One Still Living*, he had apparently not yet read any of Andersen's fairy tales, the first of which had been published three years earlier, as an inexpensive pamphlet-like volume titled *Eventyr, fortalte for Børn* (Tales Told for Children). At that time

Henriette Wulff, perhaps Andersen's closest friend, almost became an American.

Andersen once dreamed of marrying Jenny Lind, the 'Swedish Nightingale'.

Andersen himself had been far more interested in other projects, such as the success of *The Improvisatore*, and he had spoken of the tales with almost careless indifference. 'I'm beginning to write some fairy tales for children,' he wrote to Henriette Hanck in Odense on January 1, 1835. 'I want to win the next generation, you see.' In February, he told Ingemann that he had found a new form: 'I have written them completely as I would tell them to a child.' But in general he seemed to see this work as an afterthought in a career that was going in several directions, and perhaps for that very reason Andersen, for the first time in his artistic life, was able to relax. After all, critics might attack him for his novels and plays, and they had scolded him for bad grammar in an earlier attempt at a literary folktale. But why would anyone pay serious attention to stories 'told for children'?

Three of the first four stories that he published in 1835 ('The Tinderbox', 'Little Claus and Big Claus', and 'The Princess on the Pea') were retellings of folktales that Andersen had heard as a child in Fyn. The fourth, and the weakest ('Little Ida's Flowers'), was mostly Andersen's invention. Yet as Andersen published more of these tales, in the late 1830s and into the 1840s, it became clear to his Danish readers, and then to the literary world beyond, that they were something new – an original and strange and sometimes heartrending extension of German romanticism.

Jacob and Wilhelm Grimm, the German linguists and folklorists, had published their celebrated collections twenty years earlier, but the Brothers Grimm were scholars and annotators. ('The Princess on the Pea' mistakenly appeared in the 1843 edition of *Kinder-und Hausmarchen,* a collection of the Grimm brothers' fairy tales. In 1844 Andersen, by then widely known, visited Jacob Grimm, who had never heard of him and who thought that Andersen's version was an old folktale. It was removed from the next edition of the collection.) Andersen had absorbed the work of Ludwig Tieck, Friedrich von Hardenberg (Novalis), Adelbert von Chamisso, and E. T .A. Hoffmann but had managed, with irony and wit, to escape the Germans' morbid supernaturalism – at least most of the time. Andersen's strong susceptibility to superstition (which he had got from his mother) had given him a kind of firsthand experience with a world in which nonhuman entities behaved uncannily. It also gave him a curious authority.

Moreover, he wrote these stories in a new kind of Danish, utterly unlike the formal 'king's Danish' or the Germanic Danish favoured by the young Kierkegaard and the literary establishment. In much the way that Mark Twain affected American English fifty years later and Knut Hamsun (who was influenced by Twain) re-created literary Norwegian, Andersen transformed written Danish. As he had told Ingemann, he was trying to write the way that people spoke – though no one actually spoke with such effortless beauty or imaginative fun.

The critics, though, did not at first approve. Dal, Nielsen, and Hovmann, in their notes to the critical edition of Andersen's stories, recount how only two magazines even bothered to review this first quartet of tales. *Danish Literary Times* contrasted them with a new compilation of stories and poems by the formidable Christian Molbech, a professor of literary history at the University of Copenhagen and coeditor of Denmark's most influential literary magazine, *Monthly Journal for Literature.* Moreover, Molbech was the author of the *Danish Dictionary for Correct Writing and the Promotion of Proper Language.* In 1836 the *Literary Times* praised a Molbech story in which an orphaned boy and his dog save a girl from drowning and are adopted by the girl's father – a count. The same journal criticized Andersen for 'striving towards the livelier and less organized form of the spoken narrative'. By contrast, the review continued, 'Molbech's narrative is simple and calm in the highest degree.'

The reviewer in the journal *Dannora* was scathing. He believed that literature for children should instruct and edify:

> Nobody could assert that the child's sense of decency is sharpened by reading [in 'The Tinderbox'] about a sleeping princess who rides on a dog's back to a soldier who kisses her; and later, when she's wide awake, reports this lovely event as a 'strange dream', Or that the child's sense of modesty is sharpened when reading [in 'Little Claus and Big Claus'] about a farmer's wife, who, in her husband's absence, has dinner alone with the deacon . . . The tale about the princess ['Princess on the Pea'] appears to this reviewer not only indelicate but also irresponsible in the sense that the child will absorb the wrong idea that a high-born woman always has to be overly sensitive.

The review did acknowledge that Andersen had talent and a higher calling but wished that he 'would not waste his time writing fairy tales for children'. Molbech's *Monthly Journal* did not mention Andersen's collection.

These tales nevertheless quickly became enormously popular. 'It was Orpheus that he called to mind,' August Strindberg (quoted by the Andersen biographer Elias Bredsdorff) wrote many years later, 'this poet who sang in prose so that not only animals, plants and stones listened and were moved, but toys came to life, goblins and elves became real, those horrible school books seemed poetic.' A lot of Andersen's stories were also very funny – they charmed readers from the start.

What gives so many of his stories their enduring freshness is Andersen's arch, chatty, and purposefully silly voice. In 'The Nightingale' he balances affectionate, sometimes ludicrous, detail (twelve servants attach twelve silk ribbons to the nightingale's leg and walk the bird twice daily) with satirical asides about class, pretension, and art; in 'The Ugly Duckling' one duck 'has Spanish blood – that's why she's so fat'. As Andersen wrote in 1835 to Henriette Wulff, Admiral Wulff's daughter and perhaps Andersen's only real soul mate, 'My muse visits me, tells me strange fairy tales, fetches me comical figures from daily life, aristocrats and commoners, and says: Look at those people, you know them, depict them and – they shall live.'

He had appropriated a traditional form but seemed simultaneously to invent a new one, one that accommodated itself to flights of fancy and humour, social satire, and literary revenge. He was wholly aware that he was writing for adults as well as for children; indeed, even older children cannot properly understand some tales, such as the novella-length 'The Snow Queen', with its arguments about cold logic and emotional truth. 'The Little Mermaid', one of Andersen's most beautiful stories, becomes not only progressively sadder and more chilling but steadily more religious as it considers mortality and eternity. It is also full of Andersen fun, as when he writes of a dowager mermaid: 'She was a wise woman, and proud of her noble lineage, so she wore twelve oysters on her tail. (Other nobles could have only six.)' Certainly, only adult contemporaries would have recognized that Andersen was sometimes writing fairy tales à clef. 'The Shadow', published in 1847, was in large part payback to Edvard Collin for a particularly hurtful episode. (Sixteen years earlier Andersen had suggested that he and Edvard address each other with the familiar *du* – 'thou' – form. Edvard refused.) 'Sweethearts' seems to be about an early infatuation, and 'The Nightingale' is almost certainly about a later one – an almost obsessive crush on Jenny Lind, the 'Swedish Nightingale', whose musical career in many ways paralleled Andersen's literary one. (Andersen and Lind met several times in the late summer of 1843, when she made her debut in Copenhagen. He was deeply smitten and, according to his diary, actually thought of asking her to marry him.) To read the fairy tales is to get a sense of the real terrors of Andersen's life – all he left out of *The Fairy Tale of My Life*. He understood that writing honestly about heartbreak is easier if, say, the object of one's affections turns up in the form of a discarded toy ('The Sweethearts') and that he could write movingly about being misunderstood if he told the story from the perspective of a duckling who has just announced that he is eager to swim:

'Oh yes, that must be a real pleasure,' the hen said. 'You've gone mad. Ask the cat – he's the cleverest animal I know – ask him if he likes to float on the water or dive. I won't even speak about myself. Why don't you ask our mistress, the old woman? No one in the world is wiser than she is. Do you think she has the urge to swim or to dive under the water?'

Mrs Wulff, who had ridiculed Andersen's ambition seventeen years earlier, could not have said it better.

Kierkegaard was right when he said that Andersen as a novelist could not stop pleading for the reader's sympathy. But as an author of fairy tales, Andersen could take a playful step back. He could also make use of his talent for narrative and action, which, he understood, children prefer to maudlin observations. In 'Little Claus and Big Claus' Big Claus goes on a spree that includes killing four horses and putting his axe through the heads of two grandmothers. 'The Wild Swans', with its medieval atmosphere, is a perfect thriller. Yet for all that, the fairy tales still sound not quite written but almost improvised, as if Andersen were there telling them, confidingly, winkingly.

As Andersen grew older, however, he seemed to become more self-conscious about the genre that he had invented. He set the stories down at high speed, as if aware that he had only a limited time to draw from his talent. In 1836 he wrote to Henriette Wulff, 'I have perhaps four or six years left to write in, and I must grab them.' Indeed, most of the great stories were written between 1835 and 1848; *Nye Eventyr* (New Fairy Tales), perhaps his most important single collection, was published in 1845 and included both 'The Ugly Duckling' and 'The Nightingale'. But Andersen lived for another thirty-nine years and wrote many more stories, most of which had moments of brilliance. Some, such as 'Kids' Talk' and 'The Gardener and the Aristocrats', were also his responses to society and the Danish class system. Some were quite bad – filled with gooey sentimentality – and some were fascinating curiosities, such as 'By the Outermost Sea', which was prompted by Andersen's interest in the polar expeditions. But he knew when the gift was gone. In July 1874 he wrote to a friend, Dorothea Melchior, 'It's as if I've completed the circle with the fairy tales . . . I have no more new, fresh impressions, and that is sad.'

IV

Despite the popularity of the tales, Andersen was perpetually frustrated by an inability to succeed in other literary forms. For much of his life he wrote plays, such as *The Mulatto* and *The Moorish Girl*, which were unknown beyond Scandinavia and richly deserved their obscurity; his feelings were repeatedly hurt by the short runs he had at the Royal Theatre and the absence of public acclaim. The theatre, he once said, is 'the hole from which most ill winds blow over me'. He suffered personal rejection too, from Jenny Lind, who praised his 'divinely beautiful' stories but signed her letters as 'your affectionate sister'. In the winter of 1845–46 Andersen's diary recorded his hurt feelings. He had gone to Berlin, hoping to spend time with the singer, who by then had become as famous as

Marcus and Rebecca Spring, Andersen's American friends,
started a utopian community in New Jersey.

Andersen. But the trip was a horrible disappointment; although they saw one another, Andersen ended up more or less alone on Christmas Eve, suffering all the while.

He also knew that if the novels had made him a literary figure to be reckoned with, the fairy tales had made him a celebrity. And in smaller countries like Denmark, it was understood that real world fame depended first on German readers and then on English ones – usually in that order. One of his early English admirers was William Makepeace Thackeray, who in January 1847 wrote about Andersen to a friend, saying, 'I am wild about him, having only just discovered that delightful, fanciful creature.'

When Andersen made his first trip to England, in the summer of 1847, the reception overwhelmed him. To his dearest friend, Henriette Wulff, he reported on July 22 that his picture was in 'all the shop windows in London . . . I'm truly being treated like a European phenomenon. It's so wonderful for me – I get tears in my eyes.' In the margin of this letter his enthusiasm for the natives seemed to have no limits: 'The English people are the most solid, the kindest, most moral people that one can find!' At the same time he was distressed at the poverty he saw in London.

During this first visit, which lasted from late June until early September, he moved in the best circles: 'drove out to Lord Standley [*sic*], the Lady's sister spoke German; her sister's husband, Lord Hamilton, sat on the other side of me at the table and spoke good German. Several members of Parliament were there,' one diary entry noted. And another added, 'Yesterday I was invited to come into the Atheneum Club, as a 'famous traveller' . . . It's London's top club.'

The visit, in other words, could not have gone better. He saw Queen Victoria, stayed with the English writer Lady Marguerite Blessington, and was personally embraced by Dickens. A new translation of his stories, *A Christmas Greeting to My English Friends*, was effusively dedicated to 'my dear, noble Charles Dickens, who by your works had been previously dear to me, and since our meeting have taken root for ever in my heart'. If people also made a little fun of him – at his odd appearance, at his poor English – Andersen did not seem to notice. (Elias Bredsdorff recounts how one English acquaintance described Andersen in her diary as a 'long, thin, fleshless, boneless man, wriggling and bending like a lizard with a lantern-jawed cadaverous visage'.) As he wrote to Henriette Wulff, 'It's unbelievable how my writing is known and read in England and Scotland! And as one says, the masses are reading me.' His work, he told Wulff, seemed to be strangely popular in North America too, and an important chapter in Andersen's life is his relationship with the New World.

By the late 1840s the American public, like the English, knew and admired Andersen for his fairy tales. This literary preference was certainly correct, but because of the near-total separation of Andersen from his novels, plays, and travel sketches, he was inevitably seen as a genre writer. The poet Henry Wadsworth Longfellow discovered Andersen at about the time of a Mary Howitt translation called *Wonder Stories for Children* in 1846, and as the Longfellow scholar Andrew Hilen noted, 'Andersen was . . . Longfellow's favourite Danish author and he often turned to him for relaxation after the performance of scholarly and literary chores. Like many of Andersen's admirers, however, he overlooked the irony, the social import, and the deep seriousness of his work; he understood him only as a writer of fairy tales and as a man of charming imagination.'

This perception might have changed if Andersen had visited the United States. He was certainly tempted to make the trip, and he enjoyed travel; he had gone as far as Constantinople and North Africa. Henriette Wulff, who made several excursions to the New World and grew to love it, kept urging him to visit. After all, she pointed out, Jenny Lind, now world famous, had toured the States; they could meet and travel around together.

On November 30, 1850, writing from St John in the Virgin Islands (then a Danish possession), Wulff said that she had spoken with many people 'and all of them talk about Andersen – and the way he's idolized everywhere in North America . . . Why don't you travel over here? What a single woman can do alone, and easily, you can do too.'

Henriette Wulff was more than a friend. Her family – one of Copenhagen's most distinguished – had befriended Andersen during his penniless youth, and in his autobiography Andersen portrayed her as almost a muse – someone whose praise, good humour, and sense of comedy inspired him and also saved him from the bathos of which he was capable. Apparently there was no sexual chemistry between them; she was tiny, slightly hunchbacked, and, one writer said, 'had beautiful, thoughtful eyes that suggested a rich inner world'. But Jette (as her friends called her) was someone Andersen could trust completely, and he opened himself to her; his letters to her often began, 'My dear sisterly friend.' She admired Andersen as a writer, and as her English improved, she discovered her own talent as a translator; she helped translate his letters to English publishers and worked on putting Dickens's *A Child's History of England* into Danish. (Her translation was never published.) She began to fill her letters to Andersen with Americanisms – words like *of course* and *trip* – and in urging him to come to the United States, she spoke to his vanity too. 'Won't you see Niagara?' she asked in a letter in 1850. 'Not see the most beautiful landscapes on earth? Not describe them for your fellow man in your own, quite special, painterly words that make one so often see what you've described?'

When he replied, on December 18, 1851, he sounded intrigued but not yet convinced: 'It all sounds very nice, but for me it's just a beautiful fantasy. You know how you can better get me to think about travel? That's by writing: *this* is how much it costs by steamship from Europe to America, *that's* how much it costs for a day in a good hotel over there . . . I dread the long sea voyage, because I suffer. But I could get over it and bear it – yes, I'd come right away to America – if a rich man or his wife left me money in their will.'

The next year, while staying in Boston, Henriette ran into the Swedish writer and feminist Fredrika Bremer, another single woman who found it easy to travel alone. Bremer, who was born in 1801, was friendly with her compatriot Jenny Lind and shared with Lind an enthusiasm for Andersen's writing. Bremer also seems to have been someone who relished friendships with accomplished men; in the United States she had got to know Emerson, Hawthorne, and Longfellow. Jette and Fredrika had met a few years earlier in Copenhagen, where Fredrika had got to know H. C. Ørsted and H. L. Martensen, the bishop of Copenhagen. (She had also tried to meet Kierkegaard and had addressed him, flatteringly, as Victor Eremita, the pseudonym that he used for *Either/Or*. Kierkegaard wanted nothing to do with Bremer, and his journals expressed some loathing for her.) Now, in Boston, Fredrika introduced Jette to Marcus and Rebecca Spring, a couple who would become Andersen's closest American friends.

The Springs were an exceptionally interesting pair – the Americans who had introduced Bremer to Emerson, the Alcott family, and James Russell Lowell. Marcus, a wealthy New York merchant, was the founder and leader of the Eagleswood Community (also known as the Raritan Bay Union), a utopian Quaker settlement of about twenty families near Perth Amboy, New Jersey. Henry David Thoreau, a family friend who had been asked to survey the property, described Eagleswood in a letter to his sister Sophia: 'This is a queer place – There is one large stone building, which cost some $40,000, in which I do not know exactly who or how many work – (one or two familiar faces, & more familiar names have turned up – a few shops & offices, an old farm house and Mr Spring's perfectly private residence within 20 rods of the main building . . . Sunday forenoon, I attended a sort of Quaker meeting . . . (The Quaker aspect & spirit prevails here – Mrs Spring says – "does thee not?")'

Rebecca Spring's maiden name was Buffum; her father, Arnold Buffum, was president of the New England Anti-Slavery Society, and when Henriette Wulff met them in Boston in 1852, Marcus – and especially Rebecca – were active in various political causes: socialism, feminism, and, above all, abolitionism. (In 1851 Rebecca's friend Harriet Beecher Stowe published *Uncle Tom's Cabin*, which was an enormous best-seller in America and England.) Their activism would only become more pronounced in the years leading up to the Civil War.

The Springs got to meet Andersen in September 1854 during a six-day visit to Copenhagen; they were accompanied by Bremer, who by then had become a close friend and had been with them from the time of their arrival in Scandinavia. Andersen liked the Springs immensely; they apparently saw each other every day, in a social calendar that included tea with the

Dowager Queen Caroline Amalie; a political discussion with Bishop Martensen (about to become another Kierkegaard target when Kierkegaard ridiculed the idea that one may simply be born a Christian – thus skipping a 'leap of faith'); the ballet; and a trip to Roskilde, the burial place of kings. The Springs also spent an evening with Andersen at the Hotel Royal, where Jette Wulff joined them. The Springs were wild about Andersen. 'What a joy it has been to us to see you here in your own land,' Rebecca wrote to him before they left Copenhagen, 'and we hope to get to see you in our own – warm hearts will welcome you, you will find yourself at-home.' A couple of days later Jette Wulff wrote to Andersen to say how sorry she was not to have said goodbye to those 'good, friendly, people'.

During the next few weeks and months Jette wrote several times to the Springs. After Jette heard Andersen read two new stories – 'The Piggy Bank', about a get-together of toys, and 'By the Outermost Sea', about death and faith in the Arctic Circle – she asked Andersen's permission to translate them for the Springs. She sent them these two stories, along with a daguerreotype of their author; early in 1855 Jette told Andersen that the Springs had sent 'a thousand thanks' for these gifts and quoted Rebecca Spring: 'But he has so much the kind expression of his generous soul in his face that even a daguerreotype caught something of it!' The Springs had told Wulff that while Andersen's stories were read aloud at Eagleswood, his picture was on the table, and one of their children had commented that 'it was as if he was telling them stories himself!'

Jette Wulff evidently told the Springs that Andersen was finally about to make his way to America, which prompted this very American note from Marcus to Andersen in May 1856: 'I can't tell you how glad we + a great many others will be to welcome you here – + I have only 4 minutes allowed me to tell you, you must go directly to my place of business *22 Broad St* New York and get directions (if I'm not there) how to come to Eagleswood + then we will make all plans + arrangements for your future journeys. In truth + love (+ great haste).'

Someone had obviously misunderstood, but by then the Springs had taken up the cause of an Andersen visit. On July 5, 1857 (this time prompted by an erroneous newspaper story), the Springs wrote again to Andersen and tried to bring him up to date on the great issue that was dividing North America: 'How I wish you could spend part of the coming winter in the freed West Indies, and then, on your way back through our slave states, contrast the slavery of the negroes with his freedom . . . The slavery question here with us continues to occupy all our best minds, as the inevitable crisis – whatever it may be – approaches.'

Andersen, meanwhile, was making his second trip to England – this time a far less pleasant excursion than the one a decade earlier. In 1848, after Andersen had returned to Denmark, Dickens had written, 'Come over to England again soon! But whatever you do, don't leave off writing, for we cannot afford to lose any of your thoughts. They are too purely and simply beautiful to be kept in your own head.' Elias Bredsdorff recounts how, in June 1857, Dickens invited Andersen to his country house in Kent. This time they had no warm exchange of stories and compliments. Rather, Andersen stayed, maddeningly, for five weeks and seemed to have been unaware that he had become the caricature of the unwanted guest. On the day that Andersen was to leave Kent, Jette Wulff wrote to him, saying, 'What a glorious gift God has given you in having Dickens' friendship.' Dickens's daughter Kate later remembered that her father had posted a card in the guest room that said, 'Hans Andersen slept in this room for five weeks – which seemed to the family ages!' After that visit Dickens dropped him; Andersen never understood why his English friend had fallen silent.

Jette Wulff had also heard from the Springs about Andersen's alleged plans to visit the United States – 'it's in *all* the newspapers', she wrote to him, as was the detail that 'the famous H. C. Andersen' was to go directly from the ship to Perth Amboy. Jette herself was eager to return to America, and just before Christmas 1857 she told Andersen that the Springs had been expecting her since September. She said that they were worried because she had not arrived – they had '"waited, watched, and wondered,"' she said, quoting them in English.

By spring 1858 Jette's relationship with America had become more serious: she was thinking of emigrating. 'America has always been the country that I preferred, even *before* I'd seen it for myself,' she wrote. Andersen tried to talk her out of it, but she had never been more serious. On August 21, 1858, Jette wrote that she did not want to leave Europe without sending Andersen a 'last farewell', and she added that it was as if Andersen did not believe she would really do it: 'How *little* you know me!' Jette was disappointed that Andersen did not come to Hamburg to say goodbye before she sailed. She was a melancholy person anyway, and it was an especially sad time because her brother had died of yellow fever the year before (he was buried in America).

Andersen too felt bad about not saying goodbye to his closest friend; her ship, the *Austria,* left on September 13. On the twenty-fourth Andersen wrote to Jette in care of her sister, who lived in London. Jette never saw his letter; on that same day the *Austria,* less than forty-eight hours from New York, caught fire. It was not until October that Andersen heard the news: fewer than seventy of the 420 passengers aboard were saved. Andersen feared the worst, and soon enough he learned that Jette Wulff was among the missing. He was guilt-ridden at not having gone to say goodbye, and inconsolable. In a letter to Ingemann on October 12, 1858, he remembered how sad and lost his friend had been when she had returned to Denmark after her brother's death. He imagined her last moments – 'it's just unbelievable, that she, that tiny, delicate person, who had no one on board to look after her . . . it's horrible to think about her last, lost moments – what she suffered before Death ended her terrible existence!' His diary contained no entries for the rest of 1858. In the United States Marcus Spring paid for a newspaper advertisement, asking for information about the circumstances of Jette's death. Nothing was heard.

In November 1859 Rebecca Spring and her twenty-two-year-old son Edward travelled to Charles Towne, Virginia (now West Virginia), to visit the radical abolitionist John Brown in prison. 'His high white forehead expressed a sort of glory,' Rebecca wrote in a later account of the trip. 'He looked like an inspired old prophet.' In a letter of February 14, 1860, Andersen told Ingemann that Rebecca Spring had written to him about 'the noble Brown', who, in Andersen's words, 'in his eagerness to free the blacks, had been executed'. Andersen went on to tell Ingemann (and, alas, the letter from Rebecca appears to be lost) that there was something that concerned him too: 'Mrs Spring told me that Brown, whom she . . . had visited in his prison cell, read my little story, "By the Outermost Sea". That tale of death and deliverance was one of two stories that Jette Wulff had translated and sent to Marcus and Rebecca five years earlier, after their visit in Copenhagen.

After the sinking of the *Austria,* Andersen had a sharp, real fear of the journey itself – of dying horribly, as Jette Wulff had died. He kept travelling by land, however. Trains had long ago begun to replace horse-drawn coaches, and they thrilled him: 'You seem to fly, but there is no shaking, no pressure of air, nothing of what you anticipated would be unpleasant,' he wrote to a friend. In the spring of 1861, in Rome, he met the Brownings and, although he did not record it, the eighteen-year-old Henry James, who, in his 1903 biography of the American sculptor William Wetmore Story, called Andersen 'the great benefactor' whose 'private interest in children and whose ability to charm them were not less marked than his public', James went on to describe a children's party at Story's home and recalled how, after Andersen 'had read out to his young friends "The Ugly Duckling", Browning struck up with [his poem the "Pied Piper of Hamelin"]; which led to the formation of a grand march through the spacious . . . apartment, with Story doing his best on a flute in default of bagpipes.' (Mrs Browning, Andersen noted in his diary, 'looked very ill'. She died a month later.)

In January 1864, during the American Civil War, perhaps inevitably, Marcus Spring tried to enlist Andersen in a cause – helping 'wounded and dying' soldiers:

I will not doubt that your kind and generous heart will respond to the appeal I now make that you will spend an hour or two writing some autographs to be sold at this fair – also selecting from your correspondence, such notes, letters and some envelopes or scraps in the handwriting of persons of note, which would have a monetary value *here* in this far off *new* land. (+ newly renovated land, we feel that it is to be) A few words of good cheer on a little strip of paper, a few inches square, signed by your name so widely loved + cherished in thousands of households here would each sell for what would send comfort to more than one brave fellow, suffering in the cause we at least deem sacred.

In a diary entry of April 24, Andersen noted that he brought the American ambassador, Bradford R. Wood, 'autographs for Marcus Spring', along with a copy of his tale 'The Ice Maiden' for the ambassador's daughter. In August a grateful Rebecca Spring wrote to thank Andersen for helping while the 'shadow of war was darkening your own land – now so happily passed' – Denmark's second conflict with Prussia over two dukedoms in southern Jutland, which led to the forcible annexation of Schleswig to Holstein as a single Prussian province. 'We rejoice in the peace,' Rebecca went on, 'but regret that Denmark has lost so much territory. Dear Denmark is not so large that other nations need envy her any part of her soil.' Marcus also wrote, with 'apologies for not sooner acknowledging your kindness . . . May we not sometime hope to see you here?'

V

Since the early 1860s Andersen had been getting admiring letters from a rising young Boston editor and writer, Horace Scudder. Andersen did not at first reply, but in March 1868, after Scudder became the editor of the *Riverside Magazine for Young People*, the American wrote again with a proposition: if Andersen would send twelve new stories, each as long as 'The Emperor's New Clothes' (about fifteen hundred words), Scudder would be willing to pay $500 for all of them. In addition, acting on behalf of the publisher Hurd and Houghton, Scudder offered Andersen a chance to publish a complete edition of his stories. As further temptation, Scudder added this postscript: Hurd and Houghton had the posthumous writings of Fredrika Bremer, who died in 1865.

This time Andersen answered. Most of his tales were already available in English, he noted, and 'it only happens now and then that I am disposed to write new ones'. Furthermore, he was concerned that the *Riverside Magazine* appeared to be aimed at 'very young people'. His tales, he pointed out, were 'read by young and old [but the] former enjoy what I would call the exterior, the latter the inner part'. Still, he did have three new stories, which he would send over, and he would try to prevent other, competing English translations. A 'matter of much greater interest', though, was this idea of a complete and authorized edition of his stories.

When he wrote back, Scudder was a little defensive about the 'very young' character of his magazine (which he edited from 1867 until 1870). Still, the good news was that Hurd and Houghton was now interested in publishing *all* of Andersen's work – not only the tales but novels, such as *The Improvisatore*. News of this collaboration spread fairly quickly. Marcus Spring heard once more that Andersen was coming to America. He said that he was eager to 'talk over all the great and good things that have happened since we met you with those cherished friends, whom we saw with you in Denmark. Alas! Our talk of three of these' – Fredrika Bremer, Jette Wulff, and Jette's brother – 'would have a strain of sadness running through it. Remembering that we can see them no more here on this pleasant little planet.' Marcus Spring was aware of Andersen's fear of ocean travel and went on: 'Pray do not let your ancient prejudice against old Father

Neptune – a very unjust one, I assure you, still keep you from seeing our new world. For when you will have spent one week on one of our substantial and charming floating steam palaces, I am sure you will find, as I do, that you would rather take five trips across the Atlantic than one of those long rail rides, which I know you have often taken on the continent.'

The correspondence between Andersen and Scudder soon evolved into a professional and literary friendship. (The letters were found and edited by Jean Hersholt, a Danish American actor in the 1930s and 1940s, who also did a fine job retranslating all of Andersen's stories. The humanitarian award given at the annual Oscars ceremony is named after Hersholt.) The Andersen–Scudder salutations evolved from 'Dear Mr Scudder' to 'My dear, esteemed friend' and, in return, 'Dear, Honoured Friend'. Scudder himself wrote children's stories and had an ear for language; it was more than flattery when he told Andersen in 1869 that 'I find a great difference in the translations which have been made of your stories. Without reading Danish, I have frequently said – this is not like Andersen; it is fine sounding when he is simple and direct.'

Scudder and his publisher were eager to see to it that Andersen was translated properly (Scudder tried to master written Danish in order to do some himself; this made it possible for Andersen eventually to correspond in Danish). Andersen was pleased with his American partners and was willing to give them a true literary coup: the sequel to *The Fairy Tale of My Life* – the years between 1855 and 1867 – and first crack at some new stories, all of which would be published in the United States before they appeared in Denmark.

Andersen's letters to Scudder would report who the author was running into: one day it was General John Charles Frémont, the first Republican presidential candidate, and his 'charming' family; or the American ambassador; or assorted royalty. (In an 1887 memoir Jessie Benton Frémont noted that 'Hans Andersen was, with all his petty vanities and childish self-importance . . . a welcome frequent guest of royalty.') Andersen was particularly eager to cement his long-distance relationship with Longfellow, who sent him copies of his latest poems – such as *Evangeline* and *Hiawatha*. Longfellow had also advised Andersen to learn to recite three fairy tales in English – that, he promised, would make him lots of money, just like Dickens. Scudder too understood Andersen's commercial potential, and in May 1870 the young editor wrote: 'Our Mr Houghton is just now travelling across the continent to California. Think of it! Only a week from Boston to San Francisco by the great Pacific Railway. He takes his wife with him and they . . . sit down to elegant dinners in a travelling dining room! The Arabian Nights can show few things more wonderful.'

Andersen, who was fascinated by modern technology, sounded tempted when he replied that it 'must be a most interesting journey that Mr and Mrs Houghton have made. In truth, our time is a fairytale age, as peoples' lives always are. To travel from Boston to San Francisco in eight days is amazing.'

A few months later Scudder made the offer as appealing as he could: if Andersen would come over and spend at least six or eight months, Hurd and Houghton 'will most gladly charge themselves with the expense of your passage to and from America and will entertain you in their own homes in Cambridge and New York just as long as you will do them the honour to visit them.' But by then it was pretty clear that Andersen was not going anywhere. In 1872 he wrote Longfellow that 'if no great rolling ocean was between us, and I was not 67 years old, then I should arrive in your mighty country some pleasant summer day – as it is, I can only send a letter and the kind regards of your friend and admirer'.

VI

In any case, Andersen was soon too ill (he was, it turned out, suffering from liver cancer) to make such a trip. In *Century Magazine* in 1892, Hjalmar H. Boyesen, a Norwegian American and a professor at Cornell, wrote about visiting Andersen in 1873 and how he had found him 'lying on the sofa wrapped in a dressing gown. He was pale and emaciated.' And Boyesen learned that Andersen now found the idea of the United States a bit intimidating. 'Is it true,' Andersen asked, 'that the streets in New York are so crowded with wagons and trucks that you cross them only at peril of your life?' Boyesen replied that, at certain times of day, a lady would not cross Broadway without a police escort. 'I'm afraid it would not suit me,' Andersen said. 'I should be bewildered by the din, lose my wits, and be run over.'

Andersen asked whether Americans were not 'very hard and unfeeling, having regard for money and for nothing else?' Not at all, Boyesen replied, although they did have a certain fondness for money. 'But you cannot deny,' Andersen went on, 'that they have shown themselves very unfeeling towards the poor Indians. I think it is quite shocking. I assure you, I wept when I read in a German paper how the American Congress had broken all their treaties, and driven the poor red man ever farther westward, until soon he who once owned the whole magnificent continent will not have a foot of ground he can call his own.'

Boyesen wrote that he declined to 'reproduce my special plea in the case of The White Man versus The Red Man', but Andersen grew alarmed at what was certainly an exposition of social Darwinism. 'He had heard of Darwin,' Boyesen wrote, 'and took him to be a very absurd and insignificant crank who believed that he was descended from a monkey.' Before he left, Boyesen said, 'Andersen entertained me with stories and anecdotes connected with his souvenirs of celebrated people,' including a ring given to him by Queen Caroline Amalie and what Andersen called 'a little case containing the Order of the Red Eagle of the Third Class, which His Majesty King Friedrich Wilhelm IV of Prussia graciously bestowed upon me'. Boyesen confessed that, unlike Andersen, he was not excited by the sight of these objects. He was, however, moved when Andersen recited 'The Ugly Duckling' from memory and added, 'It is the story of my own life. I was myself the despised swan in the poultry-yard, the poet in the house of the Philistines.'

In August 1874, after Andersen publicly complained about the American newspaper collection for him, he made a sort of apology for his possible rudeness; at a private dinner on August 27 that included the US ambassador, Michael Cramer, Andersen toasted America and recorded the toast in his diary: 'We knew America from Washington Irving's "Columbus" and Cooper's descriptive tales. We sensed a kinship with the North in Longfellow's "Hiawatha"; and the country became dear to me through the love that flowed towards me from young hearts . . . That became a whole page in the fairy tale of my life.'

At about this time Horace Scudder wrote to Marcus Spring to seek assurance that Andersen was all right. By early 1875, though, Scudder realized that he had not heard from his Danish correspondent for a while. He wrote to Andersen, telling him about his own plans – that he was going to give up his 'business interest in order to devote myself exclusively to literature' – and, in fact, Scudder had become editor of the *Atlantic Monthly*.

When Andersen died, on August 4, 1875, at the age of seventy, he had triumphed in precisely the way that he had always hoped to. He was loved by other writers – the most important ones. He saw Odense lit up in his honour, although it was hard for him to enjoy the celebration because he was suffering from a toothache. He received a parade of visitors who paid him homage; he was still a favourite of the European royals; he posed for statues. But more than Ibsen and Strindberg, and even Hamsun, Andersen remained the most elusive of artists – a major literary figure enclosed by a minor language – and, somehow, the saddest of men, continually overwhelmed by his fearful belief in the fragility of everything that he had accomplished. On June 24, 1850, at the height of his fame, Andersen described in his diary an attack of pure panic: 'A nasty vagabond stood near the spring. I had the feeling that he might know who I was and might tell me something unpleasant, as if I were a pariah, moved up into a higher caste.'

All his life, for he had no family from the time his mother died in 1834, he felt alone, and in the months that he lay dying (he spent much of that time in the suburbs of Copenhagen, with a Jewish merchant family, the Moritz Melchiors) he seemed willing, even eager, to see almost anyone who sought him out; in the accounts of these meetings one can still sense his sweet, vain, heartbreaking thirst for recognition. In an 1890 memoir the English literary journalist and critic Edmund Gosse wrote that there was 'no man of genius in Europe so accessible as Hans Christian Andersen. He delighted in publicity and responded to the sympathy of strangers with utmost alacrity.' Gosse, who was twenty-three and barely spoke Danish when he first met Andersen, later described Andersen as having 'something like the sensitive and pathetic sweetness of a dumb animal' and said that, at first, with his height and arms of 'very unusual length', he evoked 'the usual blunt type of the blue-eyed, yellow-haired Danish peasant'. Gosse went on:

> But it was impossible to hold this impression after a moment's observation. The eyes, somewhat deeply set under arching eyebrows, were full of mysterious and changing expressions, and a kind of exaltation which never left the face entirely, though fading at times into reverie, gave a singular charm to a countenance that had no pretension to outward beauty. The innocence and delicacy, like the pure frank look of a girl-child, that beamed from Andersen's face, gave it a unique character hardly to be expressed in words.

G. W. Griffin, the American consul, seemed oblivious of Andersen's physical suffering, perhaps because Griffin was having problems of his own. In the preface to his 1875 memoir, *My Danish Days*, he explained that 'while the last Presidential campaign was pending, some evil-disposed persons, for the purpose of making political capital, sought to provoke a quarrel between Mr Cramer' – the American ambassador – 'and myself and circulated a number of contemptible falsehoods about Mr Cramer, endeavouring to trace their origin to persons in communication with me.' (This was particularly awkward because Cramer was married to Mary Frances Grant, the sister of President Ulysses S. Grant.)

Griffin visited Andersen at his residence, No. 67, in Nyhavn, the lively street along a canal close to Kongens Nytorv (the King's New Square). 'I was hardly prepared for the enthusiastic welcome he gave me the first time I saw him,' Griffin wrote. 'He seized me by the hand and led me to a chair, near his writing desk in his library. His face fairly beamed with smiles. He asked about Longfellow and other friends in America. "I should love," he said, "to go to America. I am sure it is a great and beautiful country; but I do not like sea voyages, and I fear that I shall never go there."' Andersen spoke English but 'often repeated words over and over,' and when he asked whether Griffin perhaps could speak to him in French or German, the consul told the elderly writer that his 'English was very good indeed; that I liked it better than I did anybody else's, even if he did hesitate now and then'. Andersen shook his head at this statement – was he perplexed? annoyed at being patronized? –

The world-famous Hans Christian Andersen in 1866.

and then he 'spoke of his visit to Dickens, which, he said, was one of the happiest of his life'.

The last time that Griffin saw Andersen, he was 'so ill that he refused to see me, until I sent him word that I was about to leave Denmark'. What did Consul Griffin want? 'I gave him a letter that I had received from Mr Cist' – a friend who wrote verse – 'requesting him to copy some favourite lines for his autographic collection.' Andersen scrawled something – no doubt his standard greeting – on the back of a photograph: 'To Mr L. J. Cist. Life is the most beautiful fairy-story, with the compliments of H. C. Andersen.' He then took Griffin's hand and said, 'Tell Mr Longfellow I am very ill.' Griffin describes this scene with evident, almost smug, satisfaction. Neither he nor any of the many other people whom Andersen agreed to see in those months before he died seem to have asked themselves why Andersen had bothered to take the time.

The Stories of
Hans Christian
Andersen

The Tinderbox

A soldier came marching down the highway: one, two! one, two! His rucksack was on his back and his sword was by his side, because he had been in the war and now he was on his way home. Then he met an old witch on the road; she was very ugly – her lower lip hung all the way down to her chest. 'Good afternoon, soldier,' she said.

'You have a nice-looking sword and a big rucksack – you're a real soldier, and now I'll give you as much money as you want.'

'Thanks very much, you old witch,' the soldier said.

'Do you see that big tree?' the witch asked and pointed at the tree, which was right next to them. 'It's hollow. I want you to climb to the top, and there you'll see a hole you have to slide through. It'll take you deep into the tree. I'll tie a rope around your waist, so I can pull you back up when you call.'

'What am I supposed to do in the tree?' the soldier asked.

'Get money,' the witch said. 'Let me explain: when you get to the bottom of the tree, you'll be in a big passageway. It's very bright, because there are more than a hundred lamps. You'll find three doors you can open because their keys are in the locks.

33

When you go into the first room, you'll see a big chest in the middle of the floor. There's a big dog on top of it; his eyes are as big as teacups, but don't worry about that. I'll give you my checkered blue apron, which you spread out on the floor. Then just pick up the dog, put him on my apron, open up the chest, and take as many coins as you want.

'They're all copper, but if you'd rather have silver coins, you'll have to go into the next room. The dog in there has eyes as big as mill wheels, but don't worry – put him on my apron and help yourself to the money. On the other hand, if you'd rather have gold, you can have that too – as much as you can carry – when you go into the third room. The dog who sits on that money chest has eyes as big as the Round Tower. Believe me, that's a real dog! But don't worry – just put him on my apron. Then he won't bother you, and you can take as much gold from the chest as you want.'

'Not bad,' the soldier said. 'But what do I have to give you, you old witch? Because you want something too, I'll bet.'

'No,' the witch replied, 'I don't want a single penny. Just bring me the old tinderbox that my grandmother forgot the last time she was down there.'

'Okay, then, tie the rope around my waist,' the soldier said.

'There you are,' the witch said, 'and here's my blue-checkered apron.'

Then the soldier climbed up the tree, let himself drop through the hole, and stood, as the witch had told him, in a big passageway with hundreds of lamps burning.

He opened up the first door. Uh-oh! There sat the dog, staring at him with eyes as big as teacups.

'You're quite something,' the soldier said. He put the dog on the witch's apron, took as many copper coins as his pockets would hold, closed the chest, put the dog back, and went to the next room. Ooh! There was the dog with eyes as big as mill wheels.

'Don't keep looking at me,' the soldier said. 'Your eyes might get sore.' He put the dog on the witch's apron, but when he saw all the silver in the chest, he threw away the copper coins and filled his pocket and his rucksack with silver. Then he went into the third room. It was terrifying. The dog in there really did have eyes as big as the Round Tower, and they turned like wheels in his head.

'Good evening,' the soldier said and took off his cap, because he'd never seen a dog like that before. But after he'd looked at the dog for a while, he thought: enough of that. He put him on the floor, opened the chest, and – good lord! There was so much gold. He would be able to buy all of Copenhagen and the baker ladies' sugar pigs, and every tin soldier, spinning top, and rocking horse in the world. Now this was *real* money! The soldier tossed out all the silver that had filled his pockets and rucksack and took the gold instead – yes, indeed, he filled all his pockets and his rucksack and even his boots, so he could hardly walk. Now he had money! He put the dog back on the chest, closed the door, and shouted up through the tree:

'Pull me up, you old witch!'

'Have you got the tinderbox?' the witch asked.

'Oh, right,' the soldier said. 'I completely forgot.' And he went to fetch it. The witch pulled him up, and he was back on the highway with his pockets, rucksack, boots, and cap filled with money.

'What are you going to do with that tinderbox?' the soldier asked.

'None of your business,' the witch replied. 'You've got the money, so give me the tinderbox.'

'Don't be silly,' the soldier said. 'Tell me right now what you're going to do with it, or I'll pull out my sword and cut off your head.'

'I won't,' the witch said.

So the soldier chopped off her head, and there she lay. He tied her apron around all the money, carried it in a bundle on his back, put the tinderbox in his pocket, and headed straight for the city.

It was a beautiful city. The soldier went to the most beautiful inn and ordered the very best room and his favourite food. He was rich now, because he had so much money.

The servant who was supposed to polish his boots thought that they were a peculiar pair of old boots for such a rich man, but the soldier had not got around to buying new ones. The next day he got some boots and some really nice clothes. The soldier became a distinguished gentleman, and people told him about all the attractions of their city, and about their king, and what a pretty princess his daughter was.

'How can you get to see her?' the soldier asked.

'It's not easy to get to see her,' they all told him. 'She lives in a big copper castle, surrounded by lots and lots of walls and towers. There's a prophecy that she's going to marry a simple soldier, but the king doesn't like that, so only the king dares to go in and out of her room.'

'I'd really like to get a look at her,' the soldier thought, but of course he could never get permission.

The soldier lived it up, went to the theatre, took the carriage to the King's Gardens, and gave away a lot of money to the poor – which was a nice thing to do. He remembered from the old days how awful it was not to have a penny. Now he was rich, had nice clothes, and made lots of friends. They all said that he was a good fellow, a true gentleman, and the soldier liked to hear all that. But because the money flowed out every day and nothing flowed in, he eventually had only two pennies left. He had to move out of the beautiful rooms where he had lived and into a tiny room just beneath the roof. He also had to polish his own boots and repair them with a darning needle, and none of his friends came to see him, because there were too many stairs to climb.

It was a very dark evening, and he couldn't even afford to buy a light, but he remembered that a little piece of candle was left inside the tinderbox – the one that the witch had helped him get inside the hollow tree. He took out the tinderbox and candle stump, but just as he struck the flint and sparks flew from it, the door sprang open and the dog with eyes as big as teacups, the one he had seen beneath the tree, stood in front of him and said, 'What does my master demand?'

'What on earth!' the soldier said. 'That's a funny kind of tinderbox, if I can get whatever I want. Get me some money,' he said to the dog. And in a flash the dog was gone, and in a flash he was back again, carrying a big bag of coins in his mouth.

Then the soldier realized what a wonderful tinderbox he had. If he clicked it once, the dog who sat on the chest full of copper coins showed up; if he clicked twice, the dog with the silver appeared; and if he clicked three times, there was the one with the gold. The soldier moved back into his beautiful rooms, put on good clothes, and all his friends recognized him right away – they were so fond of him.

He had this thought: It's strange that you can't get to see this princess. Everyone says she's so gorgeous, but what's the point when she's always inside the copper castle with all those towers?

Isn't there some way I can get to see her? Where's my tinderbox? He lit it and, in a flash, there was the dog with eyes as big as teacups.

'I know it's the middle of the night,' the soldier said. 'But I really, really want to see the princess – just for a moment.'

The dog was out the door instantly, and before the soldier had time to think, he was back with the princess. She slept on the dog's back and was so gorgeous that everybody could see that she was a real princess. The soldier couldn't help it: he had to kiss her, because he was a real soldier.

The dog took the princess back to the castle, but in the morning, when the king and queen poured tea, the princess said that she'd had such a strange dream during the night – about a dog and a soldier. She had ridden the dog, and the soldier had kissed her.

'Quite a story,' the queen said.

The next night one of the old ladies-in-waiting was sent to watch over the princess's bed to see whether she was dreaming or what else it could be.

The soldier longed terribly to see the beautiful princess again. During the night the dog went to the princess, picked her up, and ran as fast as he could, but the old lady-in-waiting put on her waterproof boots and ran just as quickly after them. When she saw them disappear into a big house, she thought, 'Now I know where it is,' and she made a big cross on the door with a piece of chalk. The lady-in-waiting went home and lay down, and the dog returned with the princess. But when the dog saw a cross on the door where the soldier lived, he took a piece of chalk himself and drew crosses on all the doors in the city. That was a clever thing to do, because then the lady-in-waiting could not find the right door – not when there were crosses on all of them.

Early the next morning the king and the queen, along with the old lady-in-waiting and all the officers, went to see where the princess had been.

'There it is,' the king said, when he saw the first door with a cross on it.

'No, darling, it's there,' replied the queen, who saw another door with a cross.

'But there's one – and there's one!' they all said whenever they saw a door with a cross. Then they realized that there was no point in searching.

But the queen was a very wise woman who could do more than ride around in a royal carriage. She took out her large gold scissors, cut a big piece of silk into pieces, and sewed a pretty little pouch. She filled it up with finely ground buckwheat, tied it to the princess's back, and cut a little hole in the pouch so that the buckwheat meal would sprinkle along the princess's path.

During the night the dog returned, put the princess on his back, and took her quickly to the soldier who loved her so. He wanted very much to be a prince so that she could be his wife.

The dog did not notice how the buckwheat dribbled all the way from the castle to the soldier's window, where the dog had climbed up the wall while carrying the princess. The next morning the king and queen realized where their daughter had been, and they seized the soldier and put him in jail.

There he was – ugh, it was so dark and dismal – and then they told him, 'Tomorrow you'll be hanged.' That wasn't much fun to hear, and he had left his tinderbox back at the inn. In the morning, through the iron bars of his little window, he could see people rushing out of the city to see him hanged. He heard the drums and saw the soldiers march by. Everyone was running along; among them was a cobbler boy wearing slippers and a leather apron. He hurried off at such a gallop that one slipper flew off and went all the way to the wall, where the soldier was looking out through the iron bars.

'Hey, cobbler boy, what's the hurry?' the soldier asked. 'Nothing's going to happen before I show up. If you'll run over to where I was living and pick up my tinderbox, I'll give you four pennies. But you've got to be quick.' The cobbler boy wanted the four pennies. He ran off to fetch the tinderbox, gave it to the soldier, and – now we'll hear what happened!

A large gallows had been erected outside the city, and soldiers and hundreds of thousands of people stood around it. The king and queen sat on a beautiful throne, right across from the judges and the entire council.

The soldier was already standing on the ladder, but just as they were about to put the rope around his neck, he said that before a sinner suffered his punishment, he was always allowed to make an innocent wish. He would really like to smoke a pipe, because it was the last smoke that he would be able to have in this world.

That was a wish that the king could not refuse, so the soldier took out his tinderbox and lit it – one, two, three! There were all the dogs: the one with eyes like teacups, the one with eyes like a pair of mill wheels, and the one whose eyes were as big as the Round Tower.

'Help me so I won't be hanged,' the soldier asked them, and the dogs charged the judges and the whole council, grabbing one by the legs and another by the nose, throwing them high into the air so that when they fell down, they broke into pieces.

'Not me, not me!' the king said, but the biggest dog took him and the queen and threw them into the air like all the others. The soldiers were terrified, and all the people shouted, 'Little soldier, we want you to be our king and marry the beautiful princess!'

They put the soldier into the royal carriage. All three dogs danced in front, shouting 'Hooray!' as boys whistled and soldiers stood at attention. The princess came out of the copper castle and became queen, which she liked very much. The wedding lasted eight days, and the dogs sat at the table, wide-eyed with wonder.

Little Claus and
Big Claus

Two men who lived in a certain town had the same name – both were called Claus. But one of the men had four horses, and the other only owned a single horse. To tell them apart, people called the man with four horses Big Claus, and the owner of only one horse was Little Claus. Now let's hear what happened to them, for this is quite a story.

All week long Little Claus had to plough for Big Claus and lend him his only horse. In return, Big Claus let Little Claus use his four horses but just once a week – and that was on Sunday. How Little Claus cracked his whip! because on that one day it was as if he owned all five horses. The sun shone prettily, and all the bells in the steeple rang for church; people got dressed up and carried their hymnals under their arms as they went to hear the parson preach. They looked at Little Claus, who ploughed with five horses and was in such a good mood that he cracked the whip again and shouted, 'Giddyup, all my horses!'

'Don't say that,' Big Claus told him. 'Only one of the horses is yours, you know.'

But when people passed by again on their way to church,

Little Claus forgot that he wasn't supposed to say that, and he shouted, 'Giddyup, all my horses!'

'I'm telling you to stop,' Big Claus said. 'If you say it one more time, I'll hit your horse so it falls down dead right there, and that'll be the end of him.'

'Okay, I won't say it any more,' Little Claus promised. But he was very happy when people walked by and nodded to him; he thought how impressive it looked to have five horses ploughing his field. So he cracked his whip and shouted, 'Giddyup, all my horses!'

'I'll giddyup all your horses,' Big Claus said. He picked up a mallet and clubbed Little Claus's only horse on the head, so that it fell down quite dead.

'Oh, no, now I don't have any horse at all,' Little Claus said and started to cry. Later he skinned the horse and left the hide to dry in the wind; then he put the horsehide in a sack that he slung over his shoulder, and he went to town to sell it.

It was a very long way. He had to walk through a big dark forest, and the weather turned really nasty. He completely lost his way, and before he could get back on track it was evening;

both the town and his home were too far away to reach before nightfall.

He saw a big farmhouse by the road. The shutters were closed, but a bit of light escaped at the top. Maybe they'll let me stay for the night, Little Claus thought, and went to knock on the door.

The farmer's wife answered, but when she heard what he wanted, she told him to be on his way. Her husband wasn't at home, and she didn't want strangers in the house.

'Well, then, I'll have to sleep outside,' Little Claus said, and the farmer's wife shut the door in his face.

There was a big haystack nearby, and a small shed with a flat straw roof stood between the haystack and the house.

'I can sleep up there,' Little Claus said when he saw the straw roof. 'That'll make a wonderful bed. I hope the stork won't fly down and bite my legs.' (A real stork was on the roof where it had made its nest.) Little Claus climbed up on the shed, where he kept turning around to get comfortable. He could look right into the living room because the wooden shutters were not tight at the top.

A large table had been set with wine, a roast, and some tasty-looking fish. The farmer's wife and the deacon sat at the table. No one else was there. She filled his glass, and he stuck his fork into the fish because he really liked fish.

'I'd really like some of that,' Little Claus said and put his face right up against the window. What a delicious piece of cake he saw. This was quite a feast!

Then he heard someone on horseback riding along the road towards the house. It was the woman's husband, coming home.

The husband was a good man, but he had a strange disease: he could not stand the sight of deacons. If he got a glimpse of a deacon, he became furious. That's why the deacon had stopped off to say hello to the farmer's wife, for he knew that her husband wasn't at home and that the good woman would dish up the most delicious meal she could make. As soon as they heard her husband approaching, they grew alarmed. The farmer's wife asked the deacon to crawl into a big empty chest that stood in the corner, and he did it because he knew that the poor husband couldn't bear the sight of a deacon. The farmer's wife quickly hid all the delicious food and wine in the oven, because, if her husband saw it, he would certainly ask what was going on.

'Too bad,' Little Claus sighed from the shed, as he watched the food disappear.

'Is anybody up there?' the farmer asked, looking up at Little Claus. 'What are you doing there? Why don't you come inside with me?'

Little Claus told him how he'd lost his way and asked if he could spend the night.

'Of course,' the farmer said. 'But we have to have some nourishment first.'

The farmer's wife gave both of them a friendly welcome, set the long table, and served them a big bowl of porridge. The farmer was hungry and eagerly dug into his food, but Little Claus couldn't help thinking about the wonderful roast, fish, and cake that he knew were inside the oven.

Little Claus put the sack with the horsehide under the table by his feet. As we remember, he had left home to sell the hide in town. He wasn't enjoying the porridge, and he stepped on his sack so that the dry hide inside the bag creaked loudly.

'Sssh!' Little Claus whispered to his sack, but at the same time he stepped on it again so that it creaked much louder than before.

'Hey, what do you have in your bag?' the farmer asked.

'Why, it's a troll,' Little Claus replied. 'He says that we shouldn't be eating porridge – that he's hexed the oven full of roast, fish, and cake.'

'What on earth are you saying?' the farmer asked and quickly opened the oven, where he saw all the delicious food that his wife had hidden. He thought that the troll in the bag had conjured it up, and his wife was afraid to say anything. He put the food on the table right away – and they ate fish, roast, and cake too. Then Little Claus stepped on his bag again so that the hide creaked.

'What's he saying this time?' the farmer asked.

'What he's saying,' said Little Claus, 'is that he's also conjured up three bottles of wine for us – they're in the oven too.' The farmer's wife fetched the wine that she had hidden, and the farmer drank it; he became very cheerful. He would really like to own a troll like the one that Little Claus had in his bag.

'Can he conjure up the devil too?' the farmer asked. 'I wouldn't mind seeing him while I'm feeling so good.'

'Yes,' Little Claus assured him. 'My troll can do whatever I ask him to do. Isn't that true?' he asked and stepped on the bag until it squeaked. 'Can't you hear – he's saying "yes"? But the devil looks so abominable that you're better off not seeing him.'

'Oh, I'm not afraid – how bad could he look?'

'Well, he'll look exactly like a deacon.'

'Ugh,' the farmer said. 'That *is* bad – I should tell you that I can't stand the sight of deacons. But never mind; if I know it's the devil, it'll be easier to take. I can face it now. But don't let him get too close to me.'

'I'll ask my troll,' Little Claus said, stepping on the bag and holding his ear to it.

'What's he saying?'

'He says you should open the chest over there in the corner – and you'll see the devil inside, sulking. But hold on to the lid so he can't get away.'

'Will you help me hold on to it?' the farmer asked and went to the chest where his wife had hidden the real deacon, who was very frightened.

The farmer lifted the lid slightly and peeped inside. *'Aiie!'* he shrieked, jumping back. 'I saw him – he looked just like our own deacon. It was really horrible.'

They needed a drink after that, and they drank until it was late at night.

'You've got to sell me that troll,' the farmer pleaded. 'Ask anything you want for it! I'll give you a whole bushel of money.'

'I can't do that,' Little Claus replied. 'Just think how useful that troll is to me.'

'Oh, I really, really want it,' the farmer said and continued to beg.

'Well,' Little Claus said at last. 'Since you've been nice enough to put me up for the night, it's fine with me. You can have the troll for a bushel of money, but I want the bushel filled to the top.'

'You'll get it,' the farmer promised. 'But you have to take that chest with you – I don't want it in the house for even an hour. You never know if he's still in there.'

Little Claus gave the farmer his sack with the dry hide, and in return he got a whole bushel of money – filled to the top. The farmer even gave him a big wheelbarrow to carry the money and the chest.

'Goodbye,' Little Claus said, and he carted off his money and the big chest with the deacon still inside.

On the other side of the forest was a deep river; the current was so strong that you could barely swim against it. A big new bridge had been built over the river, and Little Claus stopped halfway across and said, loud enough for the deacon inside the chest to hear: 'Now, what on earth am I going to do with this silly chest? It's as heavy as if it were filled with rocks. I'm going to get pretty tired of wheeling it any farther, so I'll just throw it in the river. If it floats home to me, that's fine; if it doesn't, I don't care.'

Then, with one hand he took hold of the chest and lifted it slightly, as if he were going to heave it into the water.

'No, don't!' the deacon shouted from inside the chest. 'Let me out of here!'

'Oooh!' Little Claus said and pretended to be afraid. 'He's still in there. I have to get it into the river right away, so he'll drown.'

'No, no!' the deacon shouted. 'I'll give you a whole bushel of money if you don't throw me in.'

'Well, that's different,' Little Claus said and opened the chest. The deacon immediately climbed out and pushed the empty chest into the water. Then they went to the deacon's home, where Little Claus got a whole bushel of money. Of course, he had already got a bushel from the farmer, so now his wheelbarrow was loaded with cash.

'Well, I got paid pretty well for that horse,' Little Claus said to himself when he got back to his own room and tipped all the money into a big pile in the middle of the floor. 'When Big Claus finds out how rich I've become from one horse, it's really going to annoy him. But I won't tell him straight out.'

He sent a boy off to borrow a bushel measure from Big Claus.

'I wonder what he wants with that,' Big Claus thought, and he smeared tar on the bottom so that some of what Little Claus wanted to measure would stick to it. Sure enough, when he got the bushel measure back, three silver coins were stuck to it.

'What on earth!' Big Claus exclaimed, running straight to Little Claus. 'Where did you get all that money?'

'From my horsehide – I sold it last night.'

'That's a pretty good price,' Big Claus said. He ran home, took an axe, knocked all four of his horses dead, skinned them, and took the hides to town.

'Hides, hides! Who wants to buy a hide?' he shouted through the streets.

All the cobblers and tanners came running up to him and asked how much he wanted for them.

'A bushel of money apiece,' Big Claus said.

'Are you crazy?' they all said. 'Do you think we have bushels of money?'

'Hides, hides, who wants to buy hides?' he shouted again. But everybody who asked what the hides cost got the same answer: 'A bushel of money.'

'He's making fun of us,' they said. Then the cobblers and the tanners began to thrash Big Claus with their straps and leather aprons.

'Hides, hides!' they sneered at him. 'Yes, we'll give you a hide that bleeds like a stuck pig! Let's run him out of town!' they shouted, and Big Claus had to rush off as fast as he could. He had never had such a whipping.

'Well, well,' he said when he got home. 'Little Claus is going to pay for this. I'm going to kill him!'

❋

Meanwhile, Little Claus's old grandmother had died. Certainly, she'd been ill-tempered and mean to him, but he was still sad; he put the dead woman in his warm bed to see if she would come back to life. He was going to leave her there all night while he slept on a chair in the corner. He had done that before.

During the night as he sat there, the door sprang open, and Big Claus came in with his axe. He knew just where Little Claus's bed was. He went straight to it and hit the dead grandmother in the head, thinking that it was Little Claus.

'Well, now,' he said. 'You're not going to fool me any more!' Then he went back home.

'What a bad, evil person,' Little Claus muttered. 'He wanted to kill me. The old woman was lucky to be dead already – or he would have killed her.'

Little Claus dressed his old grandmother in her Sunday best, borrowed a horse from a neighbour, and hitched it to the wagon. He propped his grandmother up in the back seat so she couldn't fall out when he speeded up – and they drove off through the forest. By the time the sun rose, they had come to a big inn; Little Claus stopped and went inside to get something to eat.

The innkeeper had a lot of money. He was also a very kind man but short tempered, as if he were filled with pepper and snuff.

'Good morning,' he said, greeting Little Claus. 'You're dressed up early today.'

'Yes,' Little Claus replied. 'I'm going to town with my old grandmother – she's sitting out there in the wagon. I can't get her to come in. Won't you bring her a glass of mead? But you have to speak very loudly, because she's hard of hearing.'

'Yes, I'll do that,' the innkeeper said and poured a big glass of mead. He took it to the dead grandmother, who was propped up in the wagon.

'Here's a glass of mead from your grandson!' the innkeeper said. But the dead woman didn't say a word and sat quite still.

'Can't you hear?' the innkeeper shouted as loudly as he could. 'Here's a glass of mead from your grandson!'

He shouted again and then once more, but because she didn't move an inch, he got angry – he threw the glass right in her face. The mead ran down her nose, and she tumbled backwards into the wagon, because she had only been propped up, not tied down.

'Well, now!' Little Claus shouted as he leaped through the doorway and grabbed the innkeeper by the shirt. 'You've killed my grandmother! Just look – there's a big hole in her forehead.'

'Oh, my, it was an accident!' the innkeeper shouted, wringing his hands. 'It's all because of my hot temper. Please, dear Little Claus, I'll give you a whole bushel of money and bury your grandmother as if she were my own. But don't tell anyone, or else they'll cut off my head – and that's so unpleasant.'

Little Claus got a whole bushel of money, and the innkeeper buried the old grandmother as if she were his own.

Then Little Claus went back home with all his money. He immediately sent his boy to Big Claus to ask if he could borrow the bushel measure.

'What?' Big Claus asked. 'Haven't I already killed him? I must go and see for myself.' He brought the bushel measure to Little Claus himself.

'Where on earth did you get all that money?' Big Claus asked, his eyes growing wider when he saw how the money pile had grown.

'It was my grandmother you killed, not me,' Little Claus said. 'I've just sold her and got a bushel of money.'

'That's a pretty good price,' Big Claus declared and hurried home, got his axe, and immediately killed his old grandmother. He put her in his wagon and drove her to town, where the apothecary lived; he asked him if he wanted to buy a dead person.

'Who is it, and where did you get it?' the apothecary asked.

'It's my grandmother,' Big Claus replied. 'I've just killed her for a bushel of money.'

'God help us!' the apothecary exclaimed. 'You shouldn't talk like that. If you say that sort of thing, you'll lose your head.' Then, without holding back, he told Big Claus that he had done an awful thing, that he was a bad person, and that he ought to be punished. This gave Big Claus such a fright that he jumped right from the apothecary's shop into his wagon, whipped his horses, and rushed home. The apothecary and everyone else thought that Big Claus was insane and let him go.

'You're going to pay for this!' muttered Big Claus when he reached the road. 'You're going to pay for this, Little Claus!' As soon as he got home, he grabbed the biggest sack he could find, went over to Little Claus, and said, 'Now you've fooled me again! First I killed my horses, and then my old grandmother. It's all your fault, but you're never going to fool me again.' He caught Little Claus around the waist, put him in his sack, and slung him over his shoulder. He shouted, 'Now I'm going to drown you!'

It was a long way to the river, and Little Claus was heavy. The road ran close by the church, where the organ played and the people inside sang so nicely. Big Claus put the sack down near the church door; he thought that it would be good to go in and listen to a hymn before he set off again. He knew that Little Claus could not get out of the sack and that everyone else was in church, so he went inside.

'Oh, my, oh, my!' Little Claus sighed from inside the sack. He turned and twisted, but he couldn't get the rope on the sack untied. Just then an ancient cattle herder with chalk-white hair and a large staff in his hand drove a herd of cows and bulls past the church. They bumped into the sack where Little Claus was trapped and knocked it over.

'Oh, my,' Little Claus sighed. 'I'm so young, and I'm already going to heaven!'

'Oh, poor me,' the cattle herder said. 'I'm so old and I haven't got there yet!'

'Open up the sack!' Little Claus shouted. 'Take my place in here, and you'll get to heaven right away.'

'Oh, I'd really like that,' the cattle herder said. He untied the sack for Little Claus, who instantly jumped out.

'Would you watch the cattle?' the old man asked, and he climbed into the sack, which Little Claus tied up before heading off with all the cows and bulls.

Soon after that Big Claus came out of the church. He put the sack on his back again, but, not surprisingly, it had become much lighter, because the old cattle herder weighed only half as much as Little Claus. 'He's grown so easy to carry. I'm sure it's because I listened to a hymn.' He walked to the river, which was deep and wide, and he threw the sack with the old cattle herder into the water. Thinking, of course, that it was Little Claus, he shouted, 'There – now you're not going to fool me any more!'

Big Claus walked homeward, but when he came to the crossroads, he ran into Little Claus, who was driving all the cattle.

'What on earth!' Big Claus exclaimed. 'Didn't I just drown you?'

'Yes, indeed,' Little Claus said. 'You tossed me into the river half an hour ago.'

'But where did you get all those nice cattle?' Big Claus asked.

'They're sea cattle,' Little Claus said. 'I'll tell you the whole story. I want to thank you for drowning me – now I'm doing well and, believe me, I'm very rich. I was really frightened inside the sack – the wind whistled in my ears when you threw me off the bridge into the cold water. I sank to the bottom right away, but I didn't get hurt, because the most delicate, soft grass grows down there. I landed in the grass, and right away the bag opened up. Then the loveliest maiden in snow-white clothes – with a green wreath in her wet hair – took my hand and said, "So you're here, Little Claus. First, I have some cattle for you, and then, a mile up the road, there's another whole herd I want to give you." I realized that the river was a big highway for the sea people. They travelled along the bottom of the water – from the sea, deep into the country where the river ends. It was very beautiful; it had flowers and the freshest grass, and the fish in the water whizzed past my ears just like the birds up here. The people were very nice, and cattle were walking along the hedges and ditches.'

'Why did you come back up to us so fast?' Big Claus asked. 'I wouldn't have done it if it was so nice down there.'

'Well,' Little Claus said. 'That's what was so clever of me. You heard what I said: how the sea maiden told me that a mile up the road – by the road, of course, she meant the river, because she can't go anywhere else – a whole herd of cattle waited for me. But I know how the river winds – first here, then there – it's a long way round. But you can make the trip shorter by travelling up here, on land, and cutting back to the river again. That way, I save almost half a mile and get to my sea cattle even faster.'

'Oh, you're a lucky man,' Big Claus said. 'Do you think I can get sea cattle too, if I go to the bottom of the river?'

'I certainly think so,' Little Claus said. 'But I can't carry you to the river in a sack – you're too heavy for me. If you'll walk there and crawl into the sack, it will give me great pleasure to throw you in.'

'Thank you very much,' Big Claus said. 'But if I don't get any sea cattle when I get down there, I promise you, I'm going to beat you up.'

'Please don't be so mean!' Little Claus replied, and they walked to the river. The cattle were thirsty, and when they saw the water, they ran as fast as they could to get something to drink.

'Look at what a hurry they're in,' Little Claus said. 'They can't wait to get to the bottom again.'

'But you've got to help me first,' Big Claus said. 'Or else I'll beat you up.' Then he crawled into the big sack, which had been lying across the back of one of the bulls. 'Put a rock in the bag, or I'm afraid I won't sink,' Big Claus said.

'It'll work fine,' Little Claus replied, but still he put a big rock in the sack, tied it tight, and pushed it: *splash!* There was Big Claus out in the river, and he sank to the bottom at once.

'I'm afraid he won't find any cattle,' Little Claus said, and he went home with what he had.

The Princess on the Pea

Once upon a time there was a prince who wanted to marry a princess. But she had to be a real princess. He travelled all over the world to find her, yet everywhere he went, something was the matter. There were certainly enough princesses, but he couldn't be sure that they were real princesses – there was always something that wasn't right. He came home and was very sad because he so wanted to marry a real princess.

One evening there was an awful storm, with thunder and lightning; the rain poured down. It was really terrible. There was a knock on the gate of the city, and the old king went to open it.

A princess was standing outside. Oh my, how dreadful she looked from the rain and the nasty weather. Water dripped from her hair and her clothes, and it ran in at the tip of her shoes and out at the heel. And she said that she was a real princess.

'We'll soon see about that,' the old queen thought. She didn't say anything, but she went into the bedroom, removed all the covers, and placed a pea on the bottom of the bed. Then she took twenty mattresses and put them on top of the pea and placed twenty eiderdowns on top of the mattresses.

That was where the princess was going to sleep that night.

In the morning they asked her how she had slept.

'Oh, very badly,' the princess said. 'I barely closed my eyes all night. Lord knows what was in that bed. I was lying on something hard, and my body is black and blue all over. It's just awful.'

Now they could tell that she was a real princess, because she had felt the pea through twenty mattresses and twenty eiderdowns. Only a real princess could be that sensitive.

The prince made her his wife, because he knew that he had found a real princess. And the pea was placed in the Royal Museum, where it can still be seen – that is, if no one has stolen it.

See, that was a real story!

Thumbelisa

Once there was an old woman who was eager to have a little child. But she had no idea how to get one, so she went to an old witch and said, 'I really, really want to have a little child. Won't you tell me where I can find one?'

'Of course, we'll work it out,' the witch said. 'Here's a barley seed for you, but not the sort that grows in the farmers' fields or the kind that chickens eat. Put it in a flower pot – then you'll get a surprise.'

'Thanks very much,' said the old woman, who gave the witch twelve coins, went home, and planted the barley seed. Right away a beautiful big flower came up. It looked just like a tulip, but the petals were closed as if it were still a bud.

'That's a lovely flower,' the woman said, and kissed its pretty red and yellow petals. But just as she kissed it, the flower gave a loud pop and opened up. Then you could see that it was a real tulip, but in the middle of the flower, as if on a green stool, sat a tiny girl – delicate and lovely. But she was no taller than a thumb, and that's why she was called Thumbelisa.

She was given a cradle made of a brightly lacquered walnut

shell, a mattress made from blue violets, and a rose-petal cover. That's where she slept at night, but during the day she played on the table, where the old woman had put a plate. The plate was decorated with a ring of flowers, and their stems reached into the water where a big tulip leaf floated. Thumbelisa was allowed to sit on the leaf and sail from one side of the plate to the other, rowing with two white horsehairs. It was wonderful. She sang softly and charmingly – no one had ever heard a voice like hers.

One night as she lay in her nice bed, an ugly toad hopped in through the window – a windowpane was broken. The toad was repulsive, big, and wet, and she jumped right onto the table where Thumbelisa was asleep under the red rose petal.

'She'd make a lovely wife for my son,' the toad said and grabbed the walnut shell where Thumbelisa slept. The toad took her away, hopping through the window into the garden.

A wide stream ran through the garden, but its banks were swampy and muddy; that's where the toad lived with her son. Yuck! He was ugly and disgusting, just like his mother. *Ko-ax, ko-ax, brekke-ke-kex.* That was all he said when he saw the pretty little girl in the walnut shell.

'Don't talk so loud or you'll wake her up,' the old toad said. 'She could still run away, because she's as light as swans' down. We'll put her out in the stream, on one of those big lily pads. She's so slight and small that it will be like an island for her. That way she can't run off while we fix up the parlour under the mud, where you'll live.'

There were lots of water lilies in the stream. They had broad green leaves and looked as if they floated on the water. The one farthest away was also the biggest, and the old toad swam out to it and left the walnut shell with Thumbelisa on the leaf.

The poor little girl woke up early the next morning. When she saw where she was, she began to cry bitterly, because there was water on all sides of the big green water-lily leaf. She had no way of reaching the shore.

The old toad was down below in the mud, decorating her parlour with rushes and yellow water lilies – she wanted to make it really nice for her new daughter-in-law. She and her ugly son swam out to Thumbelisa's leaf to fetch her pretty bed, which they wanted to move to the bridal chamber before Thumbelisa arrived. The old toad made a deep curtsy in the water in front of Thumbelisa and said, 'Here's my son. He'll be your husband, and the two of you will have such a nice home in the mud.'

Ko-ax, ko-ax, brekke-ke-kex. That was all that her son could say.

They took the little bed and swam away. Thumbelisa sat all alone on the green leaf and cried, because she did not want to live with the revolting toad or marry her repulsive son. The little fish in the stream had seen the toad and heard what she said; that's why they poked their heads out of the water – they were curious to see the little girl. As soon as they saw how lovely she was, it really upset them to imagine her living down there with the ugly toad. No – that was never going to happen. Under the water they gathered around the green stalk that held the leaf where Thumbelisa was standing. They gnawed through the stalk with their teeth, and the leaf floated down the stream –

taking Thumbelisa away, far away, where the toad couldn't reach her.

Thumbelisa sailed past so many places. Small birds watched her from the bushes and sang, 'What a pretty little girl!' Her lily pad floated farther and farther, and in that way Thumbelisa travelled abroad.

A white butterfly kept circling around her. Eventually, it settled on the leaf, because it liked Thumbelisa. She was happy that the toad couldn't reach her now and that everything around her was so lovely; the sun made the water shine like the prettiest gold. Thumbelisa untied the ribbon from her waist and attached one end to the butterfly and the other end to the leaf. The lily pad floated much faster, and so did she – after all, she was standing on it.

At that moment a big beetle flew by. It noticed Thumbelisa and immediately pounced; it grabbed her slender waist and flew up into a tree. But the leaf kept floating downstream, and the butterfly followed, because it was still tied to the leaf and could not get loose.

Poor Thumbelisa was frightened when the beetle carried her up into the tree, but mostly she was sad about the beautiful white butterfly that she had tied to the leaf. If it couldn't break loose, it would starve to death. But the beetle couldn't care less. He put Thumbelisa on the biggest green leaf in the tree, fed her honey from the flowers, and said that she was very pretty even if she did not look like a beetle. Later on the other beetles who lived in the tree paid a visit; they looked at Thumbelisa, and all the maiden beetles shrugged their antennae and said, 'She only has two legs – how pathetic!'

'She doesn't have antennae,' they said. 'Her waist is so thin – *ugh*!' the lady beetles said. 'She looks just like a human. She's revolting!'

Yet Thumbelisa was very pretty. The beetle who had kidnapped her thought so too, but when the others kept saying that she was ugly, he finally agreed and didn't want anything to

do with her any more. She was free to go wherever she wanted. The beetles carried Thumbelisa down from the tree and put her on a daisy. She cried, because now the beetle thought she was hideous and because the other beetles wanted nothing to do with her. But actually, she was as lovely as you could imagine – as delicate and pure as the most beautiful rose petal.

All summer long, poor Thumbelisa lived alone in the big forest. She braided a bed of grass and hung it under a large burdock leaf to keep the rain off. She ate honey from the flowers, and she drank the dew that covered the leaves every morning. Summer and autumn passed that way, but then winter came – the cold long winter. All the birds, which had sung so prettily for her, flew away; the trees and flowers withered, and the burdock leaf where she had lived curled up and became a dead yellow stalk. She was terribly cold because her clothing was torn and she was so delicate and tiny: poor Thumbelisa was going to freeze to death. It started to snow, and for Thumbelisa every flake felt as a whole shovelful of snow would to us. That's because we are big, and she was no taller than a thumb. She wrapped herself in the dead leaf, but it didn't keep her warm; she shivered with cold.

She came to a large wheat field just beyond the forest, but the wheat had been cut long ago. Only dry bare stalks stuck out of the frozen ground, and for Thumbelisa it was like walking through a forest. She was very cold. Then she came to the door of a field mouse, which was a little hole among the stubble. The field mouse's place was warm and cosy; her parlour was filled with grain, and she had a wonderful kitchen and pantry. Thumbelisa squeezed through the door, just like a poor beggar girl, and asked for a little piece of barleycorn because she hadn't had a thing to eat for two days.

'Poor dear!' the field mouse said, because at heart she was a good old field mouse. 'Come into my warm parlour and join me for a meal.'

Because the field mouse liked Thumbelisa, she said, 'You can stay here with me for the winter, but you have to keep my parlour

nice and clean and tell me stories, because I really like stories.'
Thumbelisa did what the good old field mouse wanted and was
as comfortable as could be.

'I think we'll have a visitor soon,' the field mouse said. 'My
neighbour usually comes once a week to see me. His place is even
nicer than mine – he has large rooms and wears a lovely velvety
black fur coat. If you could only marry him, you'd be set for life.
But he can't see. You'll have to tell him the most beautiful stories
you know.'

Thumbelisa didn't like that idea; she didn't want to marry the
neighbour, because the neighbour was a mole.

The mole came to call, wearing his black velvety coat. He was
very rich and very learned, the field mouse said, and his house
was more than twenty times larger than hers. He was wise too,
but he didn't like the sun or beautiful flowers; he made nasty
comments about them, because he'd never seen them. Thumbelisa
had to sing to him, and she sang both 'Beetle, Fly, Fly Away
Home!' and 'The Monk Walks in the Meadow'. At that, the mole
fell in love with Thumbelisa because of her beautiful voice. But
he didn't say anything, because he was a very cautious type.

The mole had recently dug a long passageway in the ground
from his house to theirs, and the field mouse and Thumbelisa got
permission to walk there whenever they wanted. He told them
not to be afraid of the dead bird on the path. The bird still had
its feathers and beak, and it appeared to have died quite recently,
at the beginning of winter. It was underground, right where the
mole had dug his path.

The mole picked up a piece of rotting wood, which, as you
know, can glow in the dark like fire, and put it in his mouth;
he walked ahead, lighting the long dark passageway. When they
came to the dead bird, the mole pushed his wide nose through
the earth, making a big hole to let the sun shine in. In the middle
of the floor a dead swallow lay with its beautiful wings pressed
tight against its side and its legs and head tucked under its
feathers.

The poor bird had undoubtedly died from the cold.

Thumbelisa felt very sorry for it. She loved birds, because they had chirped and sung beautifully for her all summer long. But the mole pushed away the dead bird with his short legs and said, 'Now he won't squeak any more. It must be just awful to be born a bird. Thank goodness none of my children will be birds – that sort of bird can only chirp for us, and in the winter it will starve to death.'

'You're so right, because you're a sensible man,' the field mouse said. 'What is a bird's chirping worth when winter comes? It will starve and freeze – but I suppose people think suffering makes you noble.'

Thumbelisa said nothing. But when the mole and field mouse turned their backs to the bird, she bent down, pushed aside the feathers that covered its head, and kissed its closed eyes. 'Maybe this is the bird who sang for me last summer,' she thought. 'That dear beautiful bird gave me so much joy.'

The mole plugged the hole where the light shone in and accompanied the ladies home. At night Thumbelisa couldn't sleep. She got out of bed and braided a handsome big blanket out of hay. She carried it down and spread it over the dead bird. Then she took some soft cotton wool that she'd found in the field mouse's parlour and tucked it around the bird to keep it warm in the cold ground.

'Goodbye, you beautiful little bird,' she said. 'Goodbye and thank you for your summer song when the trees were green and the sun was so warm.' She laid her head on the bird's chest but suddenly became quite alarmed, because it seemed as if something was pounding inside. It was the bird's heart. It wasn't dead; it was only numb with cold, and now it had warmed up and come to life again. (In the autumn all the swallows fly off to the warm countries. But if one of them gets a late start, it will freeze and fall down dead; it stays where it falls, and the cold snow covers it.) Thumbelisa was shaking; she had had a great fright because the bird, of course, was so big – big compared to Thumbelisa, who was no taller than a thumb. But she got up her courage, tucked the cotton wool tighter around the poor swallow, and fetched a mint leaf, which she had used as her cover, and put it over the bird's head.

The next night she crept back to the bird. It was alive but so weak that it could only open its eyes briefly to look at Thumbelisa, who stood there with a piece of glowing wood in her hand. That was all the light that she had.

'Thank you, my pretty little child,' the sick swallow said. 'I feel nice and warm again. Soon I'll be strong enough to fly into the warm sunlight.'

'Oh, no!' she replied. 'It's very cold outside – it's snowing and freezing. Stay in your warm bed, and I'll take care of you.'

She carried water to the swallow in a petal. He drank it and told her how he had torn his wing on a thornbush and couldn't fly as fast as the other swallows when they'd flown away – far away to the warm countries. In the end he had fallen to earth, but that's all he could remember. He didn't know how he had ended up here.

Thumbelisa and the swallow stayed underground for the whole winter. She was kind to the bird and loved it; neither the mole nor the field mouse knew about it, because Thumbelisa realized that they didn't like the poor little swallow.

As soon as it was spring and the sun warmed up the ground, the swallow said goodbye to Thumbelisa, who opened up the hole that the mole had made overhead. The sunlight felt wonderful, and the swallow asked Thumbelisa if she wanted to come along. She could sit on his back, and they would fly far away into the green forest. But Thumbelisa knew that the old field mouse would be very sad if she left.

'No, I can't do it,' Thumbelisa said.

'Goodbye, goodbye, you sweet, pretty girl,' the swallow said and flew into the sunshine. Thumbelisa watched it leave, and her eyes filled with tears because she was so fond of the swallow.

'*Qui-vit, qui-vit!*' the bird sang and flew into the green forest.

Thumbelisa was very sad. She wasn't allowed out in the warm sunshine; the grain, which had been sown on the field above the mole's house, grew high – it was like a thick forest for the little girl, who of course was only as big as a thumb.

'You must sew your wedding trousseau this summer,' the field mouse told Thumbelisa, because by now the neighbour, the dreary mole in the black velvety fur coat, had proposed to her. 'You need wool and linen. You need something to wear and to sleep on when you become the mole's wife.'

Thumbelisa turned the spindle, and the mole hired four spiders to spin and weave night and day. Every evening the mole paid a visit, and he always said that when summer was over, the sun wouldn't feel nearly so hot – now it scorched the earth and made it hard as rock. At the end of the summer it would be time to celebrate Thumbelisa's wedding. But she wasn't happy about it, because she didn't much like the boring mole. Every morning when the sun rose, and every evening when it set, Thumbelisa crept to the doorway; when the wind parted the grain so that she could see the blue sky, she thought how beautiful and bright it was. She so wished that she could see her dear swallow again, but it didn't return – it had probably flown far off into the great green forest.

When autumn came, Thumbelisa had finished her entire trousseau.

'Four weeks to your wedding!' the field mouse reminded her. Thumbelisa cried and said that she didn't want to marry the tedious mole.

'Nonsense,' the field mouse said. 'Don't be stubborn, or I'll have to bite you with my white teeth. You're marrying such a wonderful man! Even the queen can't match his dark velvety fur coat. He has both a kitchen and a basement. You should thank God for him.'

It was time for the wedding. The mole had already come to pick up Thumbelisa. She was going to live deep underground and never come out into the warm sun – because the mole didn't like sunlight. The poor child was miserable because she had to say goodbye to the beautiful sun; even when she'd stayed with the field mouse, she had been allowed to look at the sun through the doorway.

'Goodbye, you bright sun,' she said, stretching her arms into the air. She was able to walk a few steps from the field mouse's house, because the grain had been harvested and only dry stalks were left. 'Goodbye, goodbye,' she went on and put her arms around a little red flower that hadn't been cut down. 'Say hello to the dear swallow from me, if you happen to see him.'

All at once, right above her, she heard *'Qui-vit, qui-vit!'* She looked up and saw the swallow flying by. It was happy as soon as it saw Thumbelisa. She told the swallow how she hated the idea of marrying the ugly mole and having to live far underground where the sun never shone. The thought made her weep.

'Cold winter is coming,' the swallow said. 'I'm going to fly to the warm countries – do you want to come along? You can sit on my back – and you can tie yourself to me with the ribbon around your waist. We'll fly away from the ugly mole and his dark house – over the mountains, far away to the warm countries, where the sun shines more brilliantly than it does here and where they always have summer and beautiful flowers. Come along, dear Thumbelisa – you saved my life when I was frozen in that dark cellar underground.'

'Yes, I'll come along,' Thumbelisa said. She climbed up on the bird's back, put her feet on its outstretched wings, tied her belt to one of its strongest feathers, and then the swallow flew far up in the air. It flew over forests and lakes and above the tall mountains that always have snow on top. Thumbelisa shivered in the cold air. She crept in under the bird's warm feathers and stuck out her head only to look at all the beauty down below.

They reached the warm countries. The sun shone much more brightly than it does here, the sky was twice as high, and the most beautiful green and blue grapes grew along ditches and on fences. There were lemons and oranges in the forest, and the air smelled of myrtle and mint. Along the road the nicest children were playing with big colourful butterflies. But the swallow kept going – and everything became more and more beautiful. Beneath magnificent green trees by a blue lake was a shiny white marble castle; vines wound around the tall pillars, and at the very top were lots of swallows' nests. The swallow who carried Thumbelisa lived in one of them.

'Here's my house,' the swallow said. 'But you should go and find yourself a beautiful flower down there. I'll set you down, and you can make yourself as happy as you want.'

'That's lovely,' she said and clapped her tiny hands.

A large white marble pillar had fallen over and broken into three pieces, and among them grew dazzling white flowers. The swallow flew down and put Thumbelisa on one of the leaves – and what a surprise she got. A tiny man was sitting in the middle of the flower. He was white and transparent, as if he were made of glass; he had the prettiest gold crown on his head and the loveliest clear wings on his shoulders – he was no bigger than Thumbelisa. He was the spirit of the flowers. (A little man or woman lives in every flower, but he was the king of them all.)

'He's so beautiful!' Thumbelisa whispered to the swallow. The little prince was afraid of the swallow, because it was a giant bird compared to someone like him; he was so small and delicate. But he was delighted when he saw Thumbelisa; she was the loveliest girl he had ever seen. That's why he took off his gold crown and placed it on Thumbelisa's head. He asked her name and if she wanted to be his wife – which would make her queen of all the flowers. Yes, he was certainly different from the toad's son or the mole with the black velvety fur coat. So she said yes to the handsome prince. Then an enchanting man or woman came out of every flower, and each one brought a gift to Thumbelisa. But the best present was a pair of beautiful wings from a big white fly; they were attached to Thumbelisa's back, so that she too could fly from flower to flower. It was a very happy moment. The little swallow sat in his nest and sang for them as best he could, but in his heart he was sad, because he was very fond of Thumbelisa and didn't want to be separated from her.

'They shouldn't call you Thumbelisa,' the spirit of the flowers told her. 'It's an ugly name, and you're so beautiful. We'll call you Maya.'

'Goodbye, goodbye,' the swallow said and once more flew away from the warm countries, far away, back to Denmark. There it had a little nest above the window of the man who knew how to tell fairy tales. It sang *'Qui-vit, qui-vit!'* to him, and that's how we got this whole story.

The Little Mermaid

Far out in the ocean the water is as blue as the petals of the prettiest cornflower and as clear as the purest glass. But it is very deep, deeper than any anchor can reach. You would have to stack a lot of church steeples on top of each other to get from the bottom to the surface. The sea people live down there.

Now don't get the idea that there's only bare white sand at the bottom of the sea. No, you will find the strangest trees, and plants whose stems and leaves are so supple that, at the slightest movement of the water, they stir as if they were alive. Fish, large and small, dart among the branches just as birds up here fly through the air. The sea king's castle stands at the deepest spot. Its walls are coral, and its long pointed windows are the clearest amber. The roof is made of mussel shells, which open and close as the water moves. It looks beautiful, because in every shell there's a shiny pearl, and just one of them could be a great gem in a queen's crown.

The sea king had been a widower for many years, and his old mother kept house for him. She was a wise woman, and proud of her noble lineage, so she wore twelve oysters on her tail.

70

(Other nobles could have only six.) But apart from this she deserved a lot of credit, because she was so fond of the little sea princesses – her grandchildren. They were six delightful children, and the youngest was the prettiest of all. Her skin was as delicate and clear as a rose petal, her eyes as blue as the deepest lake, but like her sisters she didn't have any feet. Her body ended in a fish tail.

All day long the children played in the castle, in the great halls where flowers grew out of the walls. When they opened the large amber windows, fish swam in, just as swallows up here fly in when we open ours. The fish swam right up to the little princesses, ate out of their hands, and let themselves be petted.

Outside the castle was a large garden, with fiery red and dark blue trees. The fruit shone like gold, and the flowers looked like fire because their stems and leaves were constantly moving. The ground itself was the finest sand, but it was blue, like a sulphurous flame. Everything had a strange blue glow, and it was easier to believe that you were high up in the air, with sky above and below, than to think that you were at the bottom of the sea. When the water was perfectly still, you could glimpse the sun, which looked like a purple flower from whose calyx all the light streamed out.

Each little princess had her own spot in the garden, where she could dig and plant as she wished. One princess shaped her little flower patch like a whale; another wanted hers to look like a small mermaid. But the youngest princess made her garden as round as the sun, and she only planted flowers that were red like the sun. She was a strange child – quiet and thoughtful. When her sisters decorated their gardens with the wondrous objects that they had taken from sunken ships, she wanted only one thing apart from the rose-red flowers that looked like the distant sun: the beautiful marble statue of a handsome boy. He was carved out of that white, shiny stone and had ended up on the bottom of the sea in a shipwreck. Next to the statue she planted a rose-red weeping willow; it grew splendidly, and its fresh branches hung over the statue towards the blue sandy bottom, where its shadow looked purple and moved just like the branches. It looked like the top branches and the roots were pretending to kiss each other.

Nothing made the mermaid happier than to hear about the world of people up above. She wanted her old grandmother to tell everything she knew about ships and cities, people and animals. It seemed especially wonderful to her that up on earth, the flowers had a smell – they didn't on the bottom of the sea – and that the forests were green and that the fish one saw among the branches could sing loudly and prettily. Grandmother called the small birds *fish*; otherwise, the mermaids could not have understood her because they had never seen a bird.

'When you turn fifteen,' her grandmother said, 'you'll be allowed to go to the surface of the sea, sit on the rocks in the moonlight, and watch the great ships sail by – you'll see forests and cities too.'

The next year one of the sisters would be fifteen. The girls had been born a year apart, so the youngest sister still had to wait five years before she could venture from the bottom of the ocean to see how things looked up here. Each sister promised to tell the others what she had seen and liked most on her first visit; their grandmother had not told them enough, so there was a lot that they wanted to learn.

No one yearned to go as much as the youngest mermaid, the one who had to wait the longest and who was so quiet and thoughtful. On many nights she stood by the open window and looked up through the dark blue water where the fish flicked their fins and tails. She could see the moon and the stars. They were of course quite pale, but through the water they appeared much bigger than they do to our eyes. If a black cloud seemed to glide under the stars, she knew that either a whale was swimming above her or a ship with many people on board was passing by. It probably did not occur to them that a beautiful little mermaid stood beneath them, stretching her white hands towards the ship's keel.

The oldest princess turned fifteen and swam to the surface.

When she returned, she had hundreds of things to tell her sisters. But the best thing, she said, was to lie in the moonlight on a sandbank in the tranquil sea and look at the big city near the coast where the lights blinked like hundreds of stars, listen to music and the hustle and bustle of carriages and people, see the many church steeples and spires, and hear the bells ring. Because the youngest sister couldn't go there, she longed all the more for it.

How she listened! And when, later in the evening, she stood by the open window and looked up through the dark blue water, she thought about the big city and all the hustle and bustle and believed that she could hear the church bells ring all the way down to where she was.

A year later the next sister got permission to go to the surface and swim wherever she wanted. She rose from the water just as the sun was setting, and she thought that was the most beautiful sight. The whole sky, she said, looked like gold, and the clouds – actually, she couldn't even describe how beautiful they were, red and violet – sailed above her. Moving much faster, a flock of wild swans flew like a long white veil across the water towards the sun. She swam towards the sun, but it set, and its rose-red light vanished from the clouds and the surface of the sea.

The next year the third sister went up. She was the most daring of them all and swam up a wide river that ran into the sea. She saw beautiful green hills covered with grapevines; castles and farms peeped through great forests. She heard how the birds sang, and the sun was so hot that she often had to dive under the surface to cool her burning face. In a small bay she ran into a group of children; they ran about quite naked, splashing in the water. She wanted to play with them, but they were frightened and ran away. A little black animal came along; it was a dog, but she had never seen a dog before. It barked at her so frightfully that it scared her, and she headed for the open sea. But she would never forget the magnificent forest, the green hills, and the nice children, who could swim even though they did not have fish tails.

The fourth sister wasn't so daring. She stayed in the middle of the wild ocean and said that right there was best of all. She could see for miles, and the sky above was like a big glass bell. She had seen ships, but they were far away; they had looked like seagulls. Funny dolphins turned somersaults, and big whales squirted water through their nostrils so it looked as if she were surrounded by hundreds of fountains.

Then it was the fifth sister's turn. It so happened that her birthday was in the winter, and that was why she saw what none of the others had seen during their first outings. The ocean looked very green. Big icebergs floated here and there. Each of them, she said, looked like a pearl, and still they were a lot bigger than the church steeples that people built. They had the strangest shapes and glittered like diamonds. She sat on one of the biggest, and, terrified, all the ships went around the iceberg where she sat with the wind blowing through her long hair. Later in the evening the sky became overcast. There was thunder and lightning, and black waves lifted up big blocks of ice so that they gleamed in bolts of red lightning. With fear and horror, deckhands pulled in the sails on every ship, but the mermaid sat calmly upon her floating iceberg and watched blue lightning zig-zag into the shiny sea.

Whenever one of the sisters came to the surface for the first time, she would be thrilled by the new and beautiful things she had seen. But now that they were grown and were allowed to swim to the surface whenever they wished, they didn't care any more. After a month of this they wanted to be at home. They said that their own place down there was the most beautiful of all and that it was so nice to be home.

On many evenings the five sisters linked arms and rose in a straight line to the surface. They had lovely voices, more beautiful than any human voice, and when a storm was coming and they thought that ships might founder, they swam in front of the ships. They sang enchantingly about how beautiful it was on the bottom of the sea, and they told the sailors not to be afraid to go there. But the sailors didn't understand the words – they thought it was the storm. Nor did they get to see the beauty down there, for when their ships sank, the sailors drowned. When they came to the castle of the sea king, they were dead.

In the evening, when the sisters rose up through the water arm in arm, the youngest sister was left all alone, watching them go. She felt as if she were about to cry, but mermaids have no tears, so they suffer all the more.

'If only I were fifteen!' she said. 'I know that I would love the world up above and the people who live there.'

At long last she turned fifteen.

'You're on your own now,' said her grandmother, the old dowager queen. 'Come, let me dress you up like your sisters.' She put a wreath of white lilies on the youngest sister's hair. Every petal in the flower was half a pearl, and the old lady clamped eight big oysters on the princess's tail to show her high rank.

'It really hurts!' the little mermaid cried.

'Well, there's no beauty without pain,' the old woman replied.

Oh! She would have liked to shake off all that finery and remove that heavy wreath. The red flowers from her garden would have looked much better on her, but she didn't dare change anything. 'Goodbye,' she said, and light and clear as a bubble, she rose through the water.

The sun had just set when she lifted her head above the surface, but the clouds still gleamed like roses and gold. The evening star shone brightly and beautifully in the middle of the pale red sky. The air was mild and fresh, and the sea was dead calm. She saw a big ship with three masts; only one sail was up, because there was not so much as a breeze, and sailors sat around in the rigging and on the masts. There was music and song, and as the evening grew darker, hundreds of lamps in all kinds of colours were lit. It was as if the flags of all nations waved in the wind.

The little mermaid swam right up to the porthole of a cabin, and every time a wave lifted her, she could see through the clear windowpane. She saw lots of elegantly dressed people, but the most handsome of all was the young prince with big black eyes. He probably wasn't much older than sixteen. It was his birthday, and that's why there were all these festivities. As the young prince came out on deck where the sailors were dancing, more than a hundred rockets were fired into the air; they made the sky as light as day and frightened the little mermaid. She dived under water but soon poked up her head, and it was as if all the stars in the sky were falling down to her. She had never seen such fireworks. Large suns whirled around, grand fire fish glided through the blue air, and everything was reflected in the clear calm sea. The ship itself was so brightly lit that you could see every little rope – and of course the people. How handsome the young prince was! He shook hands with everybody and laughed and smiled while music filled the beautiful night.

The night wore on, but the little mermaid could not turn away from the ship and the handsome prince. The coloured lamps were extinguished; no more rockets were fired into the air, and there were no more salutes from the cannon, but deep down the ocean groaned and growled. Through it all, the little mermaid rode the waves up and down so that she could look into the cabin. But the ship picked up speed; one sail after another billowed out, and the waves rolled faster. Huge clouds gathered, and lightning flashed in the distance. Terrible weather was coming, so the deckhands took in the sails. The great ship rocked as it flew across the violent sea. The water rose like great dark mountains that could smash into the mast, and the ship dipped like a swan between the tall peaks before the towering waves lifted it again. The little mermaid thought it was fun to go so fast, but the sailors didn't; the ship creaked and groaned, and its thick planks were bent by the powerful waves. The ocean crashed against the ship, the mast snapped like a reed, and the ship rolled onto its side as water rushed into the hold.

Now the little mermaid saw that the sailors were in danger; she herself had to watch out for timber and pieces of the ship that floated on the water. One moment it was pitch dark and she couldn't see a thing; then, when lightning flashed, it got so bright that she recognized everybody on the ship. Everyone was thrashing about as best he could. Most of all, she looked for the young prince, and when the ship broke apart, she saw him sink into the deep ocean. At first she was happy, because now he was going to her world. But then she remembered that humans can't live in the water, and that he could only come to her father's castle if he were dead. No, he mustn't die; so she swam among the beams and planks that drifted about on the water, not even thinking that they could crush her. She dived deep under the water and came up again between the waves; finally she reached the young prince, who barely had the strength to keep swimming in the stormy sea. His arms and legs had begun to weaken, his beautiful eyes were closed, and he would have died if the little mermaid hadn't been there. She held his head above water, and let the waves push them along.

In the morning the nasty weather was gone. There wasn't a splinter left of the ship. The sun rose red and shiny from the water and seemed to bring colour back to the prince's cheeks. But his eyes stayed closed. The mermaid kissed his beautiful high forehead and brushed back his wet hair. She thought that he looked like the marble statue in her own little garden. She kissed him again and wished more than anything that he would live.

She saw land ahead of her – high blue mountains whose tops,

shiny with white snow, looked like swans huddled together. Down by the coast was a beautiful green forest, and in front of that was a church, or a cloister, she wasn't quite sure which – a building of some sort. Lemon and orange trees grew in the garden, and tall palm trees stood in front of the gate. Here the ocean formed a little bay; it was utterly calm but very deep right up to the rock where the fine white sand had washed ashore. The mermaid swam over there with the handsome prince, laid him down in the sand, and made sure to lift his head towards the warm sun.

The bells rang in the large white building, and a group of young girls walked through the garden. The little mermaid swam farther out, behind some tall rocks that jutted from the water; she covered her hair and chest with foam so that no one could see her face, and she watched to see who would help the poor prince.

It wasn't long before a young girl came along. She looked quite alarmed but only for a moment; then she went to fetch other people, and the mermaid saw that the prince had come to and that he smiled to everyone around him. Yet he did not smile to her, because of course he didn't know that she had rescued him. She felt very sad, and when he was led into the big building, she dived sorrowfully into the water and headed home to her father's castle.

The little mermaid had always been quiet and thoughtful, but now she was even more so. Her sisters asked what she had seen during her first time up there, but she didn't tell them anything.

Often in the evening and morning she swam to the spot where she had left the prince. She saw the fruit in the garden ripen and be picked; she saw the snow melt in the tall mountains. But she did not see the prince, which was why she always went home even sadder. Her only consolation was to sit in her little garden and wrap her arms around the beautiful marble statue that looked like the prince. She didn't take care of her flowers, which grew into a wilderness. They spread over the path and wound their long stems and leaves into the branches of the trees so that everything became quite dark.

In the end, she couldn't stand it any longer and told one of her sisters. Right away all of them knew, but nobody apart from them and a couple of other mermaids, who didn't say anything to anyone except *their* closest friends. One of them knew who the prince was; she too had seen the festive ship and knew where he came from and the whereabouts of his kingdom.

'Come along, little sister,' the other princesses said, and with their arms around each other's shoulders, they rose out of the water in a long row, where they knew the prince's castle stood.

The castle was built with a kind of pale yellow, glistening stone; it had grand marble staircases, and one went all the way to the sea. Magnificent gilded cupolas arched above the roof, and between the pillars, which surrounded the entire building, were lifelike marble statues. Through the clear glass of tall windows, you could see into majestic rooms with priceless tapestries and silk curtains; the walls were covered with large paintings, which were a pleasure to look at. A great fountain splashed in the middle of the biggest hall, and its spray reached high up towards a glass dome in the ceiling. The sun shone down to the water and on the beautiful plants that grew in the pool of the fountain.

Now the little mermaid knew where the prince lived, and she would often go there in the evening and at night. She swam much closer to land than any of the others had dared – in fact, she went all the way to a small canal under a splendid marble balcony that cast its long shadow across the water. She sat there and gazed at the young prince, who thought that he was all alone in the bright moonlight.

Many evenings she saw him sail off in his grand ship, with music playing and flags waving. She would peep through the green rushes, and if the wind lifted her long silver-white veil and you happened to see it, you would have thought it was a swan taking flight.

Often at night, when the fishermen were out at sea with their flares, she heard them say lots of nice things about the young prince. It made her happy that she had saved him when he drifted half dead upon the waves, and she remembered how his head had rested tightly against her breast and how lovingly she had kissed him. He didn't know anything about it, so he couldn't even dream about her.

The little mermaid grew fonder and fonder of human beings, and more and more she wished that she could live among them. Their world, it seemed to her, was much bigger than hers. They could fly across the ocean in their ships, climb the tall mountains far above the clouds, and their land, covered with woods and fields, stretched farther than she could see. There was so much that she wanted to know, but her sisters didn't have an answer for everything; that was why she asked her old grandmother, who knew about the world, which she quite rightly called the Lands Above the Sea.

'If people don't drown,' the little mermaid asked, 'can they live forever? Don't they die, as we do down here in the ocean?'

'Yes,' the old woman said. 'They have to die too, and their lifespan is even shorter than ours. We can live for three hundred years, but when we stop existing, we turn into foam on the sea, and we don't even have a grave down here among our loved ones. We don't have an immortal soul; we won't ever live again. We're like the green rushes: once they've been cut they can't grow again. But humans have a soul, which lives forever – it lives even after the body has turned to dust. It rises through the clear air to the shining stars. Just as we swim to the surface of the ocean and see where people live, they go up to beautiful unknown places that we'll never get to see.'

'Why didn't we get an immortal soul?' the little mermaid asked sadly. 'I would give all my three hundred years if I could be human for just one day and get a place in the heavenly world.'

'You shouldn't think about that sort of thing,' the old woman said. 'We're much happier and better off than people up there.'

'So that means I'm going to die and float like foam on the ocean – and not hear the music of the waves or see the beautiful flowers and the red sun? Can't I do something to get an immortal soul?'

'No,' the old woman said. 'Only if a human being loved you so much that you meant more to him than his father or mother – and only if all his thoughts and feelings were devoted to you and he let the vicar put his right hand in yours with the promise of faithfulness now and for all eternity. Then his soul would flow into your body, and you too could share human happiness. He would give you a soul and still keep his own. But that's never going to happen. The thing that's so wonderful in the sea, your fish tail, is considered hideous up on land. They don't know any better. To be beautiful up there, you need to have two clumsy pillars that they call *legs*.'

The little mermaid sighed and looked sadly at her fish tail.

'Let's be happy,' the old woman said. 'Let's hop and skip for the three hundred years that we get to live. When you think about it, that's enough time. After that, we'll be glad to rest in our graves. Tonight we're going to have a dance at the castle.'

Everything looked more fabulous than anything you'll ever see on earth. Inside the great ballroom the walls and ceiling were made of thick but clear glass. Several hundred colossal mussel shells, rose red and grass green, were lined up on each side, each burning with a blue flame. They lit up the whole room and shone through the walls, illuminating the ocean outside. You could see countless fish, large and small, swim towards the glass wall; some of their scales glowed scarlet, and others appeared to be silver and gold. A wide rushing stream flowed through the middle of the ballroom, and mermaids and mermen danced on the water to the sound of their own beautiful singing. No one on earth had such lovely voices.

The little mermaid sang more beautifully than anyone. They clapped for her, and for a moment her heart was joyful because she knew that she had the most beautiful voice of anyone on earth or in the sea. But soon she began to think again about the world above; she could not forget the handsome prince or her sorrow at not having an immortal soul, as he did. That was why she sneaked out of her father's castle, and while it was all song and merriment inside, the little mermaid was sad in her little garden.

She heard the sound of a horn through the water, and she thought, 'I'm sure he's out sailing – the one who means more to me than my father and mother, the one I can't stop thinking about, in whose hands I would put my life and happiness. I'd risk everything to win him and an immortal soul. While my sisters dance in my father's castle, I'll go to the sea witch. I've always been afraid of her, but maybe she can give me advice and help me.'

The little mermaid left her garden and went to where the sea witch lived, behind the roaring maelstroms. The mermaid had never gone that way before. No flowers grew there, no sea grass, nothing but the naked, grey sandy bottom stretching towards the maelstroms, where the water, like a churning waterwheel, whirled round and pulled everything it got hold of down to the depths. To reach the sea witch's district the little mermaid had to go through these crushing whirlpools, and for a long stretch the only route was over the hot bubbling mud that the sea witch called her peat bog. Her house lay behind it, in the middle of a peculiar forest. All the trees and bushes were sea polyps, half animal and half plant, and looked like hundred-headed snakes growing from the earth. The branches were long slimy arms, with fingers like slithering worms, and joint for joint they undulated from their roots to the uppermost tips. They wound themselves around everything in the sea that they could get hold of, and they never let go.

The little mermaid became frightened as she stood there; her heart pounded with fear – she almost turned back. But then she thought about the prince and the human soul, and that gave her courage. She tied her long floating hair round her head so that the sea polyps couldn't grab it; she folded both hands across her chest, and like the fish that fly through the water, she darted in among the hideous sea polyps, which stretched their sinuous arms and fingers after her. She saw that each sea polyp held on to something that it had caught – hundreds of little arms wound around their catch like strong iron bands. People who had died at sea and sunk to the bottom peeped like white skeletons through the arms of the sea polyps. The polyps held on to ship rudders, chests, the skeletons of animals, and also a small mermaid they had caught and strangled – that was almost the scariest thing for the little mermaid.

She came to a large slimy clearing in the forest, where big fat water snakes gambolled and showed off their disgusting yellow-white undersides. In the middle of the clearing was a house built out of the white bones of shipwrecked humans; that was where the sea witch sat with a toad that she let eat out of her mouth the way that people let a little canary eat a lump of sugar. She called the fat ugly water snakes her little chickens, and let them frolic on her huge spongy chest.

'I think I know what you want,' the sea witch said. 'You are being very unwise. You can have it your way, but it's going to bring you grief, my lovely princess. You want to get rid of your fish tail and replace it with two stumps to walk on, like a human, so the young prince will fall in love with you, and you will have him and an immortal soul.'

At that, the sea witch laughed so loudly and nastily that the toad and snakes fell to the ground and rolled around. 'You came just in time,' the witch said. 'After sunrise tomorrow I wouldn't have been able to help you for another year. I'll make you a drink, but before the sun comes up, you must swim to land, sit on the shore, and drink it. Then your tail will split in two and shrink into what humans call "pretty legs". But it hurts – it's like a sharp sword going through you. Everyone who sees you will say that you're the loveliest girl that they have ever seen. You will keep your gliding walk; no dancer will soar like you. But every step you take will feel like you are stepping on a sharp knife that makes you bleed. If you're willing to suffer all this, I'll help you.'

'Yes!' the little mermaid said in a quavering voice, and she thought about the prince and about winning an immortal soul.

'But remember,' the sea witch continued, 'as soon as you get a human form, you can't ever be a mermaid again. You can never swim down through the water to your sisters and your father's castle. And unless you win the prince's love so that he forgets his father and mother for your sake and thinks only about you and lets the vicar put your hands together so that you become man and wife, you won't get an immortal soul. The first morning after he has married someone else, your heart will break, and you'll turn into foam on the sea.'

'I still want to do it,' the little mermaid said. She was as pale as a corpse.

'But you have to pay me too,' the sea witch went on, 'and I ask for quite a bit. You have the prettiest voice of anyone on the bottom of the sea, and I'm sure you imagine that you'll charm him. But you have to give me that voice. I want the most precious thing you own for my precious drink. As you know, I have to add my own blood to make the drink as sharp as a double-edged sword.'

'But if you take my voice,' the little mermaid said, 'what will I have left?'

'Your beautiful figure,' the witch said, 'your soaring walk, and your eloquent eyes – with all that you can certainly enchant a human heart. Well, well – have you lost heart? Stick out your little tongue. Then I'll cut it off as payment, and you'll get my powerful drink.'

'Do it,' the little mermaid said, and the sea witch put on the kettle to cook the magic potion. 'Cleanliness is next to godliness,' the sea witch said. She scoured the kettle with one of the snakes, which she tied into a knot. Then she cut her chest and let her black blood drip down. The steam made the oddest shapes, enough to make anyone anxious and afraid. Every other moment the witch added something new to the kettle, and when it reached full boil, it sounded like a crocodile shedding tears. At last the drink was done, and it looked like the clearest water.

'Here's your drink,' the witch said and cut off the little mermaid's tongue. Now she was mute and could neither sing nor speak.

'In case the sea polyps grab you when you return through my forest,' the sea witch explained, 'just throw a single drop of this potion on them – and their arms and fingers will explode into a thousand pieces.' But the little mermaid didn't need to; when the sea polyps saw the luminous drink that glowed in her hand like a radiant star, they retreated in fear. She quickly got through the forest, the bog, and the whirling maelstrom.

The mermaid could see her father's castle; the torches in the great ballroom had been extinguished – they were probably all asleep. She didn't dare go to look for them, though – not when she was mute and was going to leave them forever. Her heart felt as if it would break from sorrow. She crept into the garden, took one flower from each of her sisters' flowerbeds, tossed a thousand kisses towards the castle, and swam up through the dark blue sea.

The sun had not yet risen when she saw the prince's castle and climbed the magnificent marble stairs. The moon was bright and clear. The little mermaid drank the fiery acrid drink, and it felt like a double-edged sword going through her delicate body. She fainted and lay there as if she were dead. When the sun shone down on the ocean, she awoke and felt a stinging pain. But right in front of her was the handsome young prince. He stared at her with his coal black eyes, and she lowered hers and saw that her fish tail was gone – that she had the prettiest slender white legs that any young girl could want. But she was naked, so she wrapped herself in her thick long hair.

The prince asked who she was and how she had got there. With a gentle yet sad expression, she looked at him with her dark blue eyes – she couldn't speak, of course. He held her by the hand and led her into the castle. Every step she took felt like stepping on piercing needles and sharp knives, as the sea witch had predicted, but she endured it gladly. With the prince holding her hand she moved as lightly as a bubble, and the prince and everyone was amazed by her lovely floating walk.

They dressed her in precious clothes made of silk and muslin.

She was more beautiful than anyone in the castle, but she was mute, could neither sing nor speak. Gorgeous slave girls, dressed in silk and gold, came out and sang for the prince and his royal parents. One sang more beautifully than all the rest, and the prince clapped his hands and smiled at her. Then the little mermaid felt sad, because she knew that she had once sung much more beautifully. She thought, 'Oh, if he only knew that I had given away my voice for all eternity just to be with him.'

The slave girls performed a charming, gliding dance to the most glorious music; the little mermaid lifted her beautiful white arms, rose up on the tips of her toes, and floated across the floor – dancing as no one had ever danced. Every movement made her loveliness more apparent, and her eyes spoke more deeply to the heart than the song of the slaves.

Everyone was enraptured by her dance, especially the prince, who called her his little foundling; she danced again and again, although every time her foot touched the ground, it felt as if she were stepping on sharp knives. The prince said that she should stay with him always, and she was allowed to sleep outside his door on a velvet cushion.

He had a boy's costume sewn for her, so that she could go riding with him. They rode through sweet-smelling forests, where green branches brushed against her shoulders and little birds sang behind new leaves. She climbed the highest mountains with the prince, and although her delicate feet bled so much that everyone could see it, she laughed it off and followed the prince until below them they saw clouds sailing by like a flock of birds on their way to foreign lands.

At night in the prince's castle, while everybody was asleep, the little mermaid went out onto the wide marble stairs. It cooled her burning feet to stand in the cold seawater. That was when she thought about those down there in the deep.

One night her sisters came to her, arm in arm; they sang sorrowfully as they swam above the water. She waved to them, and they recognized her and told her how unhappy she had made them. From then on they visited her every night, and one night, far out at sea, she saw her old grandmother, who had not come to the surface for many years, and she saw the sea king with his crown on his head. They stretched out their hands to her but didn't dare come as close to shore as her sisters had.

Day by day the prince grew fonder of the little mermaid. He loved her as one loves a dear sweet child, but it never occurred to him to make her his queen. Yet she had to become his wife to get an immortal soul, or else, on the morning of his wedding, she would turn into foam on the sea.

'Don't you love me more than anyone else?' the little mermaid's eyes seemed to ask when he took her in his arms and kissed her beautiful forehead.

'Yes, you're the one dearest to me,' the prince said, 'because you have the noblest heart of all. You're the one most devoted to me, and you remind me of a young girl I once saw but probably will never find again. I was aboard a ship that sank; the waves carried me ashore near a holy temple, where several young girls served. The youngest one found me on the beach and saved my life. I saw her twice – she's the only one in the world I could love. But you look like her, and you almost make me forget the picture I keep of her in my mind. She belongs to the holy temple – that explains the good luck that brought you to me. We'll never be separated!'

'He doesn't know that I saved his life,' the little mermaid thought. 'I carried him across the sea to the forest, where the temple stands. I sat there covered with foam and watched to see if someone would come. I saw the beautiful girl he loves more than me.' The little mermaid sighed deeply, because she couldn't cry. 'The girl belongs to the holy temple, he told me; she'll never come out into the world. They'll never meet again. I'm here with him – I see him every day, I'll take care of him, love him, devote my life to him.'

But then, people said, the prince was going to marry the beautiful daughter of the neighbouring king, which was why he was fitting out such a splendid ship. They said that the prince was going to visit the neighbour king's country but that really he was going to see the king's daughter. He took along a large entourage.

The little mermaid shook her head and laughed. She knew the prince's thoughts much better than all the rest of them.

'I have to leave,' he had said to her. 'I have to meet the beautiful princess. My parents insist on it, but they won't make me bring her back as my bride – I can't love her! She doesn't look like the beautiful girl in the temple that you remind me of. When I have to choose a bride some day, it's much more likely to be you, my silent foundling with the eloquent eyes.' He kissed her red mouth, played with her long hair, and laid his head against her heart, so that she dreamed about human happiness and an immortal soul.

'You're not the least bit afraid of the sea, my silent child,' he said, when they were aboard the great ship that was going to take him to the neighbour king's land. He told her about stormy seas and dead calm, about strange fish in the deep, and what divers had seen. She smiled at his tale, because of course she knew a lot more than anyone about the bottom of the sea.

During the moonlit night, when everyone slept except for the officer who stood at the helm, the mermaid sat by the ship's railing and stared down through the clear water, imagining that she saw her father's palace. On the top floor her old grandmother, wearing a silver crown on her head, was staring at the ship's bow through the rushing water. Then her sisters came to the surface; they stared at her sadly and wrung their white hands. She waved to them, smiled, and wanted to tell them that she was happy and everything was going well. But the cabin boy approached her, and her sisters dived down so that he would think that the whiteness he had seen was foam on the sea.

The next morning the ship sailed into the harbour of the neighbour king's magnificent city. All the church bells rang, and from high towers trumpeters played fanfares, while soldiers passed by with waving banners and gleaming bayonets. There were celebrations every day – parties and balls, one after another. But the princess had not come yet. She was being taught in a holy temple far away, people said; she was learning all the royal virtues. Finally, she arrived.

The little mermaid stood there, eager to see the princess's beauty, and she had to admit that she had never seen anyone so lovely. Her skin was soft and smooth, and a pair of deep blue, loving eyes smiled behind her long dark eyelashes.

'It's you!' the prince said, 'you who saved me when I lay half-dead by the shore.' He held his blushing bride tightly in his arms. 'Oh, I'm far too happy!' he said to the little mermaid. 'The best thing that I ever dared to hope for has been granted to me. You will be happy that I'm so happy, because you love me best of all.'

The little mermaid kissed his hand and felt that her heart was ready to break. His wedding morning, of course, would mean her death, and she would turn into foam on the sea.

The church bells rang, and heralds rode through the streets and announced the engagement. On every altar sweet-scented oil burned in precious silver lamps; priests swung their censers, and the bride and bridegroom held each other's hands and received the bishop's blessing. The little mermaid, dressed in silk and gold, held the bride's train. But her ears didn't hear the festive music, her eyes didn't see the holy ceremony. She thought about the night of her death and about everything in this world that she had lost.

That very evening the bride and bridegroom went aboard the ship. Cannons boomed, flags waved, and in the middle of the ship was a grand tent of purple and gold, with the finest cushions. That was where the newlyweds were to sleep in the silent cool night.

The sails swelled in the wind, and the ship glided smoothly over the glassy sea.

When it got dark, lamps in many colours were lit, and the sailors danced merry reels on deck. The little mermaid couldn't help thinking about the first time she had swum up through the ocean and seen the same splendour and gaiety. She whirled into the dance, gliding like a swallow when it's being pursued. Everyone cheered and applauded with admiration. She had never danced so gloriously. It was as if sharp knives were cutting her delicate feet, but she didn't feel it; the pain that pierced her heart was far worse. She knew that this was the last night that she would see the prince – the one for whom she had left her family and her home, given up her beautiful voice, and suffered endless torment every day without his knowing it. It was the last night that she would breathe the same air as he, that she would see the deep ocean and the starry blue sky. Eternal night, without thoughts or dreams, awaited her, she who didn't have a soul and could not win one. Aboard the ship merriment and celebration continued long past midnight. The mermaid laughed and danced, her heart filled with thoughts of death. The prince kissed his lovely bride, and she played with his black hair. Arm in arm, they went to rest in the magnificent tent.

The ship fell silent and still; only the officer stood by the helm. The little mermaid rested her white arms on the railing and looked for dawn in the east, knowing that the sun's first ray would kill her. Then she saw her sisters rise out of the sea. They were as pale as she was; their long beautiful hair no longer waved in the wind. It had been cut off.

'We gave it to the witch so she could help you, so that you don't have to die tonight. She gave us a knife – here it is. Do you see how sharp? Before the sun rises, you must stab the prince's heart with it. When his warm blood spatters on your feet, they'll grow together into a fish tail, and you'll become a mermaid again, dive into the water with us, and live your three hundred years before you turn into dead salty foam on the sea. Hurry up – he or you must die before the sun rises. Our old grandmother is so grief-stricken that her white hair has fallen out, just as ours fell to the witch's scissors. Kill the prince and come back! Hurry – do you see the red streak in the sky? In just a few minutes the sun will rise, and you will die.' They let out a strangely deep sigh and sank down into the waves.

The little mermaid pulled aside the tent's purple curtain and saw the beautiful bride asleep with her head on the prince's chest. She bent down, kissed his handsome forehead, and looked up, where the red sky of morning became brighter and brighter.

Then she looked at the sharp knife and fastened her eyes again on the prince, who, as he dreamed, said his bride's name aloud. She was the only one in his thoughts. The knife trembled in the mermaid's hand – but then she threw it far out into the waves, which glowed red where it fell, and it looked as if drops of blood were bubbling up through the water. Once more she looked at the prince, her eyes dying, and then she leaped from the ship into the sea and felt her body dissolve into foam.

The sun rose from the sea, its rays falling with mildness and warmth on the dead-cold sea foam. The little mermaid did not feel death; she saw the bright sun, and hundreds of beautiful transparent beings floated above her. She could see them through the ship's white sail and the red clouds in the sky. Their voices were a melody, but so spirit-like that no human ear could hear them, just as no earthly eye could see them. They soared through the air without wings, on their own lightness. The little mermaid saw that she had a body like theirs; it rose higher and higher from the foam.

'To whom am I coming?' she asked, and her voice sounded like the other beings', so spirit-like that no earthly music could sound like it.

'To the daughters of the air,' the others replied. 'A mermaid has no immortal soul and can never get one unless she wins the love of a human being. Her eternal life depends on another power. The daughters of the air don't have immortal souls, either, but they can earn them through their good deeds. We fly to hot countries where warm pestilential air kills people; we fan in coolness there. We spread the scent of flowers through the air and bring relief and healing. When we've struggled for three hundred years to do what good we can, we'll get an immortal soul as people do and enjoy eternal happiness. You poor little mermaid – you've struggled with your entire heart for the same thing we have. You've suffered and endured, and you've come to the world of spirits of the air. By doing good deeds, you too can win an immortal soul in three hundred years.'

The little mermaid lifted her clear arms towards God's sun, and for the first time she felt tears.

On the ship noise and life had returned; the mermaid saw that the prince and his beautiful bride were looking for her, staring sadly at the frothy foam, as if they knew that she had thrown herself into the waves. The mermaid, invisible, kissed the bride's forehead, smiled to the prince, and, with the other children of the air, rose into the pink clouds, which sailed across the sky.

'In three hundred years we will sail like that into God's kingdom.'

'We might get there sooner,' one of them whispered. 'We float invisibly into people's houses, where children live. Every time we find a good child who makes his parents happy and deserves their love, God will shorten our trials. A child won't know when we fly through the room, but if we can smile with joy at the child, a year will be taken away from the three hundred. But when we see a naughty and mean child, it makes us cry tears of sorrow – and every tear adds a day to our trials.'

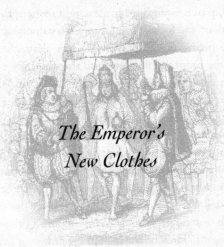

The Emperor's
New Clothes

Many years ago there was an emperor who was so fond of beautiful new clothes that he spent all his money on being stylishly dressed. He didn't care about his soldiers or about the theatre, and he didn't enjoy going out unless he could show off his new clothes. He had an outfit for every hour of the day, and just as people say that 'the king is in a meeting', in his case people always said, 'The emperor is in his closet.'

In the big city where the emperor lived there were lots of amusements and many foreign visitors. One day two swindlers arrived. They pretended to be weavers and said they knew how to make the most wonderful cloth that anyone could imagine. Not only were the colours and patterns unusually beautiful, but the clothes made from this material had the amazing quality of being invisible to anyone who was no good at his job or to people who were just stupid.

'Clothes like that would be wonderful,' the emperor thought. 'If I wore them, I'd find out which men in my kingdom weren't cut out for their work, and I'd know who was clever and who was stupid. Yes, indeed, they've got to weave that cloth for me right away!' He gave the two impostors lots of money so that they could get started.

They set up two looms and pretended to work. But there was nothing at all on the loom. Right away, they demanded the finest silk and the purest gold. They stuffed this into their bags and worked on the empty looms late into the night.

'I wonder how far they've got with the fabric,' the emperor thought, but he felt a little uneasy when he considered that stupid people, or people unsuited for their jobs, could not see it. Of course, he thought, he had no reason to worry, but first he wanted to send someone to find out how things were going. Everyone in town knew what strange power the cloth possessed, and everyone was eager to learn how incompetent or dim-witted his neighbours were.

'I'm going to send my honest old minister to the weavers,' the emperor thought. 'He'll be the best judge of how it looks, because he's intelligent and no one is better at his job than he is.'

The kindly old minister went to the room where the two swindlers were working on the empty loom. 'Good lord,' the old minister thought, opening his eyes wide. 'I can't see anything!' But he didn't say that out loud.

The swindlers invited him to come closer and asked if he didn't agree that it was a beautiful pattern with lovely colours. They pointed to the empty loom, and the poor old minister opened his eyes even wider. But he could not see anything, because there was nothing to see. 'Oh, my lord,' he thought. 'Could I possibly be stupid? I never thought so. No one must know. Am I incompetent? I'm afraid to admit that I can't see the cloth.'

'Hmm, you're not saying anything,' the man at the loom said.

'Oh, it's pretty – quite charming,' the old minister said and looked through his glasses. 'That pattern – those colours! Oh, yes, I'll tell the emperor how much I like it.'

'Ah, we're glad to hear that,' both weavers said and went on to speak about the colours and the mysterious design. The old minister listened carefully, because he had to repeat what they'd said when he returned to the emperor. And that was what he did.

The swindlers demanded more money and more silk and gold that they needed for their weaving. They pocketed all of it. There wasn't a scrap on the loom, but they kept working with the empty loom as they had before.

Soon the emperor sent another gentle bureaucrat to find out how the weaving was going and whether the fabric was close to being finished. Like the minister before him, he looked and looked, but because there was nothing on the loom, he couldn't see anything.

'Isn't that a beautiful piece of material?' both swindlers asked, and they described the lovely pattern that didn't exist at all.

'I'm not stupid,' the man thought. 'It must be that I'm not good at my job. It's quite odd – but one can't let on.' He praised the cloth that he could not see and said how pleased he was with the pretty colours and the exquisite design. 'It's ravishing,' he told the emperor.

Everybody in town talked about the wondrous cloth.

Then the emperor wanted to see it for himself, while it was still on the loom. Accompanied by a host of distinguished men – among them, the two kindly old officials who had been there before – he approached the sly impostors. They were weaving as fast as they could but without any yarn or thread.

'Isn't it *magnifique?*' both kindly officials said. 'Won't it please Your Majesty to see such patterns, such colours?' They pointed to the empty loom, because they were sure that the others could see the cloth.

'What on earth!' the emperor thought. 'I can't see anything. This is terrible. Am I stupid? Am I not qualified to be the emperor? This is the worst thing that could happen to me.'

Then the emperor said, 'Oh, it's very beautiful. It has my very highest approval.' And he nodded with satisfaction and regarded the empty loom. He didn't want to say that he couldn't see anything. The entire entourage, the one that he had brought along, looked and looked but saw no more than the rest of them. Still, like the emperor, they said, 'Oh, it's very beautiful.' They advised him to wear his splendid new outfit for the first time in the big parade that was coming up. They were all very pleased, and their praise went from mouth to mouth: 'It's *magnifique*, charming, excellent!' The emperor gave each swindler a medal to hang from his buttonhole and the title of Knight of the Loom.

The night before the parade the two swindlers stayed up, working in the light of more than sixteen candles. People could see that they were busy finishing the emperor's new clothes. They pretended to take the fabric from the loom; they cut the air with big scissors; they sewed with a needle that had no thread, and in the end they said, 'See, now the clothes are finished.'

The emperor himself arrived with his most distinguished lords-in-waiting, and each swindler held up an arm, as if lifting something, and said, 'Look, here are the trousers. Here's the coat. And here's the cape,' and so on. 'It's as light as a spider web, as if you had nothing on. But that's what makes it so special.'

'Yes,' all the lords-in-waiting said, but they couldn't see anything, because there was nothing to see.

'May we most graciously ask Your Imperial Majesty to please take off his clothes?' the swindlers asked. 'Then we'll help you into the new ones – over here, in front of the big mirror.'

The emperor took off all his clothes, and the charlatans acted as if they were handing him each piece of the new costume that they were supposed to have made. They reached around his waist, as if attaching something – it was his train – and the emperor looked at himself, front and back, in the mirror.

'That looks really good on you, it fits so beautifully,' they all said. 'What pattern, what colour! It's a priceless outfit.'

'They're waiting outside with the canopy to shade Your Majesty during the parade,' the chief master of the ceremonies said.

'I'm all ready,' the emperor announced. 'Doesn't it fit well?' He turned once more in front of the mirror to suggest that he was really looking at himself in all his finery.

The lords-in-waiting, who were supposed to carry the train, fumbled along the floor, as if they were picking it up; they walked along, holding the air, and they dared not let on that they couldn't see a thing.

So the emperor walked in the parade under the beautiful canopy, and all the people in the street and in the windows said, 'Oh, my, aren't the emperor's new clothes magnificent? What a beautiful train on his coat! How divinely it fits.' No one would admit that he couldn't see anything, because then he'd either be no good at his job or else very stupid. None of the emperor's other clothes had ever been such a success.

'But he hasn't got anything on!' a little child said.

'Dear me, listen to that innocent voice,' the child's father said, and people whispered to one another what the child had said: 'But he's got nothing on – a little child says he's got nothing on.'

'He's really got nothing on!' everybody finally shouted. The emperor cringed, because he realized that they were right. But this is what he thought: 'I must see this through.' He walked ever more proudly, and the lords-in-waiting walked behind him, carrying the train that wasn't there at all.

The Wild Swans

Far away, where the swallows go when it's winter here, there lived a king who had eleven sons and one daughter, Elisa. The eleven brothers – they were princes – went to school with stars on their chests and swords at their sides. They wrote on gold slates with diamond pencils and knew their lessons inside and out. You knew right away that they were princes. Elisa, their sister, sat on a little stool made of mirrored glass and had a picture book that cost half the kingdom.

Those children really had a good life, but it wouldn't always be like that.

Their father, who was king of the whole country, married an evil queen, who was not the least bit nice to the poor children. They noticed that from the first day. During the wedding festivities at the castle, the children played Company's Coming. They were used to getting all the cakes and baked apples that they could eat, but this time the queen gave them only sand in a teacup and told them to pretend.

A week later the queen took Elisa away to live with some peasants in the country. It didn't take long for the queen to get the king to believe so many things about the poor princes that he just didn't like them any more.

'Fly out into the world and take care of yourselves,' the evil queen told the princes. 'Fly away as big silent birds.' But she couldn't hurt them as much as she had wanted to, and they turned into eleven beautiful wild swans. With a strange cry they flew away, out of the castle windows, above the park and the forest.

It was still early in the morning when they reached the peasant's little house, where their sister, Elisa, slept. As they hovered over the roof, they turned their long necks and beat their wings, but no one heard or saw them. They had to leave again – way up to the clouds, far out in the wide world, and into a big dark forest that reached all the way to the shore.

Inside the peasants' house poor Elisa played with a green leaf – she didn't have any other toys. She poked a hole in the leaf and peered through it at the sun; it was like seeing her brothers' bright eyes. When the sun's warm rays shone on her cheek, she thought about all their kisses.

One day was just like the next. The wind blew through the large rose hedges outside the house and whispered to the roses, 'Who could possibly be more beautiful than you?' The roses shook their heads and replied, 'Elisa.' On Sundays, when the old wife sat in the doorway and read her hymnbook, the wind turned the pages and said to the book, 'Who could be more devout than you?' 'Elisa,' the hymnbook replied. What the roses and hymnbook said was definitely true.

When Elisa was fifteen, she had to go home. When the queen saw how beautiful Elisa had become, she became angry and full of hate. She wanted to change Elisa into a wild swan just like her brothers, but she was afraid to do it straight away, because the king of course wanted to see his daughter.

Early in the morning the queen went to the baths, which were made of marble and decorated with soft cushions and the most beautiful carpets. She took three toads, kissed them, and said to the first one, 'Hop onto Elisa's head when she gets into the bath, so she'll be as sluggish as you.'

'Hop onto her forehead,' the queen told the second toad, 'so she'll be as ugly as you and her father won't recognize her.'

'Lie down by her heart,' she whispered to the third one, 'and let her become so mean-spirited that she torments herself.'

Then the queen put the toads into the clear water, which immediately turned greenish. She called Elisa, undressed her, and let her step into the bath. As Elisa soaked herself, one toad climbed into her hair, another onto her forehead, and the third onto her chest. But Elisa didn't seem to notice. As soon as she stood up, three red poppies floated on the water. If the toads had not been poisonous and the witch had not kissed them, they would have been turned into red roses. But by resting on Elisa's head and heart, at least they turned into flowers. She was too devout and too innocent for the spell to have any power over her.

When the evil queen saw what had happened, she rubbed Elisa with walnut juice until she turned dark brown. She spread stinky ointment on her pretty face, and let her beautiful hair get matted. It was impossible to recognize the beautiful Elisa, and her father became quite frightened when he saw her and said that she wasn't his daughter. No one but the watchdog and the swallows wanted anything to do with her, but they were lowly animals and didn't matter.

Poor Elisa cried and thought about her eleven brothers, who were gone. Downhearted, she crept out of the castle and walked all day through fields and fens, into the great forest. She had no idea where to go. But she felt sad and longed for her brothers, who had probably been driven away too. She wanted to find them.

Elisa had been in the forest for only a short time before night fell, and she had walked far away from roads and paths. She lay down on the soft moss, said her evening prayers, and leaned her head against a tree stump. It was quiet, the air was very mild, and scattered around in the grass and on the moss were more than a hundred glowworms, shining like green fire. When she gently touched a branch with her hand, the shining insects fell like shooting stars.

All night long she dreamed about her brothers: once more they played like children; they wrote on golden slates with diamond pencils and looked at the beautiful picture book that cost half a kingdom. But they didn't just draw circles and lines as they had once done – they wrote about their most daring deeds and everything that they had seen and been through. Everything was alive in the picture book; birds sang, and people walked out of the book and talked to Elisa and her brothers. But when she turned the page, they jumped back in so that the pictures wouldn't get mixed up.

When Elisa woke up, the sun was already high in the sky. She couldn't actually see it, because the tall trees spread their dense branches, and the sun's rays flickered through the trees like glistening golden gauze. There was a fresh smell of green, and birds were just about to settle on her shoulders. She heard the sound of splashing water – lots of large springs flowing into a pond with the most beautiful sandy bottom. Thick bushes grew around the pond, but deer had made a large opening in one spot.

That's where Elisa went down to the water, which was so clear that if the wind hadn't moved the branches and bushes, she might have thought that they were painted on the bottom. Every leaf was reflected perfectly – the leaves that the sun shone through and the ones completely in the shade.

As soon as Elisa saw her own face in the water, she was frightened at how brown and ugly it was, but when she wetted her little hand and rubbed her eyes and forehead, her pale skin shone through again. She took off her clothes and went into the cool water. It would be impossible to find a more beautiful royal child in all the world.

When Elisa had dressed again and had braided her long hair, she went to the sparkling spring, drank from her cupped hands, and wandered farther into the woods without knowing where she was heading. She thought about her brothers, and about merciful God, who, she was sure, wouldn't abandon her. He had made wild apples to feed the hungry, and he showed her a wild apple tree, its branches weighed down with fruit. That was where she had her dinner. Afterwards, she propped up the branches and walked into the darkest part of the forest. It was so quiet that she heard her own footsteps – heard every little dry leaf crushed under her foot. There wasn't a bird to be seen; not a ray of sunshine could get through the huge dense branches. The tall tree trunks were so close together that when she looked straight ahead, it was as if the trunks, one after the other, were a fence that surrounded her. This was a loneliness that she had never known before.

The night became very dark; not a single glowworm glimmered on the moss. Dejected, Elisa lay down to sleep. Then, suddenly, it was as if the branches overhead opened up – and God looked at her with gentle eyes, and small angels peeped out above his head and below his arms.

When Elisa woke up in the morning, she didn't know if she had dreamed it or if it had really happened.

She had gone only a few steps when she met an old woman with a basket of berries. The old woman gave her some, and

Elisa asked if she had seen eleven princes riding through the woods.

'No,' the old woman said. 'But yesterday I saw eleven swans with gold crowns on their heads. They were floating down the river close by.'

She led Elisa a little farther until they came to a steep hillside. Down below was a winding river, where the trees on both banks stretched their long leafy branches towards each other. Wherever their limbs couldn't reach across, the trees had torn their roots out of the earth, and they leaned over the water, their branches entangled.

Elisa said goodbye to the old woman and walked along the river to where it flowed into the sea.

The beautiful ocean lay in front of the young girl, but not so much as a single sailor was out there, and there wasn't a boat to be seen. So how could she get any farther? She looked at the countless pebbles on the beach; the water had worn them round and smooth. The water had shaped pieces of glass, iron, rocks – everything that had washed up on the beach – although the water was much softer than her delicate hands. 'It keeps rolling and never gets tired, and it smooths out whatever is hard. I want to be just as untiring! Thank you for your lesson – you clear, rolling waves. My heart tells me that some day you'll take me to my dear brothers.'

Eleven white swan feathers lay on top of some seaweed that had washed ashore, and Elisa gathered them into a bouquet. There were drops of water on the feathers – whether it was dew or tears, she couldn't tell. It was lonely out there by the sea, but she didn't feel it, because the sea was constantly changing; it changed more in a few hours than lakes do in a whole year. If a big black cloud covered the sun, it was as if the sea wanted to say, 'I can also look dark,' and then the wind blew and the waves turned white. But if the clouds were red and the wind was sleeping, the sea was like a rose petal. At one moment the sea was green, then white, but no matter how quietly it rested, there was nonetheless a slight movement by the shore. The ocean swelled gently, like the chest of a sleeping child.

When the sun was about to set, Elisa saw eleven white swans with gold crowns flying towards land, one behind the other. They looked like a long white ribbon. Elisa climbed up the steep bank and hid behind a bush. The swans settled near her and flapped their great white wings.

As the sun disappeared into the sea, the swans' feathers suddenly dropped away, and there stood eleven handsome princes – Elisa's brothers. She let loose a loud scream, because although they had changed a lot, she knew it was them – and felt that it *must* be them. She jumped into their arms and called them by name; they were overjoyed when they recognized their little sister, now so grown-up and beautiful. They laughed and cried, and soon they learned from each other what their stepmother had done to all of them.

'We brothers,' the oldest said, 'are wild swans as long as the sun is up. When it sets, we get our human shape back. That's why we always have to make sure that we have solid ground underfoot when the sun sets. If we were flying among the clouds, we would, as human beings, plunge into the deep. We can't stay here, but there's a country as beautiful as this one on the other side of the ocean. It's a long distance. We have to cross the big ocean, and there are no islands on the way where we can stay for the night – only a solitary little rock juts up in the middle of the sea. It's just big enough for us to rest on side by side, and when the sea is rough, the water sprays high above us.

'Still, we thank God for that spot where we can spend the night in our human shape. Without that rock we could never visit our beloved native land because it takes the two longest days of the year to fly here. We can visit the home of our ancestors only once a year, and we daren't stay here more than eleven days. That's when we can fly over the big forest and see the castle where we were born, where our father lives, and see the tower of the church where our mother is buried. Here it feels as if the trees and bushes are part of us. Here the wild horses run across the plains, as we saw when we were children. Here's where the charcoal maker sings the old songs that we danced to as children. This is our country – it draws us and we've found you here, you dear little sister. We can stay for another two days – then we have to go away across the sea to the beautiful country. But it's not *our* country. How can we take you with us? We have neither ship nor boat.'

'How could I save you?' the sister asked.

They talked the whole night through and slept for only a few hours.

Elisa woke up at the sound of swans' wings, which whooshed above her. Her brothers were transformed again, and they flew around in large circles until at last they were gone. But one of them – the youngest – stayed behind; the swan put his head in her lap, and she patted his white wings. They stayed together all day. Towards evening the others came back, and when the sun went down, they stood in their human shapes.

'Tomorrow we fly away – we don't dare return for a whole year. But we can't leave you like this. Are you brave enough to come too? If my arm is strong enough to carry you through the forest, wouldn't all our wings be strong enough to carry you across the ocean?'

'Yes, take me with you!' Elisa said.

They spent the whole night braiding supple willow bark and tough rush into a net, which they made big and strong. Elisa lay down on it, and when the sun came out and the brothers were transformed into wild swans, they took hold of the net with their beaks and flew high up towards the clouds with their beloved sister, who was still sleeping. Because the sun's rays shone right in her face, one of the swans flew above her head to shade her with his wide wings.

They were far from land when Elisa woke up. She thought that she was still dreaming – that's how odd it was for her to be carried across the sea, high up in the sky. A branch with delicious ripe berries lay by her side, along with a bunch of tasty roots. The youngest brother had gathered them and put them beside her, and Elisa smiled gratefully to him because she knew he was flying above and shading her with his wings.

They were so high up that the first ship that they saw below looked like a white seagull floating on the water. A large cloud rose behind them. It was as big as a mountain, and as they flew, Elisa saw her shadow, and the shadows of the eleven swans, looking enormous against it. It was a more glorious picture than anything she'd ever seen. But as the sun rose higher, and the cloud fell farther behind, the floating shadow picture disappeared.

They flew all day, like an arrow rushing through the air. Yet they moved more slowly than usual now that they had to carry their sister. Bad weather threatened; evening approached, and with dread Elisa saw the sun set. There was still no sign of the solitary rock in the ocean, and it seemed to Elisa that the swans beat their wings faster and faster. She felt that it was her fault that they couldn't travel fast enough; when the sun was down, the swans would become humans, plunge into the sea, and drown. She prayed to God with all her heart, but she still couldn't see the rock. The black cloud was coming closer, and strong gusts of wind warned of a storm. Clouds gathered in a single huge, threatening wall that rushed ahead, as solid as lead. Lightning bolts flashed.

The sun had reached the edge of the ocean. Elisa's heart fluttered with fear. The swans dived down so fast that she thought they were falling. But they floated again. The sun was halfway into the water, and that was when she spotted the rock below. It looked no bigger than a seal poking its head out of the water. The sun set so rapidly that now it was no bigger than a star. When her foot touched solid ground, the sun was gone, like the last ember of burning paper. Elisa saw her brothers standing around her, arm in arm, and the rock had just enough room for all of them. The sea crashed against the rock and drenched them like a rain shower. The sky glowed with fiery flashes, and rolling thunder crashed, but Elisa and her brothers held hands and sang a hymn that gave them comfort and courage.

By dawn the air was clear and still; as soon as the sun rose, the swans flew with Elisa from the tiny island. The sea was still rough, and from far up in the air the white foam on the dark green sea looked like a million swans floating on the water.

When the sun rose higher, Elisa saw a mountain range shimmering in the air. Its peaks were covered with ice, and in the middle was a castle that might be miles long, with rows of audacious colonnades, one on top of the other. Forests of palm trees swayed down below, and she saw gaudy flowers as big as mill wheels. Elisa asked if that was the country where they were going; the swans shook their heads, because what she saw was Fata Morgana's beautiful, ever-changing castle in the air, and they didn't dare take a person there. As Elisa stared at it, the mountains, the forests, and the castle disintegrated, and in their place were twenty stately churches, which all looked alike, with tall towers and pointed windows. She thought that she could hear the sound of an organ, but it was only the sea. When she was very close to the churches, they became a whole flotilla sailing towards her; she looked down, but what she saw was sea mist rushing across the water. Everything was constantly changing in front of her, and then, finally, she saw the actual country where she was going. Beautiful blue mountains with cedar forests, cities, and castles rose up in front of her. Long before the sun set, she sat on a mountain slope by a large cave. It was covered with delicate green creepers that looked like embroidered tapestries.

'Let's see what you'll dream about here tonight,' the youngest brother said and showed her the bedchamber.

'Oh, I wish I could dream how to rescue you,' she said. She thought about it all the time. She prayed to God and asked for his help, and she continued to pray even when she was asleep. It seemed to her that she was flying far up, to Fata Morgana's castle in the clouds. A fairy, beautiful and dazzling, came out to meet her, but at the same time she looked just like the old woman in the woods who had given her berries and told her about the swans with gold crowns.

'Your brothers can be saved,' she said, 'but do you have the courage and perseverance that it takes? The sea may be softer than your delicate hands, but it can still change the shape of hard stones; the sea doesn't feel the pain that your fingers will feel. The sea doesn't have a heart and doesn't have to suffer the fear and anguish that you'll have to endure. Do you see this stinging nettle I'm holding in my hand? Lots of these grow around the cave where you sleep. You can only use those – and the ones that grow on the graves in the churchyard. Don't forget! You have to pick them even though they'll burn blisters on your skin. Crush the nettles with your feet, and you'll get flax; you have to spin and weave the flax into eleven armoured shirts with long sleeves. When you throw the shirts over the eleven wild swans, the spell will be broken. But remember: from the moment you begin this task until the moment it's done – even if it takes years – you must not speak. The first word you utter will pierce your brothers' hearts like a deadly knife. Their lives depend on your silence. Remember everything I have said.'

At that moment she touched Elisa's hand with the nettle. It was like burning fire, and it woke her up. The day was bright, and close to where Elisa had been sleeping was a nettle like the one she had seen in her dream. She fell to her knees, thanked God, and left the cave to begin her work.

She took hold of the horrible nettles with her soft hands; they felt like flames and left big blisters on her hands and arms. But she suffered it gladly, if only she could save her beloved brothers. She crushed every nettle with her bare feet, and spun the green flax.

When the sun had set, her brothers returned; they were alarmed at finding Elisa so quiet. They thought that their wicked stepmother had cast another spell. When they saw her hands, they understood what she was doing for their sake. Her youngest brother cried, and where his tears fell, she felt no pain and the burning blisters disappeared.

She worked all through the night, because she could not rest until she had rescued her dear brothers. The next day, while the swans were away, she sat alone, yet time had never passed so swiftly. The first shirt was already done, and she started the next one.

Hunting horns sounded in the mountains. It frightened Elisa. The sound came closer; she heard dogs barking. Terrified, she went into her cave; she tied the nettles that she had gathered and hackled, put them in a bundle, and sat down on it.

Suddenly, a big dog jumped out from the brush and one right after that and then another. They barked loudly, ran off, and came back again. Soon hunters were standing outside the cave. The most handsome among them was the king of the country. He approached Elisa – he had never seen a more beautiful girl.

'How did you get here, you beautiful child?' he asked. Elisa shook her head, for of course she was afraid to talk; her brothers' lives and freedom were at stake. She hid her hands so that the king could not see what she was forced to endure.

'Follow me,' he said. 'You can't stay here. If you're as good as you are beautiful, I'll dress you in silk and velvet, put a gold crown on your head, and you'll live in my grandest castle.' He lifted her onto his horse. She wept and wrung her hands, but the king said, 'I only want you to be happy. The day will come when you'll thank me.' Then he hurried off between the mountains, holding Elisa in front of him on his horse, with the hunting party galloping behind.

By the time the sun went down, the magnificent royal city, with churches and domes, lay in front of them. The king led Elisa into the castle, where huge fountains were splashing inside enormous marble halls, and the walls and ceilings were lavishly covered with paintings. But she hardly noticed; she cried and grieved. She didn't resist when women dressed her in royal robes, braided pearls into her hair, and pulled thin gloves over her burned fingers.

When she stood there in all her splendour, she was so blindingly beautiful that the entire court bowed even deeper for her. The king chose her as his bride, although the archbishop shook his head and whispered that the beautiful girl from the woods was probably a witch who dazzled their eyes and had stolen the king's heart.

But the king didn't listen. He ordered the music to play, the most delicious food to be brought, and the loveliest girls to dance. Elisa was led through fragrant gardens and into majestic halls. But there was no smile on her lips or in her eyes – just sorrow, as if that were her everlasting inheritance. The king opened a small room, close to where she was supposed to sleep. It was decorated with priceless green tapestries and looked exactly like the cave where she had lived. The bundle of flax that she had spun from the nettles lay on the floor, and under the ceiling hung the armoured shirt that she had finished knitting. One of the hunters had brought all this along as a curiosity.

'Here you can dream yourself back to your former home,' the king said. 'Here's the work that kept you busy. In the midst of all this splendour, it will amuse you to think about that time.'

When Elisa saw these things that were so close to her heart, a smile played on her lips and colour returned to her cheeks. She thought about rescuing her brothers and kissed the king's hand. He pressed her to his heart and let the church bells announce the wedding feast. The beautiful mute girl from the wood was to be the queen of the land.

The archbishop whispered dark words into the king's ear, but they didn't reach his heart; the wedding would go forward. The archbishop himself had to place the crown on Elisa's head, and he maliciously pushed it down over her forehead until it hurt. Yet her heart hurt more – from sorrow for her brothers – and she didn't feel the pain in her body. Her lips were silent, for of course a single word would end her brothers' lives, but her eyes shone with deep love for the good handsome king who had done everything to make her happy. Every day she became more devoted to him. If only she dared to confide in him, tell him about her suffering, but she had to stay silent and silently finish her work. At night she crept from the king's side, went into her own little room, which was decorated like the cave, and finished knitting one armoured shirt after another. But when she began the seventh shirt, she had no more flax.

She knew that the nettles she needed grew in the churchyard. But she had to pick them herself, and how was she going to get there?

'What is the pain in my fingers compared to the agony in my heart?' she thought. 'I have to risk it – God won't let me down.' Fearfully, as if she were about to commit an evil deed, she sneaked out into the moonlit night, went down to the garden, and walked along tree-lined promenades into the empty streets towards the churchyard. There, on one of the widest gravestones, she saw a circle of vulture-like demons – hideous witches. They removed their rags as if they were about to bathe; then with long bony fingers they dug down into the fresh graves, pulled out the corpses, and ate their flesh. Elisa had to pass close by. They fastened their evil eyes on her, but she said her prayers, gathered the stinging nettles, and carried them back to the castle.

Only one person had seen her – the archbishop. He was awake while others slept. Now he knew that he was right to have suspected her; something about the queen wasn't right. She was a witch, and that was how she had beguiled the king and his people.

In the confessional the archbishop told the king what he had seen and what he feared. As those harsh words passed his lips, the carved images of saints shook their heads as if to say it's not so, Elisa is innocent! But the archbishop had another explanation; he thought that they were bearing witness against her and that they shook their heads at her sin. Two heavy tears rolled down the king's cheeks, and he went home, his heart filled with doubt. He pretended to sleep at night, but he never really rested; he sensed Elisa getting up night after night. Each time he followed her quietly and saw her disappear into her little room.

Every day he looked grimmer, but Elisa couldn't understand why. Still, she noticed it, and it worried her – and how she suffered for her brothers already. Her salty tears fell onto royal purple velvet, lying there like glistening diamonds, and everyone who saw all that rich splendour wished that they could be queen.

Soon Elisa would be done with her work; she had only one armoured shirt left to finish. But she had no more flax nor a single nettle. So once more – one last time – she had to go to the churchyard to pick a handful or two. With dread she thought about her solitary journey and the horrible witches. But her determination was as firm as her trust in God.

Elisa left, but the king and the archbishop followed. They saw her disappear behind the iron gate to the churchyard; when they approached the gate, the vulture-like demons were sitting on the gravestone, as they had when Elisa saw them. The king turned away because he imagined Elisa among those creatures – Elisa, whose head had rested on his chest that very evening.

'The people must judge her,' the king said, and the people passed judgment: 'She must burn in the fiery flames.'

Elisa was taken from the grand royal halls to a dark, damp cell where the wind whistled through barred windows. Instead of velvet and silk, they gave her the bundle of nettles that she had collected. That was where she was to rest her head. The rough stinging armoured shirts that she had knitted served as covers and blankets. But they could not have given her anything more precious. She started to work again and prayed to God. Outside, boys in the street sang mocking songs about her. Not a soul comforted her with a kind word.

Towards evening the whoosh of a swan's wing passed close by the iron bars. It was the youngest brother – he had found their sister. She sobbed with joy, although she knew that the next night would be her last night alive. Still, her work was almost done, and her brothers were here.

The archbishop arrived to spend the last hour with her, for that's what he had promised the king. But she shook her head, and with looks and gestures she begged him to go away. This was the night that she had to finish her work or else it would all have been in vain – everything, the pain, the tears, the sleepless nights. The archbishop went away, cursing her, but poor Elisa knew that she was innocent and continued her work.

Small mice ran across the floor; they dragged the nettles to her feet to help, if only a little. A thrush alighted by the bars of the window and sang all night, as cheerfully as it could, so that she wouldn't lose courage.

It was barely daybreak; the sun wouldn't rise for another hour. Her eleven brothers were already standing by the gate of the castle, demanding to be taken to the king. But that was impossible, they were told; after all, it was night still, the king was asleep, and no one dared wake him. They pleaded, they threatened; the guard arrived and even the king came out and asked what this was all about. At that instant the sun rose and the brothers were gone – but eleven wild swans flew above the castle.

Everybody streamed out of the city gate. They wanted to see the witch burn. An emaciated horse pulled the cart. Elisa had been dressed in a smock of coarse burlap; her beautiful long hair was untied and hung loosely around her lovely face. Her cheeks were pale as death; her lips moved softly, while her fingers twisted the green flax. Even on the way to her death, she didn't let go of the work that she had started. Ten armoured shirts lay by her feet; she was still knitting the eleventh. The mob jeered.

'Look at the witch, how she mumbles! She doesn't even have a hymnbook in her hands – she's sitting there, working on her loathsome witchcraft. Rip it away from her – in a thousand pieces!'

They pushed forward against her, wanting to destroy the shirt. But then eleven swans appeared. They settled around her on the cart and beat their huge wings. The frightened mob fell back.

'It's a sign from heaven – she must be innocent!' many of them whispered, but they didn't dare to say it out loud.

Now the executioner grabbed her hand. Quickly, she threw the eleven shirts over the swans – and there stood eleven handsome princes. But instead of one arm, the youngest had a swan's wing, because a sleeve in his armoured shirt was missing; she hadn't finished it.

'Now I can speak!' she said. 'I'm innocent.'

When people saw what happened, they bowed in front of her,

as they would for a saint. But she collapsed lifelessly in her brothers' arms. That's what the strain, the fear, and the pain had done to her.

'Yes, she's innocent,' the oldest brother said, and he told them everything that had happened. While he spoke, there was a sweet smell as if from a million roses, because every log on the stake had taken root and grown branches. They had become a fragrant hedge, very tall and dense with red roses. On top was a flower – white and shining and as radiant as a star. The king broke it off and put it on Elisa's chest. She woke up with peace and happiness in her heart.

Church bells rang, all by themselves, and birds came flying in great flocks. The return to the castle was a wedding procession – grander than any king had ever seen.

The Swineherd

Once there was a poor prince. He had a kingdom, which was quite small but still big enough to make him worth marrying. And marriage was what he wanted.

Of course, it was pretty bold of him to ask the emperor's daughter, 'Will you marry me?' But he wasn't afraid, because his name was known far and wide, and there were hundreds of princesses who would have said yes and thanked him too. But not her.

Now we'll hear what happens:

A rosebush grew on the grave of the prince's father – and what a lovely rosebush it was. It bloomed only every fifth year and then with just one rose, but that rose smelled so sweet that you forgot all your worries and cares. The prince also had a nightingale, which sang as if it kept every lovely melody in its throat. He wanted to give the rose and the nightingale to the princess, so he put them in big silver boxes and sent them off to her.

The emperor ordered the gifts to be carried ahead of him into the great hall where the princess was playing Company's Coming with her ladies-in-waiting. That was all they ever did, and when she saw the big boxes, she clapped her hands for joy.

'Oooh, if only it were a little pussycat!' she said. But then out came the beautiful rose.

'Oh, it's so nicely made,' all the ladies-in-waiting said.

'It's more than nice,' the emperor said. 'It's pretty.'

But the princess touched it and looked as if she were about to cry.

'Ugh, Daddy,' she complained. 'It's real.'

'Ugh,' all the ladies-in-waiting said. 'It's real.'

'Let's see what's in the other box before we get upset,' the emperor suggested, and out came the nightingale. It sang so beautifully that it was hard to find anything bad to say about it right away.

'*Superbe! Charmant!*' the ladies-in-waiting said, for all of them spoke French, one worse than the other.

'How that bird reminds me of the dear departed empress's music box,' an elderly courtier said. 'Oh, yes. It has just the same tone, the same expression.'

'Yes,' the emperor said. And then he cried like a little child.

'I refuse to believe that it's real,' the princess said.

'But it *is* a real bird!' said the messengers who had delivered it.

'Then let it fly away,' the princess said. There was no way she'd allow the prince to call on her.

But the prince didn't let that stop him. He smeared his face brown and black, pulled his cap down over his face, and knocked on the door.

'Hello, Emperor,' he said. 'Is there any chance of getting a job here at the castle?'

'Well, so many people apply,' the emperor told him. 'But let me think – I'm looking for someone to take care of the pigs. We have lots of those.'

So the prince was hired as an imperial swineherd. He got a miserable little room down by the pigpen, and that was where he had to stay. He worked all day, and by evening he had made a pretty little pot with bells around the top. As soon as the pot boiled, the bells chimed beautifully as they played the old song:

> *Ach, du lieber Augustin,*
> *Alles ist gone, gone, gone.*

But the most ingenious thing was that, as soon as you held your finger over the steaming pot, you could smell what people were cooking all over town. Now *that* was something different from a rose.

The princess went walking with all her ladies-in-waiting, and when she heard the tune, she stopped and looked very pleased; for she too could play 'Ach, du lieber Augustin'. It was the only song she knew – but she could play it with one finger.

'Oh, that's the one I know!' she said. 'He must be a cultured swineherd. Listen. Go and ask him what that instrument costs.'

So one of the ladies was obliged to go in, but first she put on her wooden clogs.

'How much do you want for that pot?' the lady-in-waiting asked.

'I want ten kisses from the princess,' the swineherd replied.

'Good lord!' the lady-in-waiting said.

'I won't take less,' the swineherd declared.

'Well, what does he say?' the princess asked.

'Oh, I really can't say,' the lady-in-waiting said. 'It's too horrible.'

'Whisper it, then.' And so she whispered.

'That's indecent!' the princess exclaimed and left right away. But she'd gone only a short distance when the bells chimed beautifully:

> *Ach, du lieber Augustin,*
> *Alles ist gone, gone, gone.*

'Listen,' the princess said. 'Ask him if he'll take ten kisses from my ladies-in-waiting.'

'No, thanks,' the swineherd said. 'Ten kisses from the princess – or I keep the pot.'

'That's really too bad,' the princess declared. 'But you have to shield me so no one can see.'

The ladies-in-waiting surrounded her, spreading out their skirts. Then the swineherd got his ten kisses, and she got the pot.

Oh, they had lots of fun! All evening and all the next day the pot boiled; they knew what people were cooking all over town, from the chamberlain's to the shoemaker's. The ladies-in-waiting danced and clapped their hands.

'We know who's going to have sweet soup and pancakes. We know who's going to have porridge and cutlets. It's so interesting.'

'Most interesting,' the mistress of the royal pantry said.

'Yes, but watch what you say, because I'm the emperor's daughter.'

'So help us,' they all said.

The swineherd, which is to say the prince – but they didn't know any better; they thought he was a genuine swineherd – didn't let a day pass without inventing something. Next he made a rattle; when you swung it, it played all the waltzes, jigs, and polkas known since the beginning of time.

'But that's *superbe*!' the princess said as she walked by. 'I've never heard a more lovely composition. Listen. Go in and ask him what that instrument costs. But I won't kiss him.'

'He wants a hundred kisses from the princess,' reported the lady who had gone to ask.

'He's crazy!' the princess said, and then she left. But when she'd gone just a short distance, she stood still. 'One must encourage the arts,' she added. 'I'm the emperor's daughter. Tell him he can have ten kisses, just like yesterday. The rest he has to get from my ladies-in-waiting.'

'But we really don't want to,' the ladies-in-waiting said.

'Nonsense,' the princess told them. 'If I can kiss him, you can too. And don't forget, I pay for your food and lodging.' So the lady-in-waiting had to go back.

'A hundred kisses from the princess,' he insisted. 'Or everybody keeps what they have.'

'Hide me!' the princess commanded. All the ladies took up their positions, and then he kissed her.

'What's that commotion down by the pigpen?' asked the emperor, who had stepped out onto the balcony. He rubbed his eyes and put on his glasses. 'It must be the ladies-in-waiting who are up to something. I'd better get down there.' He pulled on his slippers, which were actually shoes that he had flattened at the heel.

Whew! How he hurried.

As soon as he got to the pigsty, he walked very quietly. The ladies-in-waiting were so busy counting kisses to keep it honest – making sure that the swineherd didn't get too many or too few – that they didn't notice the emperor. He stood on tiptoe.

'What's *that*?' he exclaimed, when he saw that they were kissing, and he hit them on the head with his slipper just as the swineherd got his eighty-sixth kiss. 'Out!' the emperor ordered, for he was angry, and he banished both the princess and the swineherd from his empire.

There she was: the princess cried while the swineherd scolded, and the rain came pouring down.

'Oh, I'm so miserable,' the princess said. 'If only I'd married the handsome prince. I'm so unhappy.'

The swineherd went behind a tree, wiped the black and brown off his face, threw his filthy clothes away, and stepped forward in his princely outfit. He looked so handsome that the princess had to curtsy at the sight of him.

'I've got nothing but contempt for you,' he said. 'You didn't want an honest prince. You didn't understand the rose and the

nightingale, but you were willing to kiss the swineherd for a plaything. You're on your own.'

Then he went into his own kingdom, closed the door, locked it, and she was left outside to sing:

Ach, du lieber Augustin,
Alles ist gone, gone, gone.

The Nightingale

You know of course that in China, the emperor is a Chinaman, and everyone around him is Chinese. This all happened many years ago, but that's why we should listen to this story – before we forget it.

The emperor's castle was the most magnificent in the world. From top to bottom it was made of fine porcelain – so expensive, so fragile, that you really had to be careful if you touched it. You could see the most amazing flowers in the garden, and the prettiest were trimmed with silver bells that chimed so that you had to notice the flower when you went by. Yes, indeed, everything was very clever in the emperor's garden, which stretched so far that even the gardener didn't know where it ended. If you kept walking, you'd come to a delightful forest, with tall trees and deep lakes. The woods reached all the way to the ocean, which was blue and deep; great ships could sail right under the branches, and that was where a nightingale lived. It sang so joyfully that even the poor fisherman, who had so much work to do, would pause when he was pulling up his nets at night and listen to the nightingale. 'Oh, that's beautiful!' the fisherman said, but then he had to attend to his chores, and he forgot the bird. The next night, when the fisherman came out again, and the bird sang, he said the same thing, 'Oh, that's really beautiful!'

People travelled from all over the world to the emperor's city, where they admired the castle and the garden. But when they heard the nightingale sing, they said, 'That's the best of all.'

When the travellers came home, they talked about everything that they had seen. Wise men wrote many books about the city, the castle, and the garden, but they did not forget the nightingale – in fact, they mentioned it first. And poets – those who could write – wrote the most beautiful poems, all about the nightingale in the woods by the deep sea.

People all over the world read these books, and some of them even reached the emperor. He sat in his gold chair and read and read, nodding his head constantly, because he enjoyed the splendid descriptions of his city, his castle, and his garden. 'But the nightingale is the best thing of all,' the books said.

'What on earth?' the emperor asked. 'The nightingale? I've never heard of it! Is there a bird like that in my empire – even in my own garden? No one ever told me – I had to find out by reading about it.'

He called one of his courtiers, who was so refined that when someone of a lesser station dared to speak to him or ask a question, he answered only 'P!' – and that meant nothing at all.

'There's supposed to be a very remarkable bird here called a nightingale,' the emperor said. 'People say that it's the very best thing in my kingdom. Why hasn't anyone said anything about it to me?'

'I've never heard anyone talk about it,' the courtier said. 'It's never been presented at the imperial court.'

'I want it to come here tonight and sing for me,' the emperor said. 'The whole world knows what's in my kingdom – but I don't.'

'I've never heard anyone talk about it,' the courtier said again. 'But I will search for it, and I shall find it.'

But where could it be? The courtier ran up and down all the stairs, through halls and corridors, but nobody he met knew anything about the nightingale. The courtier hurried again to the emperor and said that it must be a tale dreamed up by people who write books. 'Your imperial majesty mustn't believe everything that they write. It's all made up – it's what's called the black art.'

'But the book where I read it was sent to me by the great and mighty emperor of Japan,' the emperor said. 'So it must be true. I *want* to hear the nightingale! I want it here tonight! I've granted it my highest imperial favour. If it doesn't appear, I'll have the whole court pounded on the stomach as soon they have eaten dinner.'

'*Tsing-pe!*' the courtier said, and once more he ran up and down all the stairs and through all the rooms and corridors. Half the court ran along, because the courtiers did not want to be pounded on the stomach. Everyone asked about the mysterious nightingale, the one that everyone in the world knew about but nobody at the court had heard of.

Finally they ran into a little girl in the kitchen who said, 'Oh, yes, the nightingale. I know all about it. It really can sing! Every night I'm allowed to take a few leftovers home to my poor sick mother. She lives down by the sea, and when I go home and rest in the woods, I hear the nightingale sing. I get tears in my eyes – it's just as though my mother kissed me.'

'Little kitchen maid,' the courtier said, 'I'll get you a steady job in the kitchen and permission to watch the emperor eat if you can lead us to the nightingale. It has been summoned to perform tonight.'

Then they all set out for the forest, where the nightingale usually sang; half the court came along. As they walked along, a cow began to moo.

'Oh!' the young lords said. 'There we have it. The voice is remarkable for such a little creature. I'm quite certain that I've heard it before.'

'No, it's the cows mooing,' the kitchen maid explained. 'We still have a long way to go.'

Then the frogs started to croak in the pond.

'That's lovely!' the imperial Chinese chaplain declared. 'I can hear her now – it's like little church bells.'

'No, those are frogs,' the little kitchen maid said. 'But I think we'll hear the nightingale soon.'

Then the nightingale began to sing.

'That's it,' the little girl said. 'Listen, listen – there it is.' She pointed to a little grey bird sitting in the tree.

'Really!' the courtier said. 'I never thought that the bird would look like that. It's so plain. Maybe the bird turned pale at having to meet all these distinguished people who've come to hear it.'

'Little nightingale!' the kitchen maid shouted quite loudly. 'Our gracious emperor would really like you to sing for him.'

'With the greatest pleasure,' the nightingale replied, and sang, delighting everyone.

'It sounds just like crystal bells,' the courtier said. 'And look at the exercise it's giving its throat. It's amazing that we've never heard it before. It will be a huge success at court.'

'Do you want me to sing again for the emperor?' asked the nightingale, who thought that the emperor was right there.

'My splendid little nightingale,' the courtier said. 'It's my great pleasure to summon you to a court soirée tonight, where you may enchant his imperial grace with your charming voice.'

'It sounds best in the green out-of-doors,' the nightingale said. But the bird nevertheless went along when it heard that the emperor wanted it.

The palace had been all polished up. The walls and floors, made of porcelain, glinted in the light of thousands of golden lamps. The prettiest flowers, trimmed with little bells, were in the corridors. There was a lot of running about, and the draught made all the bells ring so that you couldn't hear a word.

A gold perch for the nightingale had been set up in the centre of the great hall, where the emperor sat. The entire court was there. The little kitchen maid was allowed to stand behind the door, because she had been given the title of Real Kitchen Maid. People wore their fanciest clothes, and when the emperor nodded to the little grey bird, everyone looked at it.

Then the nightingale sang so beautifully that the emperor had tears in his eyes; tears rolled down his cheeks. When the nightingale began to sing even more beautifully, its song went straight to his heart. It made the emperor so happy that he awarded the nightingale his gold slipper, to be carried around its neck. The nightingale thanked the emperor but said that he already had his reward.

'I've seen tears in the eyes of the emperor. To me, that's the greatest treasure. The tears of an emperor have astonishing power. God knows, you've given me enough.' The nightingale then sang once more with its sweet joyful voice.

'We've never seen such sweet coquetry,' the ladies said. They filled their mouths with water so that they could cluck when someone spoke to them. They thought that they too were nightingales. Even the footmen and the chambermaids reported that they were satisfied, and that means a lot, because they are the most difficult ones to please. The nightingale was definitely a great success.

It was decided that the nightingale would remain at court and have its own cage, as well as the freedom to go outside twice a day and once at night. It was accompanied by twelve servants, each of whom held tight to a silk ribbon attached to the bird's leg. An outing like that was no fun at all.

The whole city talked about the remarkable bird. Whenever two people met, the first one needed only to say 'Night – !' before the other said 'Gale!' and then they sighed and understood each other. What's more, eleven grocers named their children after the nightingale, but every one of them had a tin ear.

One day the emperor received a big package, and on the outside was written the word *Nightingale*.

'Here's a new book about our famous bird!' the emperor declared. But it was not a book; it was a work of art. Inside a box lay an artificial nightingale; it was supposed to look like the real one, but it was covered with diamonds, rubies, and sapphires. As soon as you wound it up, it sang one of the melodies that the real one sang, and its tail went up and down, gleaming of silver and gold. Around its neck was a little ribbon that said: 'The Japanese emperor's nightingale cannot compare with the emperor of China's.'

'It's lovely,' all the courtiers said, and the person who delivered the artificial bird was immediately given the title of Supreme Imperial Nightingale Bringer. 'They must sing together – what a great duet it will be.'

So they had to sing together, but it didn't quite work because the real bird had its own style, and the artificial bird had only its mechanical parts. 'You can't blame it for that,' the imperial music master said. 'It keeps perfect time, just as I like it.' Then the artificial bird had to sing by itself. It was just as popular as the real one, but of course it was also much prettier to look at: it glittered like brooches and bracelets.

The mechanical bird sang the very same tune thirty-three times, and still it was not tired. People would have liked to hear it all over again, but the emperor thought it was time for the real bird to sing a little. Where was it? No one had noticed that the nightingale had flown through the open window, far away to its green forest.

'What's going on here?' the emperor called out. All the courtiers, sounding annoyed, thought that the nightingale was a most ungrateful creature. 'Luckily, we have the best bird,' they said, and the artificial nightingale had to sing once more. They had by now heard the same tune thirty-four times, but they did not yet know all of it by heart, because it was difficult. The imperial music master lavished praise on the bird – assured everyone that it was better than the real nightingale, not only because of its apparel with all those beautiful diamonds but also because of its inner qualities.

'You see, ladies and gentlemen – and, above all, the emperor – with the real nightingale you can never know what's going to come next, but with the artificial bird it's all set. That's the way it is, and that's the way that it's always going to be. You can explain it, you can open it up and see the human ingenuity – how the pieces are put together, how they work, and how one thing follows another.'

'My very thoughts,' they all said, and the next Sunday the music master was allowed to show the mechanical bird to the public. The people ought to hear that bird sing too, the emperor said, and they heard it. It made them as happy as if they'd got tipsy on tea. Everybody said 'Oh!' and raised a finger – the one you use to point with – and nodded their heads, which is so very Chinese. But the poor fisherman, who had heard the real nightingale, said, 'It sounds pretty enough, and it's close, but it's missing something – I don't know what.'

The real nightingale was banished from the entire imperial realm.

The mechanical bird took up its place on a silk pillow close to the emperor's bed, and it was surrounded by gifts that it had received – gold and precious stones. Its title had been upgraded to Supreme Imperial Bedside Table Singer of the First Rank to the Left, because the emperor considered the left side, where the heart lies, to be nobler, and even an emperor's heart is on the left side. The music master wrote twenty-five volumes about the mechanical bird, which were so scholarly and so lengthy and so filled with the most difficult Chinese words that everybody said that they had read them and understood every bit. Otherwise, people would think they were stupid and they would get pounded on the stomach.

A whole year went by. The emperor, the court, and all the Chinese people knew every little cluck in the song of the mechanical bird by heart – and that was precisely why they liked it so much. They could sing along, and they did. The boys in the street sang, 'Zizizi! Cluck-cluck-cluck!' and the emperor sang too. They really enjoyed it.

But one night, as the mechanical bird was singing away and the emperor lay in bed and listened, the bird went 'Boing!' Something snapped. 'Bzzzzzz!' – all the wheels spun round, and then the music stopped.

Right away, the emperor jumped out of bed and summoned his royal physician. But what good was he? Then they called for the watchmaker, and after a lot of talk and looking-into-it, he got the bird more or less mended. But he said that it could not be used too much, because the pins were very worn, and if you replaced them, the music wouldn't sound the same. It was terribly sad; they were afraid to let the mechanical bird sing more than once a year, and even that was almost too much. But the music master gave a little speech filled with difficult words and said that everything was just as good as ever, and then it *was* just as good as ever.

Five years passed, and the entire country was in mourning, because, when it came right down to it, they were all fond of their emperor. But now he was ill and not expected to live, they said. A new emperor had already been chosen, and people waited in the street and asked the courtier how their emperor was doing.

'P!' he said, and shook his head.

The emperor, cold and pale, lay in his huge magnificent bed. The entire court thought he was dead, and every one of the members ran out to greet the new emperor. The footmen hurried outside to talk about it, and the imperial servant girls gossiped over coffee. They laid cloth down on the floors in all the rooms and corridors, so that you couldn't hear anyone walking, and that was why it was so still, so very still. But the emperor was not dead yet; he lay rigid and pale in his grand bed, with its long velvet curtains and its heavy gold tassels. High above him was an open window, and the moon shone in upon the emperor and the mechanical bird.

The poor emperor could hardly breathe – it was as if something was sitting on his chest. He opened his eyes, and then he saw that it was Death, sitting on his chest. Death had put the emperor's gold crown on his head; he was holding the imperial gold sword in one hand and the emperor's grand banner in the other. All around the folds of the great velvet bed curtains were strange faces, some quite nasty-looking and others sweet and gentle. They were the emperor's good and bad deeds, which stared at him now that Death sat upon his heart.

'Do you remember that?' one after the other whispered. 'Do you remember that?' They told him so many things that sweat gushed from his forehead.

'I never knew about that,' the emperor said. 'Music, music! Bring the big Chinese drum,' he cried, 'so I can't hear what they're saying.'

They kept on, and Death nodded just like a Chinaman who knows everything that's being said.

'Music, music!' the emperor shouted. 'You sweet, blessed bird! Sing – please sing! I've given you gold and jewels, I've even hung my gold slipper around your neck, so please sing!'

But the bird didn't move. No one was there to wind it up, and without that, it couldn't sing. Death kept staring at the emperor with its large empty eye sockets, and the room was silent – terrifyingly silent.

Then all at once the most beautiful song came from just

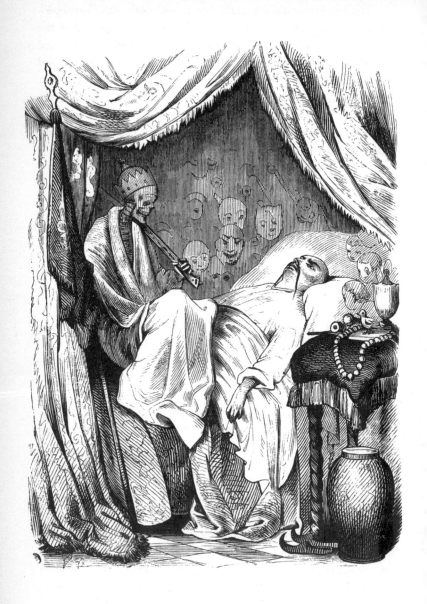

outside the window. It was the tiny nightingale – the real one – that sat there on the branch. It had heard about the emperor's suffering and had come to sing to him – to give him solace and hope. As the nightingale sang, the shapes became fainter and fainter, and blood flowed faster and faster through the emperor's weak body. Death itself listened and said, 'Keep singing, little nightingale. Keep singing!'

'Yes, if you'll give me the imperial gold sword, if you'll give me the grand banner, and if you'll give me the emperor's crown.'

Death gave up each precious object for another song, and the nightingale kept singing. It sang about the quiet churchyard where the white roses grow – where there's a scent of elderberry and fresh grass is watered by the tears of those left behind. Death began to long for his garden and drifted like a cold white fog out of the window.

'Thank you, thank you!' the emperor exclaimed. 'You heavenly little bird – I recognize you, of course. I chased you from my realm, but you sang anyway – until the evil visions and Death himself were gone from my bed and from my heart. How shall I reward you?'

'You have given me my reward,' the nightingale said. 'I saw tears in your eyes the first time that I sang – I'll never forget you. Those are the treasures that make a singer happy. But please sleep now, and get strong and well – I'll sing for you.'

Then the nightingale sang, and the emperor fell into a sweet sleep – a peaceful and refreshing sleep.

The sun was shining through the window when the emperor woke up, strong and healthy. None of his servants had yet returned, because they thought he was dead. But the nightingale was still singing.

'You must always stay with me,' the emperor said. 'You need only sing when you want to, and I'll smash the mechanical bird into a thousand pieces.'

'Don't do that,' the nightingale said. 'It has done as well as it could – and you should keep it. I can't live in your palace, but let me come for a visit when I feel like it. In the evening I'll sit on a branch outside your window and sing for you – and bring you joy and wisdom as well. I'll sing about people who are happy and people who are suffering. I'll sing about good and evil, which nobody tells you about. But a little songbird gets around – to the poor fisherman, to the farmer's house, to everyone far away from you and your court. I love your heart more than I love your crown, but still, there's something sacred about the crown. I'll come and sing for you, but you must promise me one thing.'

'Anything,' the emperor said. He stood there in his imperial robe, which he had put on, and held his heavy gold sword against his heart.

'I'll ask only one thing: don't let anyone know that a little bird tells you everything. It will all be much better that way.'

Then the nightingale flew away.

The servants came back to look at their dead emperor. Yes, there they were – and the emperor said, 'Good morning!'

The Sweethearts

The Top and the Ball shared a drawer with other toys, and the Top said to the Ball: 'How about us being sweethearts? After all, we're here together in a drawer.' But the Ball, who was made of Moroccan leather and imagined herself to be a lady, didn't want to answer that sort of thing.

The next day the little boy who owned the toys painted the Top red and yellow and drove a brass nail into its middle. The Top looked magnificent when it spun around.

'Look at me!' he said to the Ball. 'What do you say now? Don't you want to be sweethearts? We're made for each other. You jump and I dance. Nobody could be happier than the two of us.'

'That's what you think,' the Ball said. 'You don't seem to realize that my father and mother were Moroccan leather slippers and that I have a cork inside me.'

'Okay, but I'm made of mahogany,' the Top said. 'The mayor himself turned me on his lathe – he really enjoyed it.'

'Oh, really?' the Ball said.

'Let me never be whipped again if I'm lying,' the Top replied.

'You're very persuasive,' the Ball said. 'But I still can't – I'm as good as half engaged to a swallow. Every time I jump up there, he sticks his head out of the nest and says, "Will you? Will you?" and I've already told myself that I will. That's as good as a half engagement. But I promise I'll never forget you.'

'A lot of good that'll do me,' the Top said, and they didn't speak to each other again.

The next day the Ball was taken out of the drawer. The Top saw how she bounced high in the air, just like a bird, until you couldn't see her any more. She came back each time, but whenever she touched the ground, she jumped high up again – either because she longed for the swallow or because she had a cork inside. On the ninth bounce the Ball did not come back. The boy looked and looked, but she was gone.

'I know where she is,' the Top said with a sigh. 'She's in the swallow's nest and married to the swallow.'

The more the Top thought about it, the more infatuated he became with the Ball. Just because he could not have her, he

loved her even more; it seemed odd to him that she had gone and chosen someone else. The Top danced and spun around, but he always thought about the Ball, who became more and more beautiful in his thoughts. It went on like that for a long time – and in the end it was nothing but an old love story.

The Top wasn't young any more. Then one day he was gilded from top to bottom. He had never looked so good; he was now a golden top and spun until he hummed. It was really something! Then suddenly he jumped too high – and was gone.

Everyone looked and looked, even down in the basement. But no one could find him.

Where was he?

The Top had jumped into the dustbin, which was full of all kinds of things: cabbage stalks, dust from the floor, and stuff that collected in the gutter under the roof.

'What a fine place I'm in. My gold paint won't last long here – and what is this rabble around me?' He stole a sideways glance at a long cabbage stalk, which had been scraped a little too clean, and then towards a strange round thing that looked like an old apple. But it was no apple – it was the old ball, which had been lying in the roof gutter for years and become waterlogged.

'Thank goodness,' the Ball said, 'there's someone who's my social equal – someone you can talk to!' She looked at the gilded Top. 'I'm actually made of Moroccan leather, sewn by virgin hands. I have a cork inside me, but nobody can tell. I was just about to marry a swallow, but then I fell into the gutter and I was there for five years, getting soaked. That's a very long time for a young lady, you know.'

The Top said nothing. He thought about his old sweetheart, and the more he heard, the clearer it was to him that this was she.

When the servant girl went to empty the rubbish, she said, 'Goodness, there's the gold top!'

The Top was returned to the parlour and treated with honour and respect. But no one heard another word about the Ball. The Top never talked about his old love again. Love tends to fade when your beloved has lain in a gutter for five years, getting soaked. You would never recognize her if you met her in a dustbin.

The Ugly Duckling

It was so lovely out in the country – it was summer! The wheat was yellow, the oats were green, the hay was stacked in green meadows, and the stork walked about on his long red legs speaking Egyptian, because he had learned that language from his mother. The fields and meadows were surrounded by large forests, and there were deep lakes in the middle of the woods.

Yes, it was really nice out there in the country. And right in the middle of the sunshine was an old castle. It had deep moats, and burdocks that grew on the bank, from the walls down to the water; the burdocks were so big that small children could stand under the leaves of the tallest ones. It was a wilderness – like the thickest forest – and that's where a duck had her nest. She was sitting on her eggs, but she'd had just about enough of it because they took so long to hatch and she rarely had visitors. The other ducks would much rather swim in the moats than sit under a burdock and gossip with her.

Finally, one egg after another creaked 'Pip! Pip!' and all the egg yolks came to life and stuck out their heads.

'Quack! Quack!' she said, and the ducklings looked around quickly from under the green leaves. Their mother let them look as much as they liked, because green is good for the eyes.

'The world is so *big*!' all the ducklings said, because they had a lot more room here than inside the eggs.

'I don't want you to think that's the whole world,' their mother told them. 'No, it stretches far beyond the other side of the garden, straight into the vicar's field. But I've never been there . . .'

She got up. 'Is everybody here? No, not everyone. The biggest egg is still in the nest. How much longer can it take? I'm pretty tired of this already.' Then she sat down again.

'So how's it going?' asked an old duck who came to visit.

'This one egg is taking so long,' the mother duck complained while she sat on it. 'It won't hatch. But take a look at the others. They're the loveliest ducklings I've ever seen. They all look like their father – that rascal! He never comes to see me.'

'Let me have a look,' the old duck said. 'It's probably a turkey's egg. I was fooled like that once, and, believe me, I had my problems with those youngsters because they're afraid of the

water. I couldn't get them to go in. I quacked and snapped at them, but it didn't help. Let me see the egg. Yes, it's a turkey egg. Just leave it alone and teach the other children how to swim.'

'I think I'll sit on it a little longer,' the mother duck replied. 'I've been sitting this long, I might as well sit a bit more.'

'Suit yourself,' the old duck said, and then she left.

Finally, the big egg cracked. 'Quack! Quack!' the hatchling said and tumbled out. He was so big and ugly. The mother duck looked at him. 'That's an awfully big duckling, that one,' she murmured. 'None of the others looks like that. It couldn't be a turkey chick, could it? Well, we'll find out soon enough. He's going into the water even if I have to kick him in.'

The next day the weather was blessedly lovely. The sun shone on the green burdocks, and the mother duck and her whole family came down to the moat. Splash! She jumped in. 'Quack, quack!' she called, and one duckling after another plopped into the water. It closed over their heads, but they came up to the surface right away and floated very nicely. Soon, all of them were in the water, their legs moving quite naturally. Even the ugly grey one swam along.

'No, he's not a turkey,' the mother duck thought. 'Just look at how beautifully he uses his legs and how proudly he carries himself. My very own! Actually, he's quite handsome, when you really look at him. Quack. Quack! – come along, and I'll take you out into the world and introduce you to the duck yard. But keep close to me so no one steps on you, and watch out for the cat.'

They entered the duck yard. There was a terrible noise there, because two duck families were fighting over an eel's head, and then the cat got it after all.

'That's what the world is like,' the mother duck said and licked her beak, because she wanted the eel's head too. 'Use your legs!' she commanded. 'Now hurry up, and bob your heads for the old duck over there. She's more distinguished than anyone here. She has Spanish blood – that's why she's so fat, and you can see that she has a red cloth around her leg. That really means a lot. It's the greatest honour a duck can get. It means so much that nobody wants to let her go – that animals and people all know who she is. Quickly now, and no pigeon toes! A well-brought-up duckling holds his legs far apart, just like Mum and Dad. Okay. Bow your heads and say quack!'

And they did. But all the other ducks looked at them and said, loudly, 'Oh, well. Now we're stuck with that crew – as if there weren't enough of us already. And, yuck – *that* duckling is disgusting. We can't stand him.' Straight away, a duck flew over and bit his neck.

'Leave him alone,' his mother said. 'He's not bothering anyone.'

'But he's so big and strange-looking,' the duck who'd bitten him replied. 'It just makes you want to pick on him.'

'You have good-looking children,' said the elderly duck, the one with the red cloth around her leg. 'They're all beautiful, with one exception. He didn't come out too well. I wish you could do that one over again.'

'That isn't possible, as we know, your grace,' the mother duck replied. 'He's not handsome, but he's really a good soul, and he swims as well as anyone – even a little better, I'd say. I expect he'll grow up to be handsome, or he might get smaller as time goes by. I think he stayed in the egg too long, and that's why he isn't the right shape.' She picked a loose feather from his neck and stroked his back. 'Besides, he's a drake, so his looks don't matter very much.' She went on, 'I think he'll be strong and he'll succeed.'

'The other ducklings are pretty,' the old duck said. 'Make yourselves at home, and if you find an eel's head, you can bring it to me.'

They made themselves at home.

But the poor duckling – the last one to hatch, the one who looked so awful – was bitten, pushed, and teased by the other ducks and chickens. 'He's too big!' they all said, and Tom Turkey, who was born with spurs and therefore believed that he was the emperor, puffed himself up like a ship in full sail and went straight at him. He gobbled and became quite red in the face. The poor duckling did not know where to stand or where to go – he was unhappy because he looked so ugly and because the whole duck yard made fun of him.

That's how the first day went, and after that it just got worse. All of them chased the poor duckling around, and even his siblings were mean to him. They kept saying, 'If only a cat would get you, you ugly thing!' Their mother said, 'I wish you were far away.' The ducks bit him, the chickens nipped him, and the girl who fed the animals kicked him.

Finally he fled and flew over the fence, frightening small birds in the bushes, who leaped into the air. 'It's because I'm so ugly,' the duckling thought. He closed his eyes but kept running until he came to a large swamp, where the wild ducks lived. He lay there all night, very tired and sad.

In the morning the wild ducks took to the air and looked at their new companion. 'What kind of duck are you?' they asked. The duckling turned and greeted each of them as best he could.

'You're really ugly,' the wild ducks said. 'But we don't care as long as you don't marry into our family.' The poor thing. He certainly wasn't thinking about marriage; the best he could hope for was to lie in the rushes and drink a little swamp water.

He lay there for two whole days, and then two wild geese – or, rather, two wild ganders, for they were males – turned up. These youngsters hadn't been out of their eggs for long, which is why they were so cocky.

'Hey, you!' they called out. 'You're so ugly that we like you. How about coming with us and being a bird of passage? There's another swamp close by, with lots of sweet, precious wild geese, all of them maidens who can quack. You just might be ugly enough to impress them.'

At that same moment they heard 'Bang! Bang!' and both wild geese fell dead into the rushes. The water turned blood red. Then another 'Bang! Bang!' and whole flocks of wild geese flew up from the rushes. There was another blast – a big hunt was on. Hunters were hiding all over the marsh; some sat up in trees whose

branches reached across the rushes. Blue smoke drifted like clouds among the dark trees and floated far across the water. Hunting dogs came through the mud, splash-splash. Rushes and reeds swayed in every direction. The poor duckling was frightened – he turned his head and wanted to hide it under his wing. Just then a horribly big dog appeared close by, with its tongue hanging out of his mouth and his eyes shining hideously. With his jaws close to the duckling, he showed his sharp teeth – and splash! he left.

'Thank God,' the duckling sighed. 'I'm so ugly that even the dog doesn't want to bite me.'

He lay quite still while buckshot whistled in the reeds and shot after shot boomed through the air.

It didn't grow quiet until late in the day, but even then the poor duckling was afraid to get up; he waited for several more hours before looking around. Then he hurried from the swamp as fast as he could, running over the fields and meadows. It was so windy that he had a hard time getting anywhere.

Towards evening he came to a small, rundown farmhouse. It was in such poor shape that it didn't know what side to fall to, so it kept standing. The wind whooshed so hard that the duckling had to sit on his tail just to stay in one spot, and it got worse and worse. Then he noticed that the door had come off a hinge and was hanging crookedly, leaving enough of an opening for him to slip through. And that's what he did.

As it turned out, an old woman lived there with her cat and her hen. The cat, which she called Sonny, could arch his back and purr, and if you rubbed him the wrong way, his fur gave off sparks. The hen had very small, short legs and was therefore called Cockadoodleshortlegs. It laid a lot of eggs and the old woman loved the hen as if it were her child.

In the morning they noticed the strange duckling right away, and the cat began to purr and the hen to cluck.

'What on *earth!*' the woman said and looked around. But she didn't see well, so she thought that the duckling was a fat duck that had got lost. 'Oh, that's a nice catch,' she said. 'Now I can have duck eggs – if it's not a drake. We'll have to find out.'

The duckling was put on probation for three weeks, but he produced no eggs. The cat was master of the house and the hen was the mistress. They always said, 'We and the world,' because they believed that they were half of it – and the best part too. The duckling thought that it might be possible to have another opinion, but the hen wouldn't hear of it.

'Can you lay eggs?' she asked.

'No.'

'Well, be quiet, then.'

The cat asked, 'Can you arch your back, purr, and make sparks?'

'No.'

'Then you shouldn't contradict sensible people.'

The duckling sat in a corner, quite depressed. He started to think about fresh air and sunshine and had such a strange desire to float on the water that, finally, he could not stop himself. He had to tell the hen.

'What's the matter with you?' she asked. 'You have nothing to do, and that's why you're getting ideas. Lay eggs or purr – and you'll get over it.'

'But it's so nice to float on the water,' the duckling said. 'It's so nice to have the water cover your head and to dive to the bottom.'

'Oh yes, that must be a real pleasure,' the hen said. 'You've gone mad. Ask the cat – he's the cleverest animal I know – ask him if he likes to float on the water or dive. I won't even speak about myself. Why don't you ask our mistress, the old woman? No one in the world is wiser than she is. Do you think she has the urge to swim or to dive under the water?'

'You don't understand me,' the duck said.

'You're right, we don't understand you. But who could understand you? I'm sure you're not trying to be wiser than the cat or the old woman, not to mention me. Stop making a fuss, child, and thank your creator for all the good things that have come your way. Don't you have a warm room and people like us who can teach you something? But you're silly, and it's not much fun being with you. Trust me. I'll say nasty things to you, but it's for your own good – that's how you know your true friends. Now get going – lay eggs and learn how to purr.'

'I think that I'll go out into the wide world,' the duckling said.

'Fine, go ahead,' the hen replied.

So the duckling left. He floated on the water, he dived, but all the other animals ignored him because he was so ugly.

Autumn came, and the leaves in the woods turned yellow and brown. The wind got hold of them, so they danced about, and the very air looked cold. The clouds grew heavy with hail and snow, and a raven sat on the stone wall and shrieked, 'Ow! Ow!' from sheer cold. Just thinking about the cold was enough to freeze you through and through. The poor duckling really suffered.

One evening, during a beautiful sunset, a whole flock of magnificent big birds flew out of the bushes. The duckling had never seen birds so beautiful. They were shiny white all over and had long slender necks. They were swans. They spread their great wings and, with wondrous calls, flew away from the cold to warmer places and clear lakes. They were flying far up, and this had a strange effect on the ugly little duckling. He spun around in the water, like a wheel, and stretched his neck towards them and let loose a cry so loud and unusual that he frightened himself. He could not forget those beautiful birds – those lucky birds. As soon as he lost sight of them, he dived straight to the bottom, and when he came up again he was beside himself. He didn't know what those birds were called or where they were off to, but he felt attached to them – more attached than he'd ever felt towards anyone. It wasn't envy that he felt – how could he have imagined wanting such beauty? He would have been happy if only the ducks had let him be – the poor and ugly creature.

The winter was very, very cold; the duckling had to keep moving to keep his swimming hole open. But every night it got smaller and smaller; it was so cold that the ice creaked, and the duckling had to use his legs all the time to keep the ice from closing in on him. In the end, he was exhausted, lay quite still, and became stuck – frozen in the ice.

Early in the morning, a farmer came along and saw the duck. He went out on the pond, broke up the ice with his wooden shoe, and carried the duckling home to his wife. There it came to life again.

The children wanted to play with it, but the duckling thought they were going to hurt him and he rushed into the milk pan so that milk splashed onto the floor. The farmer's wife shrieked and waved her hands, and the duck flew into the butter churn, then down into the flour barrel and out again. That was quite a sight. The farmer's wife shrieked again and tried to smack the duckling with the fire tongs, and the children tumbled over each other trying to catch him. They laughed and they shouted – it was a good thing that the door was open. The duckling rushed out into the bushes and the new-fallen snow, where he lay as still as if he were taking his winter sleep.

It would be much too sad to describe all the misery and hardship he had to endure that bitter cold winter. He was lying in the marsh, among the rushes, when the sun began to shine warmly again. The skylarks sang – it was lovely springtime once more.

Then all of a sudden he lifted his wings; they felt much stronger than before. With powerful strokes, they beat the air and carried him along. Before he even realized it, he found himself in a big garden where apple trees bloomed and fragrant lilac flowers hung from long, green branches that stretched towards winding canals. It was a place as lovely and fresh as spring itself. And right in front of him three beautiful white swans came out of the thicket; they rustled their feathers as they floated on the water. The duckling recognized these magnificent creatures and was overcome with a strange sort of melancholy.

'I want to fly to them, those royal birds! Yet they would bite me to death if I did – if someone as ugly as me dared to approach them. But I don't care. It's better to be killed by them than to be nibbled by ducks, pecked by hens, kicked by the girl who takes care of the chicken yard, or to suffer through another winter.' He landed on the water and swam towards the majestic swans. They rushed towards him with ruffled feathers. 'Go ahead and kill me,' the poor creature said and bowed his head, expecting the end. But what did he see on the clear surface of the water? He saw his own image, and he was no longer an awkward black-grey bird, ugly and nasty. He was a swan.

It doesn't matter if you're born in a duck yard if you've lain in a swan's egg.

He felt immensely happy to have gone through all his hardship and suffering. Now he could appreciate his good fortune and all the wonderful things that were in store for him. The great swans swam around him and stroked him with their beaks.

Several children came into the garden. They threw bread and grain into the water, and the youngest one shouted, 'It's a new one!' The other children joined in, cheering, 'Yes, there's a new one!' They clapped their hands and danced as they ran to their mother and father. They all threw bread and cake into the water and said, 'The new one is the most beautiful – so young and handsome.' And the old swans bowed to him.

At that moment he felt quite bashful – although he did not know quite why – and hid his head behind his wings. He was just much too happy but not at all proud, because a good heart is never vain. He remembered how he had been persecuted and scorned, and now he heard everyone say that he was the most beautiful of all the beautiful birds. The lilacs bent their branches down to the water, and the sun shone warmly. He rustled his feathers, lifted his long neck, and exulted, 'I never dreamed of so much happiness when I was the ugly duckling!'

The Snow Queen

A TALE IN SEVEN STORIES

All right, let's get started! When we're at the end of the story, we'll know more than we do now, because there was an evil troll, one of the worst – it was the devil. One day he was in a really good mood; he had made a mirror that had special qualities: it would shrink everything that was good and beautiful to almost nothing, and it would magnify whatever was worthless and ugly and make it seem even worse. The most beautiful landscapes looked like boiled spinach, and the nicest people appeared loathsome, or they seemed to stand on their heads with their stomachs missing and their faces so twisted that you couldn't tell who they were. If someone had a freckle, you can be sure that it would spread over his nose and mouth. It was great fun, the devil said. If someone had a good, pious thought, the mirror would show a grin – the troll-devil just could not stop laughing at his clever invention.

Everyone who was enrolled in troll school (for the devil ran a troll school) spread the word that a miracle had happened. For the first time, they believed, you could see what people and the world were really like. The troll students ran all over the place with the mirror. In the end there wasn't a country or a person that it hadn't distorted; and now they wanted to fly up to heaven and make fun of the angels and God himself. The higher they took the mirror, the harder they laughed; they could barely hold on to it. They flew higher and higher, closer to God and the angels. Suddenly, the mirror, which was still grinning, shook so violently that it slipped from their hands and fell to earth, where it broke into a hundred million, billion, and even more pieces. From that moment the mirror spread more unhappiness than ever.

Some splinters were hardly as big as a grain of sand, and they flew around the whole wide world. If a splinter got into somebody's eye, it stayed there and made everything look bad. People would see only what was wrong, because every little speck was as powerful as the whole mirror. In fact, some people even got a small piece in their hearts. That was really awful – their hearts then became as hard as chunks of ice. Some pieces of the mirror were so big that you could use them as window-panes, but you wouldn't want to look at your friends through a window like that. Other pieces were used for eyeglasses, and when people put them on to see or to decide a question fairly, things really went wrong. The devil laughed until his sides split – that tickled pleasantly – while tiny pieces of glass kept flying through the air. Now let's see what happens.

SECOND STORY

A Little Boy and a Little Girl

In the big city, where there are so many houses and people and not enough room for everyone to have his own little garden, most people must settle for a flowerpot. Two poor children, who nevertheless had a garden a little bigger than a flowerpot, lived there too. They were not brother and sister, but they were as fond of one another as if they were. Their parents lived next to each other; each family had a room right under the roof, where one house almost bumped into the other. A rain gutter ran between the houses, under the eaves, and each had a window that faced the other. You could go across the rain gutter from window to window in a single stride.

Outside the window each family put a large wooden box for growing herbs and a little rosebush too. One rosebush grew in each box, and they thrived. The parents had set the boxes across the rain gutter so that they almost reached from window to window. The boxes looked like flowering walls; sweet-pea vines hung over the sides, and the long branches of the rosebushes wound around the windows and grew into one another. It was almost like an archway of greenery and flowers. Because the boxes were so high up, the children knew that they shouldn't climb out of them, but they were often allowed to sit on their little stools under the roses. They played so beautifully there.

In winter, of course, that sort of fun was over. The windows were often frosted over. But the children heated copper coins on the stove, pressed them against the frozen windowpanes, and the coins made perfect round peepholes. Through the opening in each window was an affectionate eye belonging to the little boy and the little girl. His name was Kai, and she was Gerda. In the summer they could get together in one leap, but in the winter they had to climb lots of steps down and lots of steps up. Outside, the snow drifted.

'The white bees are swarming,' Grandmother said.

'Do they also have a queen?' the little boy asked, because he knew that real bees had one.

'Yes, they do,' Grandmother said. 'She flies where the swarm is thickest. She's the biggest one of all, and she never stays on the ground. She flies up again into the black clouds. On lots of winter nights she flies through the streets and looks through the windows, and then they freeze over very strangely – as if they were covered with flowers.'

'Yes, I've seen that,' both children said, for they knew that it was true.

'Can the snow queen come inside?' the little girl asked.

'Let her just come,' the boy said. 'I'll put her on the hot stove, and she'll melt.'

Grandmother smoothed his hair and told more stories.

In the evening, when Kai was half undressed, he climbed up on the chairs by the window and looked through his little peephole. A couple of snowflakes fell outside, and one of them – the largest – stayed on the edge of a flower box. The snowflake grew bigger and bigger until, at last, it turned into a woman; she wore the finest white gauze made of millions of starlike flakes. She was delicate and beautiful but made of blinding, glimmering ice. Yet she was alive. Her eyes stared out like two bright stars, but there was no calm or peace in them. She nodded towards the window and waved her hand. The little boy was frightened and jumped down from the chair; just then a large bird flew past the window.

The next day it was freezing. Then the thaw came and then spring – the sun shone, green sprouts peeped out of the ground, swallows made their nests, windows were opened, and the two children sat once more in their little garden over the rain gutter, up above the top floor.

The roses bloomed unusually well that summer. The little girl had learned a hymn that mentioned roses, which made her think about her own. She sang it for the little boy, who joined in:

> *In the valley, the roses grow wild,*
> *There we can speak to the Christ child!*

The children held hands, kissed the roses, and looked into God's clear sunshine; they talked to it as if the baby Jesus were there. The summer days were so lovely, and it was heavenly to be out among the fresh rosebushes, which never seemed to stop blooming.

Kai and Gerda were looking at their picture book filled with animals and birds, and then – precisely as the clock on the big church steeple struck five – Kai said, 'Ouch! Something stung my heart, and I've got something in my eye!'

The little girl pulled him close; he blinked, but no, there was nothing to see.

'I think it's gone,' he said, but it wasn't gone. It was, in fact, one of those glass splinters from the mirror – the troll's mirror. Of course, we all remember that ghastly mirror, which could shrink everything big and beautiful down to something tiny and hideous and could magnify whatever was evil and bad, making every flaw stand out. Poor Kai, he had got a tiny piece of it right in his heart. Soon it would be like a lump of ice. It didn't hurt any more, but the splinter was still there.

'Why are you crying?' Kai asked. 'You look so ugly! There's nothing wrong with me. Ugh!' he suddenly shouted. 'That rose has been chewed by a worm. And look, it's quite crooked. When you think about it, those roses are disgusting. They look like the boxes they grow in.' He kicked the box hard and tore two roses from the bush.

'Kai, what are you doing?' the little girl shouted. When he saw how alarmed she was, he ripped off another rose and ran inside through the window, away from Gerda.

From then on, whenever she turned up with the picture book, he said it was for babies. When Grandmother told them stories, he always had to say 'but' – and if he had the chance, he would follow her, put on her glasses, and imitate the way she spoke. It was exactly like her, and it made people laugh. Kai soon learned how to walk and talk like everybody on their street and how to imitate everything that was different and unattractive about them. People said, 'That boy certainly has a good head on his shoulders.' But because of the glass splinter in his eye and in his heart, he even teased little Gerda, who loved him with all her heart.

The little boy's games became quite different from what they had been. They were so clever now: one winter day, as the snow-flakes came flying down, Kai went outside with a big magnifying glass, spread out the corner of his blue coat, and let the snow fall on it.

'Look through the glass, Gerda!' he said. Every snowflake became much bigger and looked like a dazzling flower or a star with ten points; it was beautiful.

'Look how well designed they are,' Kai said. 'They're much more interesting than real flowers. There's not a single flaw; they're absolutely perfect as long as they don't melt.'

A little later Kai showed up with big gloves; he was carrying a sledge on his back. 'They're letting me go to the big square, where the other children play!' he shouted right in Gerda's ear. And off he went.

The most daring boys on the square often tied their sledges to the farmers' wagons and rode along for a while. It was great fun. Right in the middle of their games, a large sleigh showed up. It was white all over, and in it sat someone wrapped in thick white fur and a fleecy white hat; the sleigh went twice around the square, and Kai quickly managed to tie his little sledge to it and ride along. It went faster and faster, right into the next street; then the person steering the sleigh turned round and gave Kai a friendly nod – as if they knew one another. Each time Kai wanted to unhook his little sledge, the person in the sleigh would nod again, and Kai stayed put. They drove right through the gates of the town.

By now the snow was coming down so thickly that the little boy could barely see a thing as he sped along. Quickly, he let go of the rope to get loose from the sleigh, but it didn't do any good. His tiny sledge was stuck, and it went as fast as the wind. He shouted very loudly, but no one heard him, and the snow drifted and the sleigh flew along. Occasionally, the sledge jumped while rushing across ditches and fences. He was scared; he wanted to say the Lord's Prayer, but all he could remember was his multiplication tables.

The snowflakes got bigger and bigger, and in the end they looked like big white chickens. Suddenly, they jumped out of the way, the big sleigh stopped, and the person in it got up. It was a woman. Her fur coat and the hat were made of pure snow; she stood very tall and straight, brilliantly white. It was the snow queen.

'We've arrived safely,' she said. 'But if you think that this is cold, crawl into my bear fur.' She invited him into her sleigh and wrapped him in the fur, which felt as if he were sinking into a snowdrift.

'Are you still cold?' she asked and kissed him on his forehead. Oh! Her kiss was colder than ice; it went through him, right to his heart, which, as you know, was almost a lump of ice already. It was as if he were going to die – but only for a moment, and then it felt good. He no longer sensed the cold.

'My sledge! Don't forget my sledge!' That was the first thing that he remembered. It was tied to one of the white chickens, which flew behind them with the sledge on its back. The snow queen kissed Kai again, and at that moment he forgot all about Gerda, Grandmother, and everyone at home.

'Now you won't get any more kisses,' she said. 'Because then my kisses would kill you.'

Kai looked at her – she was so beautiful. He could not imagine a wiser, lovelier face. She didn't appear to be made of ice, as she had when she was outside his window, waving to him. In his eyes she was perfect, and he was no longer afraid. He told her that he was good at arithmetic – even fractions – and knew how many square miles there were in the country and 'how many inhabitants'. She always just smiled, and he realized that he didn't know enough. He looked at the great big sky, and she flew off with him – far up to the dark cloud. The wind whistled and roared – as if it were singing old songs. They flew over forests and lakes, over oceans and land. Below, the cold wind shrieked, wolves howled, the snow glistened, and black screeching crows flew past. But above them the moon shone big and bright, and Kai could tell that it would be a very long winter night. During the day he slept at the feet of the snow queen.

THIRD STORY

The Flower Garden and the
Woman Who Knew Sorcery

How was Gerda doing now that Kai was gone? Where was he? No one knew, and no one could tell her. The other boys could say only that they had seen him tie his little sledge to a magnificent big one that went down the street and out through the gate of the city. Nobody knew where he was, lots of tears were shed, and Gerda wept despairingly for a long time. People said that Kai was dead, that he had drowned in the river close to town. Oh, those were long dark winter days.

Then spring came, with a warmer sun.

'Kai is dead and gone,' Gerda said.

'I don't think so!' the sunshine said.

'He's dead and gone,' she said to the swallows.

'I don't think so!' they replied, and in the end Gerda didn't think so either.

'I'll put on my new red shoes – the ones Kai hasn't seen,' she said one morning. 'Then I'll go down to the river and ask what it knows.'

It was very early. She kissed old Grandmother, who was still sleeping, put on her red shoes, and walked alone through the gate to the river.

'Is it true that you've taken my friend? I'll give you my red shoes if you'll give him back to me.'

She thought that the waves nodded strangely, so she took off her red shoes, the most precious thing she owned, and tossed them into the river. But the shoes landed close to the bank, and straight away small waves carried them back to her. It was as if the river would not take her most precious possession because it had not taken Kai. She began to worry that she hadn't thrown the shoes far enough, and she crawled into a boat that lay among the reeds. From the far end of the boat she tossed her shoes overboard, and because the boat wasn't tied up, that movement was enough to make it push off from the riverbank. When she felt the boat move, she hurried to get off. But before she could, the boat was already two feet from shore and sailing rapidly away.

Gerda became quite frightened and began to cry, but no one heard her except the sparrows, and they couldn't carry her ashore. Still, they flew along the riverbank and sang as if to comfort her. 'Here are we! Here are we!' The boat was carried along by the current; Gerda, in her stocking feet, sat very still. Her little red shoes floated behind, but they could not reach the boat, which was going faster now.

Both sides of the river were beautiful, with lovely flowers, old trees, sheep, and cows on the steep slopes – but not a single person in sight.

'Maybe the river will take me to Kai,' Gerda thought, and that made her feel better. She stood up and looked for hours at the beautiful green riverbank. She came to a big cherry orchard with a little house that was all thatched roof and a few strange red and blue windows. Outside stood two wooden soldiers who presented arms to everyone who sailed by.

Gerda called out to them – she thought they were alive – but of course they didn't answer. She got quite close to them; the river pushed the boat right up to the shore.

Gerda shouted even louder, and an old, old woman came out of the house. She was leaning on the crook of her cane and wore a big sun hat with beautiful flowers painted on it.

'You poor little child!' the old woman said. 'How did you get out there on that big strong river and drift so far into the wide world?' The old woman waded into the water, grabbed the boat with the crook of her cane, pulled it to shore, and lifted little Gerda out.

Gerda was happy to be on dry land but still a bit afraid of this strange old woman.

'Come here and tell me who you are and how you got here,' the woman said.

Gerda told her everything, and the old woman shook her head and said, 'Hmm. Hmm.' When Gerda had told her all there was to tell and asked if she had seen Kai, the old woman said that he hadn't come past. But, she continued, he probably would, and Gerda shouldn't be so sad; she ought to taste her cherries and look at the flowers. They were far prettier than in any picture book, and each of them had a story to tell. Then she took Gerda by the hand; they went into the little house, and the old woman locked the door.

The windows were set curiously high, and the light shone very strangely through their red, blue, and yellow panes. The most delicious-looking cherries sat on the table, and Gerda wasn't afraid to eat as many as she wanted. While Gerda was eating, the old woman untangled her hair with a golden comb. Her shiny yellow hair curled beautifully, and her friendly round face looked like a rose.

'I've always longed for such a sweet little girl,' the old woman said. 'You'll see – the two of us are really going to get on well.' As the old woman combed Gerda's hair, Gerda thought less and less about Kai, who was like a brother to her. The old woman knew witchcraft, but she wasn't an evil witch; she just did a little sorcery for her own amusement – and now she wanted to keep Gerda. So she went into the garden, pointed her cane at the rosebushes, and, although they were in beautiful bloom, they sank into the black earth so that nobody could see where they'd been. The old woman was afraid that if Gerda saw them, she would think about her own roses, remember Kai, and run away.

She led Gerda into the flower garden. It was very beautiful and fragrant. Every flower imaginable from every season was at its peak at the same time. No picture book could be more colourful and beautiful. Gerda jumped with happiness and played until the sun sank behind the tall cherry trees. Then she got into a lovely bed with red silk covers that were filled with blue violets. She slept, and her dreams were as pleasant as a queen's on her wedding day.

The next day in the warm sunshine Gerda played with the flowers. Many days passed. She recognized every flower, but no matter how many there were, she thought that one was missing. Yet she didn't know which one. Then one day she was looking at the old lady's big sun hat – the one with flowers painted on it. The most beautiful flower was a rose; the old woman had forgotten to remove it from her hat when she made the others disappear into the ground. That's what happens when you're not paying attention.

'Of course!' Gerda said. 'There aren't any roses!' She jumped around the flowerbeds and looked and looked, but there were none to be found. Then she sat down and cried, but her hot tears fell just where the rosebush had vanished. When her warm tears soaked into the earth, a rosebush suddenly shot up. It was in full bloom, just as it had been when it disappeared. Gerda hugged it, kissed the roses, and thought about the beautiful roses at home, which made her think of Kai.

'I've been here too long,' the little girl said. 'I've got to find Kai.' She asked the roses, 'Do you know where he is? Do you think he's dead and gone?'

'He's not dead,' the roses replied. 'We've been under the ground, where all the dead people are, but Kai wasn't there.'

'Thank you,' Gerda said. She went to the other flowers and looked into their blossoms and asked them, 'Don't you know where Kai is?'

All the flowers stood in the sunlight and dreamed their own fables or fairy tales. Gerda had to listen to many of their stories, but none of the flowers knew anything about Kai.

What did the orange lily say?

'Do you hear the drum – *boom boom?* It only has two notes – *boom boom!* Listen to the sad song of the women – listen to the shouts of the priests. The Hindu wife, in her long red robes, stands on the funeral pyre. Flames leap around her and her dead husband. But the Hindu wife thinks about who is living inside the circle – he whose eyes burn hotter than the flames, whose fiery eyes touch her heart more than the flames that will turn her body into ash. Can the fire in the heart die in the flame of the pyre?'

'I don't understand that at all,' Gerda said.

'It's my fairy tale,' the tiger lily replied.

What does the morning glory say?

'An old castle hangs over a narrow mountain road. Bindweed grows along its old red walls, leaf by leaf, all the way to the balcony, and a beautiful girl stands there, bending over the railing, looking down the road. No rose looks fresher – no apple blossom floating in the wind is lighter than she is. Her gorgeous silk robe rustles, "When is he coming?"'

'Is it Kai you mean?' Gerda asked.

'I'm just talking about my own fairy tale, my dream,' the morning glory replied.

What does the little daisy say?

'A wide board hangs on ropes between the trees – it's a swing. Two sweet little girls are swinging; their dresses are white like snow, and long green silk ribbons flutter from their hats. Their brother, who's older, stands on the swing, holding on with his arm twisted around the rope. In one hand he holds a little bowl, and in the other a clay pipe; he's blowing soap bubbles. The swing goes back and forth, and the bubbles, with beautiful changing colours, fly off. The last bubble clings to the pipe, shaking in the wind. The swing moves back and forth. Their little black dog, as light as the bubbles, stands on its hind legs and wants to climb onto the flying swing. The dog falls down and yelps angrily, the children laugh, the bubble pops. A swing, a reflection in a bursting soap bubble – that's my song!'

'What you're telling me may be beautiful, but you're saying it so sadly, and you haven't mentioned Kai at all. What do the hyacinths say?'

'There were three beautiful sisters, so transparent and delicate. One had a red dress, the other a blue, and the third sister's was all white. They danced hand in hand by the smooth lake in the clear moonlit night. They weren't elves; they were human children. The air smelled very sweet, and the girls disappeared into the woods. The smell got stronger. Three coffins (and inside them lay the beautiful girls) glided out of the woods and across the lake. Glowworms moved around like small floating lights. Were the dancing girls asleep or were they dead? The fragrance of the flowers tells us they're dead, and the evening bell tolls for the dead.'

'You're making me quite sad,' Gerda said. 'You have such a strong smell that I can't stop thinking about the dead girls. Is Kai really dead? The roses had been under the ground, and they said no.'

'Ding-dong,' the hyacinth bells rang. 'We're not ringing for Kai – we don't know him. We sing our own song – it's the only one we know.'

Gerda went over to the buttercup, which shone among the glistening green leaves.

'You shine like a little sun,' Gerda said. 'Tell me: do you know where I can find my friend?'

The buttercup shone brightly and looked at Gerda again. What song did the buttercup know? Its song was not about Kai, either:

'On the first day of spring, God's warm sun shone on the little courtyard. Its rays shimmered against the white wall of the house next door, and the first yellow flowers, like gold in the warm sunshine, grew nearby. Old Grandmother was outside in her chair; her granddaughter, a poor and pretty servant girl, had come home for a short visit. She kissed her grandmother. There was gold in that blessed kiss – gold from the heart. There was gold in her eyes, gold in the ground where it lies, and gold in the sky at sunrise. There you go – that's my little story,' the buttercup said.

'My poor old grandmother!' Gerda sighed. 'I'm sure she misses me and weeps for me just as she did for Kai. But I'll be going home again soon, and then I'll have Kai with me. Asking the flowers isn't helping me – they only sing their own songs and don't tell me anything.' She gathered up her skirt so she could run faster, but the narcissus smacked her on the leg as she jumped over it. She stopped and looked at the tall flower, asking, 'Maybe you know something?' She bent all the way down to it, and what did it say?

'I can see myself! I can see myself!' the narcissus said. 'Oh, how good I smell! In a small attic room a ballerina, half dressed, stands on one foot, then two, and kicks at the whole world. But she's an illusion. She pours water from the teapot onto some cloth that she's holding – it's the bodice of her dress. Cleanliness is next to godliness. Her white ballet skirt hangs from a peg; it was also washed in the teapot and dried on the roof. She puts on the skirt and ties a saffron yellow scarf around her neck to make the skirt appear even whiter. Lift your leg high! See how she shows off her stem! I can see myself! I can see myself!'

'I don't like that at all,' Gerda said. 'You don't need to tell me that.' Then she ran to the edge of the garden.

The garden gate was locked, but she jiggled the rusty handle until it shook loose and the gate sprang open. Then Gerda ran barefoot into the wide world. She looked back three times, but no one followed her. At last, when she couldn't run any more, she sat down on a big rock. When she looked around, summer was gone – it was late autumn. But you couldn't tell what season it was in the beautiful garden where the sun always shone and all the flowers bloomed the year around.

'Oh, my – all the time I've wasted!' Gerda said. 'It's already autumn. I daren't rest any longer' – and she got up to leave.

Oh, how sore and tired her little feet were. All around her it had become raw and cold. The long willow leaves had turned completely yellow; fog dripped off them, and one leaf fell after another. Only the blackthorn bush still had berries, which were sour enough to make your mouth pucker. How grey and hard the wide world was!

FOURTH STORY

The Prince and the Princess

Gerda needed to rest again. Just across from where she sat, a big crow hopped on the snow. It had been watching her for some time when it wiggled its head and said, 'Caw, caw – hellaw!' He couldn't pronounce it any better than that, but he was feeling kindly towards the little girl and asked where in the world she was going all alone. *Alone:* Gerda certainly understood that word and knew all too well what it meant to her. She told the crow her whole life story and asked whether it had seen Kai.

The crow nodded thoughtfully and said, 'Could be, could be!'

'What? Really?!' she shouted, and she nearly squeezed the crow to death – that's how hard she kissed him.

'Take it easy! Take it easy!' the crow said. 'I think I've seen Kai, but because of the princess he's probably forgotten you.'

'He's staying with a princess?' Gerda asked.

'Yes, but listen,' the crow said. 'It's hard for me to speak your language. If you spoke Crowish, it would be easier to explain.'

'I haven't learned it,' Gerda said. 'But Grandma knew it. She also spoke Snobbish. If only I had learned it.'

'Never mind,' the crow said. 'I'll tell you everything as well as

I can, but it's sure to be bad anyway.' Then he told her what he knew:

'In this kingdom there's a princess who's so incredibly intelligent that she's read every newspaper in the world and forgotten all of them – that's how intelligent she is. The other day, when she was sitting on her throne – and that's not a lot of fun, they say – she started to hum a song. To be precise, it went like this: "Why shouldn't I get married?" And she said, "Why not?" Then she decided to get married, but she wanted to find a husband who knew what to say when someone spoke to him – not someone who just stood there looking dignified, because that's so boring. She called all her ladies-in-waiting together, and when they heard what she wanted, they thought it would be great fun. "Oh, I like that idea!" they all said. "I had almost the same idea the other day."

'Believe me, everything I tell you is true,' the crow went on. 'My sweetheart is a tame bird who's allowed to go anywhere in the castle, and she's told me everything.'

Naturally, his fiancée was a crow, because birds of a feather flock together.

'The next day's newspapers had a border of hearts, along with the princess's initials, and they announced that every attractive young man was invited to come to the castle to talk to the princess. She would choose the one who sounded most at home and spoke the best. Yes, indeed!' the crow said. 'This is as true as the fact that I'm sitting here. People streamed to the castle – it was a mob scene – but nobody was chosen, not on the first day or on the second. In the street, people were all well-spoken, but the moment that they came through the castle gate and saw guards in the courtyard wearing silver, and footmen on the stairs wearing gold, they were stunned. They stood in front of the throne where the princess sat, and they didn't know what to say, so they repeated the last thing she had said – and she didn't want to hear that again. It was as if the suitors inside had fallen asleep with snuff spilling down their fronts. It wasn't until they got out into the street again that they could talk. There was a line of people from the city's gate all the way to the castle. I saw it with my own eyes,' the crow continued. 'They were hungry and thirsty, but at the castle they didn't get even a glass of luke-warm water. Of course, some of the cleverest had brought sandwiches, but they didn't share with their neighbour, because this is what they thought: If he looks hungry, the princess won't choose him.'

'But Kai, little Kai?' Gerda asked. 'When did he come? Was he in the crowd?'

'Be patient, be patient – we're almost there. On the third day a short person without a horse or carriage marched boldly right up to the castle. His eyes shone like yours, and he had nice long hair, but his clothes were shoddy.'

'It was Kai,' Gerda said excitedly. 'Oh, I've found him!' She clapped her hands.

'Did he have a little rucksack on his back?' the crow asked.

'No, it was probably his sledge,' Gerda said, 'because he was on a sledge when he went away.'

'You may be right,' the crow said. 'I didn't look very carefully. But my tame sweetheart told me all about it. When he came through the castle door and saw the guards dressed in silver and the footmen on the stairs dressed in gold, he wasn't the least bit daunted. He just nodded and said, "It must be really boring to stand there on the stairs – I'd rather go inside." Inside, the royal rooms were all lit up; the king's councillors and various excellencies went around barefoot and carried golden plates. It was enough to make anyone solemn. His boots creaked very loudly, but he still wasn't afraid.'

'I'm sure it's Kai!' Gerda said. 'I know he had new boots – I heard them creak at Grandmother's.'

'Oh, yes, they certainly creaked,' the crow said. 'But he was bold and went straight to the princess, who sat on a pearl as big as a spinning wheel. All the ladies-in-waiting with their servant girls, and the servant girls with *their* servant girls, and all the lords-in-waiting with *their* servants and their servants' servant boys – all stood at attention around the castle. The closer they stood to the door, the prouder they looked. And the servants' servants' servant boy, who always wears slippers, was so proud that you could hardly bear to look at him.'

'That must have been awful,' Gerda said. 'But Kai got the princess anyway?'

'If I hadn't been a crow, I would have won her – although I'm engaged. People say that he spoke as well as I speak when I'm speaking Crowish – or that's what my tame sweetheart says. He was bold and charming. He wasn't there to propose, only to listen to the wisdom of the princess. He liked what he heard, and she liked him too.'

'Yes, that was certainly Kai,' Gerda said. 'He was so clever he could do numbers in his head – with fractions! Oh, please, won't you take me to the castle?'

'That's easy for you to say,' the crow said. 'But how do we do it? I'll talk to my tame fiancée; she can probably give us advice. But I've got to tell you, a little girl like you will never get permission to get all the way in.'

'Yes, I will!' Gerda said. 'When Kai finds out that I'm here, he'll come out and fetch me right away.'

'Wait for me by the fence there,' the crow said, wiggled his head, and flew off.

As soon as it got dark, the crow came back. 'Caw, caw!' he said. 'My fiancée sends you many greetings, and here's a little piece of bread for you. She got it in the kitchen – there's enough bread there – and you must be hungry. Anyway, you can't get inside the castle; after all, you're barefoot, and the guards dressed in silver and the footmen in gold won't allow it. But don't cry; we'll get you there. My fiancée knows a small back staircase that leads to the bedroom, and she knows where to get the key.'

They went into the garden, past the trees along the wide path, where one leaf fell after another. At the castle, when the lights were put out, one after another, the crow led Gerda to the back door, which stood ajar.

Gerda's heart beat with dread and yearning. It was as if she were about to do something bad, but all she wanted to know was where Kai was. It must be him. In her mind she could see his wise eyes, his long hair; she could vividly remember the way he had smiled when they had sat under the roses at home. She thought he would be happy to see her – to hear how far she had come for his sake and to know how sad everyone at home had been when he did not return. She felt dread and longing.

Then they were on the staircase; a small lamp burned on a cupboard. The tame crow stood in the middle of the floor. She turned her head every which way and looked at Gerda, who curtsied as Grandmother had taught her.

'My fiancé has said so many nice things about you, Miss Gerda,' the tame crow said. 'Your vita, as we say, is very touching. If you'll take the lamp, I'll lead the way. We'll go straight there. That way we won't run into anyone.'

'I think someone is following right behind us,' Gerda said, and something rushed by her like shadows on a wall: horses with flying manes and thin legs, gamekeepers, and ladies and gentlemen on horseback.

'Those are just dreams,' the tame crow said. 'Dreams take the royaltys' thoughts out to the hunt, and that's good, because they can see it all better from bed. I want to be sure that if you reach a position of honour and respect, you'll show heartfelt gratitude.'

'Don't mention it,' the crow from the woods said.

They went into the first room. It was all rosy satin with artificial flowers on the walls. Here the dreams rushed by but so quickly that Gerda was not able to catch sight of royalty. Each room was more magnificent than the one before – it was amazing – and then they were in the bedroom. The ceiling there looked like a great palm tree made of glass – precious glass. In the middle of the floor two beds that resembled lilies hung on stems of gold. One was white, which is where the princess slept; the other was red, and that was where Gerda looked for Kai. She pushed one of the red petals aside and saw a brown neck. 'Oh, that's Kai!' She shouted out his name, held the lamp close, and dreams galloped into the room again. He woke up, turned his head, and – it was not Kai.

It was only the prince's neck that looked like Kai's, but nevertheless the prince was young and handsome. The princess peeped out from her white lily bed and asked what was going on. Gerda began to cry. She told her entire story and all that the crows had done for her.

'You poor thing!' the prince and the princess said. They praised the crows and said that they weren't the least bit angry with them but that they shouldn't do it again. Meanwhile, the crows would get a reward.

'Do you want freedom?' the princess asked. 'Or would you rather have steady jobs as court crows, with benefits – whatever is left over in the kitchen?'

Both crows curtsied and asked for jobs at the court, for they were thinking about their old age and said, 'It's so nice to have something for our golden years,' as they called it.

The prince got out of his bed and let Gerda sleep in it, but that was all he could do for her. She folded her hands and thought, 'How good the people and the animals were.' Then she closed her eyes and slept very soundly. All the dreams came flying in, and they looked like God's angels, pulling a little sledge. Kai sat on the sledge and nodded to her, but it was only a dream, and it was gone again as soon as she woke up.

The next day Gerda was dressed from top to toe in silk and velvet. They invited her to stay at the castle and live in comfort, but all she asked for was a horse, a little carriage, and a pair of small boots. Then she would head out into the wide world again and look for Kai.

She got boots and a fur muff. She was dressed very nicely, and when she wanted to leave, a new coach of pure gold was waiting at the door. The prince and princess's coat of arms shone like a star from the carriage. The coachman, servants, and postilions – for there were postilions too – wore gold crowns. The prince and princess helped Gerda into the coach themselves and wished her good luck. The wild crow, who by now was married, accompanied her inside the coach for the first three miles; he sat next to her, because riding backwards made him sick. The tame crow stood on the castle gate and flapped her wings. She did not come along because she'd had a headache ever since she'd got a steady job and too much to eat. The coach was lined with sugar pretzels, and the seats were filled with fruit and cookies.

'Goodbye, goodbye!' the prince and princess called. Gerda cried; the crow cried – that is how the first few miles passed. Then the crow said goodbye too, and it was the saddest parting. He flew up into a tree and flapped his black wings for as long as he could see the coach, which shone like the bright sunshine.

FIFTH STORY

The Little Bandit Girl

They drove through a dark forest, but the coach was bright like a flame. It hurt the bandits' eyes – they couldn't stand it.

'It's gold, it's gold!' the bandits shouted as they rushed forward and took hold of the horses. They killed the postilions, the coachman, and the servants, and yanked Gerda out of the coach.

'She's plump, she's lovely, she's fattened up with nuts,' said the old bandit hag, who had a long bristly beard and eyebrows that covered her eyes. 'She's as good as a little fat lamb – oh, she'll taste so good.' She pulled out her shiny knife – the way it glinted was terrifying.

'Ouch!' the hag said suddenly. She had been bitten on the ear by her own daughter, who clung to her back and looked so unruly and wild that it was sheer pleasure for a bandit. 'You nasty brat!' the mother said and didn't have the time to chop up Gerda.

'I want her to play with me,' the bandit girl insisted. 'I want her to give me her muff, her beautiful dress, and I want her to sleep next to me.' She bit her mother again, which made the bandit hag jump up and spin around. All the bandits laughed and said, 'Look how she dances with her kid!'

'I want to get into the coach,' the bandit girl said. She had to have her way because she was so spoiled and stubborn. She and Gerda sat in the coach, and they drove over brambles and thorns, deep into the woods. The bandit girl was no bigger than Gerda, but she was stronger – her shoulders were broader and her skin was darker. Her eyes were quite black – they looked almost sad. She hugged Gerda and said, 'They won't chop you to pieces as long as I don't get mad at you. I suppose you're a princess?'

'No,' Gerda said and told her all that had happened to her and how fond she was of Kai.

The bandit girl looked solemn, nodded slightly, and said, 'I won't let them chop you up, and even if I do get angry with you, I'll do it myself.' She dried Gerda's eyes and warmed her hands in the beautiful muff, which was very soft and warm.

The coach stopped. They were in the middle of the courtyard of the bandits' castle, which had a crack that ran from top to bottom. Ravens and crows flew out of holes in the wall, and big bulldogs – each of them looked as if it could swallow an entire person – jumped high in the air. But the dogs didn't bark, because it was forbidden.

A big fire burned on the stone floor in the middle of an enormous old sooty room. Smoke drifted towards the ceiling and had to find its own way out. Soup was cooking in a large vat, and hares and rabbits turned on spits.

'You'll sleep here with me and all my little animals,' the bandit girl said. They ate and drank and went to a corner that was covered with blankets and straw. Above them, perched on pegs and rafters, were nearly a hundred tame pigeons. They seemed to be asleep, but they stirred slightly when the little girls approached.

'They're all mine,' the bandit girl said and quickly grabbed one of the pigeons. She held it by the feet and shook it until it flapped its wings. 'Kiss it!' she shouted, and it flapped in Gerda's face. 'The wild wood pigeons are up there,' she continued and pointed high up the wall to bars that covered a hole. 'Those two are wood pigeons – they'll fly off in a second if you don't lock them up properly. And here's my dear old Baa!' she said, yanking the antlers of a reindeer who was tied by a shiny copper ring around his neck. 'We have to watch him carefully too or he'll run off with the pigeons. Every single evening I tickle his neck with my sharp knife – he's afraid of that.' The little bandit girl pulled a long knife from a crack in the wall and let it slide across the reindeer's neck. The poor animal kicked; the bandit girl laughed and dragged Gerda to bed.

'Do you keep the knife with you when you sleep?' Gerda asked and looked at it a little fearfully.

'I always sleep with the knife,' the bandit girl replied. 'You never know what might happen. But tell me again what you told me before about Kai and why you went out in the wide world.'

Gerda started from the beginning, while the wild pigeons cooed in their cage, and the tame pigeons slept. The little bandit girl put her arm around Gerda's neck and held the knife in her other hand. She made a lot of noise when she slept. Gerda could not close her eyes, for she didn't know if she was going to live or die. The bandits sat around the fire singing and drinking, and the bandit hag did somersaults – oh, it was a terrible sight for a little girl to see.

Then the wood pigeons said, 'Grrgh, grrgh! We've seen Kai. A white hen pulled his sledge – he sat in the carriage of the snow queen. When we were still in our nest, her carriage flew by above the forest. Her ice-cold breath killed all the baby birds except the two of us. Grrgh, grrgh!'

'What are you two saying up there?' Gerda shouted. 'Where did the snow queen go? Have you any idea?'

'She probably went to Lapland, because there's always snow and ice there. Just ask the reindeer who's tied up over there with a rope.'

'Yes,' the reindeer said. 'There's ice and snow, and it's wonderful and good. You can jump all around the big shiny valleys. The snow queen has her summer tent there, but her permanent castle is up by the North Pole on the island called Spitsbergen.'

'Oh, Kai, little Kai,' Gerda sighed.

'Now lie still,' the bandit girl said. 'Or else I'll poke you in the stomach with my knife.'

In the morning Gerda told her everything that the wood pigeons had reported, and the bandit girl looked quite serious. She nodded her head and said, 'It doesn't matter, it doesn't matter. Do you know where Lapland is?' she asked the reindeer.

'Who would know better than me?' the reindeer replied, and his eyes sparkled. 'I was born and brought up there, and I played there in the snowy fields.'

'Listen,' the bandit girl said to Gerda. 'You can see that all the men are gone. But Ma is still here, and she'll stick around. Late in the morning she'll start to drink from the big bottle. After that, she'll take a little nap, and that's when I can help you.' She jumped out of bed, rushed to give her mother a hug, pulled her mother's beard, and said, 'Good morning, my own sweet goat!' Her mother pinched her nose so that it turned both red and blue, but she did it all out of love.

When her mother had drunk from her bottle and was taking her nap, the bandit girl went to the reindeer and said, 'I really wish I could keep tickling you with my sharp knife, because it's so funny. But never mind. I'll untie your rope and help you get outside, so you can run away to Lapland. But you must hurry and take this little girl to the snow queen's castle, where her friend lives. You know her story, because she talked loud enough and you listened in.'

The reindeer jumped for joy. The bandit girl lifted Gerda onto its back, took care to tie her down, and even gave her a little pillow to sit on. 'While we're at it,' she said, 'here are your fur boots, because it will get cold. I'll keep the muff because it's much too pretty, but you won't freeze. Here are my mother's big mittens – they'll reach all the way to your elbow. Put them on. Now your hands look like my horrid mother's.'

Gerda was so happy that she cried.

'I don't like it when you whine,' the bandit girl said. 'Just look happy now! And here are two loaves of bread and a ham so you won't starve.' The bread and the ham were tied behind Gerda. The bandit girl opened the door, coaxed all the big dogs inside, and cut the rope with her knife, telling the reindeer, 'Now run! But take care of the little girl.'

Gerda stretched her big mittens towards the bandit girl and said goodbye. Then the reindeer rushed off through bushes and stubble, through a big forest, across swamps and steppes, as fast as it could go. Wolves howled, ravens shrieked, and the sky made a noise like 'achoo, achoo' – as if it had sneezed itself red.

'Those are my old Northern Lights,' the reindeer said. 'Look how they shine!' It ran farther, through night and day. The bread was eaten, the ham too, and then they were in Lapland.

SIXTH STORY

The Lapp and the Finn

They stopped at a small house. It looked wretched; the roof almost touched the ground, and the doorway was so low that the people who lived there had to crawl on their stomachs to get in or out. No one was in except for an old Lapp woman who was frying fish next to a whale-oil lamp. The reindeer told her Gerda's whole story, but first he told his own because it seemed much more important; besides, Gerda was so worn out by cold that she could not speak.

'Oh, you poor things,' the Lapp woman said. 'You still have a long way to go. You have to travel more than a hundred miles into

Finnmark because the snow queen has her country house there; she sends up blue light every single night. I'll write a few words on a dried codfish, because I haven't any paper. You can give it to the Finn woman up there – she knows more about it than I do.'

When Gerda had warmed up and had something to eat and drink, the Lapp woman wrote a few words on the dried codfish and told Gerda to keep it safe. She tied Gerda to the reindeer again, and he bounded off. There was a sound of 'phst, phst!' in the air, and all night the most beautiful blue Northern Lights burned in the sky. Then they arrived in Finnmark, where they knocked on the Finn woman's chimney, because she did not even have a door.

It was so hot inside that the Finn woman walked around almost naked. She was tiny and sort of grimy. She helped Gerda out of her clothes and took off her mittens and boots – otherwise Gerda would be far too hot – and put a piece of ice on the reindeer's head. Then she read what was written on the dried fish. She read it three times. By then she knew it by heart and put the dried codfish into the pot. You could still eat it; she never wasted anything.

The reindeer told his own story first and then Gerda's. The Finn woman blinked her wise eyes but said nothing.

'You're so wise,' the reindeer said. 'I know that you can tie up all the winds of the world with a thread. When a sailor unties one knot, he'll get a good breeze. If he unties a second, it will blow hard, and when he unties a third and fourth, it'll be so stormy that the trees in the forest will blow down. Won't you give the little girl a drink so she'll get the strength of twelve men and overpower the snow queen?'

'The strength of twelve men?' the Finn woman said. 'A lot of good that will do!' She went over to a shelf, took down a big rolled-up hide, and unfolded it. The hide was covered with strange letters. The Finn woman read until sweat poured from her forehead.

Once again the reindeer begged the Finn woman to help Gerda. Gerda looked at her pleadingly, her eyes filled with tears.

The Finn woman's eyes fluttered again, and she pulled the reindeer into a corner. As she put another piece of ice on his head, she whispered, 'It's all true. Kai's with the snow queen – where he can have everything he wants or imagines. He believes it's the best place in the world, but that's because he has a splinter from the mirror in his heart and a little speck of glass in his eye. Unless they come out, he'll never be human again, and the snow queen will keep her power over him.'

'But can't you give Gerda some kind of potion to give her power over everything?'

'I can't give her any more power than she already has. Can't you see how much that is? Don't you see how people and animals feel they must help her – how far she's come on just her bare feet? But we mustn't tell her about this power. It's in her heart because she's a sweet innocent child. If she can't get to the snow queen herself and get rid of Kai's glass splinters, there's nothing we can do. The snow queen's garden starts two miles from here. You must carry Gerda over there and set her down in the snow by the big bush with red berries. Don't dawdle – and hurry back.' The Finn woman lifted Gerda onto the back of the reindeer, and he ran as fast as he could.

'I forgot my boots! I forgot my mittens!' Gerda shouted. The cold stung her, but the reindeer did not dare stop. He ran until he came to the big bush with red berries, where he set her down. He kissed her on the mouth, and big shiny tears ran over the animal's cheeks. Then he ran back as fast as he could. There she was, poor Gerda, without shoes, without gloves, in the middle of the fearsome, ice-cold Finnmark.

She ran on as quickly as she could, but a whole regiment of snowflakes came towards her. These snowflakes did not fall from the sky – it was quite clear and glowed with the Northern Lights. They rushed along the ground, and the closer they came, the bigger they got. Gerda remembered how big and strange snowflakes had looked when she had seen them through a magnifying glass, but here they were altogether different – big and scary. They were alive – they were the snow queen's guard –

and had the most peculiar shapes. Some looked like big ugly hedgehogs, and others were like snakes knotted together, jabbing with their heads. Some looked like small chubby bears whose hair stood up. They were all shining white; they were all living snowflakes.

Gerda said her prayers, and it was so cold that she could see her own breath – it came out of her mouth like smoke from a chimney. Her breath got denser and denser until it turned into small transparent angels who grew larger and larger when they touched the ground. They all wore helmets, they all carried spears and shields, and they kept coming. By the time Gerda had finished her prayers, a legion of angels surrounded her. They stabbed the terrible snowflakes with their spears, and they splintered into hundreds of pieces. So Gerda could move on, cheerful and safe. The angels rubbed her feet and hands so that she didn't feel so cold, and she walked quickly towards the snow queen's castle.

But before we go on with Gerda's story, we need to see how Kai is doing. He certainly wasn't thinking about Gerda, and he never imagined that she was just outside the castle.

SEVENTH STORY

What Happened in the Snow Queen's Castle and What Happened Later

The walls of the castle were made of drifting snow, the windows and doors of cutting winds; depending on how the snow drifted, the castle had more than a hundred rooms. They were very bright, lit by the strong Northern Lights. The biggest room stretched for miles, and all the rooms were so large, so empty, so shiny, and so icily cold. No one ever had any fun there – there wasn't even a dance for the polar bears, where the wind made the music and small bears got up on their hind legs to show how refined they were. There were no card games with paw-smacking and backslapping or even a ladies' tea party for the white foxes. The snow queen's rooms were empty, enormous, and cold. The Northern Lights flared so regularly that you could calculate the exact moment when they would be at their brightest and at their dimmest. In the middle of this empty, endless, icy room was a frozen lake; it had cracked into a thousand pieces. Amazingly, each piece looked exactly like every other piece. When the snow queen was at home, she sat in the middle of this lake. It was the Mirror of the Mind, she said – unique and the best thing in the world.

Kai had become quite blue with cold – almost black, in fact – but he did not feel it, because the snow queen had kissed away his shivers, and his heart had nearly become a lump of ice. Kai was dragging sharp flat pieces of ice, which he put together in all sorts of ways – as we use pieces of wood in Chinese puzzles. He was trying to work something out, making most ingenious patterns: an ice puzzle of the mind. To Kai his design seemed wonderful and very important – but that was only because of the glass splinter in his eye. He had been struggling to shape the pieces of ice into a word – *eternity* – but could not work out how to do it. The snow queen had said, 'If you can make

that design for me, you'll be your own master, and I'll give you the entire world and a pair of new skates.' But he could not do it.

'I must rush off to the warm countries,' the snow queen told him. 'I want to take a look at the big black pots' – she was referring to the volcanoes Etna and Vesuvius. 'I want to give them a coat of whitewash. They need it, and it will look good after the lemons and grapes have been harvested.' Then the snow queen flew away, and Kai was left all alone in the big, empty, icy room that was miles long. He looked at the pieces of ice and thought and thought until his head ached. He was so stiff and still that you would think he had frozen to death.

That was when Gerda came into the castle, through the big gate made of stinging winds. But she read an evening prayer, and the winds calmed down as if they were going to sleep. She stepped into the big, empty, cold room and saw Kai. She recognized him, rushed to him, hugged him, held him tight, and cried, 'Kai, dear Kai! Now I've found you!'

But he sat very still, stiff and cold. Gerda started to cry hot tears. Her tears fell on his chest and reached his heart – thawing out the lump of ice and melting the piece of mirror lodged in it. He looked at her as she sang the hymn:

> *In the valley, the roses grow wild,*
> *There we can speak to the Christ child!*

Kai burst into tears. He cried so hard that the splinter washed right out of his eye. He recognized her and let out a shout: 'Gerda, sweet Gerda! Where on earth have you been? And where have I been?' He looked around. 'It's really cold in here! And how big and empty it is!' He held on to her, and she laughed and cried with joy. It was so wonderful that even the pieces of ice danced happily around. When they got tired, they lay down, forming just the word that the snow queen had asked Kai to guess. Now he was his own master, and the snow queen would give him the whole world and a new pair of skates.

Gerda kissed his cheeks, and they turned red; she kissed his eyes, and they shone like hers; she kissed his hands and feet, and he became healthy and fit. It was all right for the snow queen to come back now. His freedom was written on the floor in shining pieces of ice.

Kai and Gerda held hands and wandered out of the big castle. They talked about Grandmother and about the roses on the roof, and wherever they went, the winds were quiet and the sun broke through. When they reached the bush with the red berries, the reindeer was waiting. Another young reindeer had come with him; her udder was full, and she gave the children warm milk and kissed them on the mouth. The reindeer carried Kai and Gerda to the Finn woman, where they warmed up in her hot room and got directions for reaching home. Then they went to the Lapp woman, who had sewn them new clothes and had got her sledge ready.

The reindeer – with its young companion jumping alongside –

followed the children all the way to the border, where they saw green sprouts for the first time. There they said goodbye to the reindeer and Lapp woman. 'See you!' they shouted. The first little birds began to chirp, and green buds covered the forest. Then a young girl wearing a shiny red hat and holding two pistols came out of the woods on a magnificent horse. Gerda recognized the horse; it was one of those that had pulled her golden carriage. The rider was the bandit girl. She was bored at home and wanted to go north, and if that did not amuse her, she would go somewhere else. She immediately recognized Gerda, and Gerda recognized her – a happy moment.

'You're quite a fellow, the way you get around,' Gerda said to Kai. 'We've gone to the end of the world for your sake. I wonder if you deserve it.'

Gerda patted the bandit girl on the cheek and asked after the prince and princess.

'They've travelled to foreign countries,' the bandit girl told her.

'What about the crow?' Gerda asked.

'Well, the crow is dead,' she replied. 'His tame sweetheart is a widow. She walks around with a piece of black wool tied to her leg. The way that she complains is pathetic, but it's all nonsense. Tell me what happened with you – how you managed to find him.'

Gerda and Kai told her.

'So that's it,' the bandit girl said. She grabbed their hands and promised that if she ever came through their town, she would come to see them. Then she rode away into the wide world as Kai and Gerda walked off hand in hand. As they walked, it turned into a beautiful spring day, all green and filled with flowers. Church bells rang, and they recognized the tall towers, the great city. That was where they lived. They went straight to Grandmother's door – up the stairs to the living room where everything was just as it had been. The clock said tick-tock, the hands turned, and as they walked through the door, they realized that they were grown-ups now. The roses on the roof bloomed in the open windows. There were their small chairs. Kai and Gerda sat down and held each other's hands. They had forgotten, as if it were a bad dream, the cold empty splendour of the snow queen's castle. Grandmother sat in God's clear sunshine and read aloud from the Bible: 'Unless you become like children, you cannot enter the Kingdom of God.'

Kai and Gerda looked at each other and suddenly understood the old hymn:

> *In the valley, the roses grow wild,*
> *There we can speak to the Christ child!*

There they sat, the two of them. They were grown-ups, and yet they were children – children in their hearts. And it was summer – warm, wonderful summer.

The Red Shoes

Once there was a little girl – so delicate and pretty. Because she was poor, she had to go barefoot in the summer, and in the winter she had to wear big wooden shoes that rubbed against her instep until her little feet became quite red. It was awful.

Old Mother Shoemaker lived in the middle of the village and used strips of old red cloth to sew a small pair of shoes as best she could. They were crudely made, but she meant well, and she wanted the little girl to have them. The little girl's name was Karen.

On the very day that her mother was buried, Karen wore these red shoes for the first time. Of course, they were not the right thing to wear for mourning, but she did not have any other shoes. So she put them on her bare feet and followed the lowly straw coffin.

At that moment a large old carriage passed by, with a large old woman inside. She looked at Karen and felt sorry for her. She said to the vicar, 'Listen, let me have the little girl and I'll be good to her.'

Karen thought that all this happened because of the red shoes, but the old lady said that they were hideous. The shoes were burned and Karen was given neat, clean clothes. Now she had to learn to read and sew, and people said that she was pretty. But the mirror said, 'You're much more than pretty – you're beautiful!'

One day the queen travelled through the country with her little daughter, who was a princess. People swarmed outside the castle – Karen was there too – and the princess, dressed in fine white clothing, stood in a window and let people admire her. The princess did not have a train or a gold crown, but she did have lovely red shoes, made of fine leather. They certainly looked a lot nicer than the ones that Mother Shoemaker had made for Karen. There was really nothing in the world like red shoes.

Eventually, Karen was old enough to be confirmed. She got new clothes and was supposed to get new shoes. The rich shoemaker, who lived in town, measured her little foot; his shop was in his house, where large glass cases were filled with pretty shoes and shiny boots. It looked very nice, but the old woman could not see very well, so she got no pleasure from it. Among the shoes was a red pair, just like the ones the princess had worn. They were exquisite! And sure enough, the shoemaker said that he had sewn them for a nobleman's daughter. But they hadn't fitted.

'It must be patent leather,' the old lady said. 'They're so shiny!'

'Yes, they're shiny,' Karen said. They fitted her, and they bought them, but the old lady didn't realize that they were red. She would never have allowed Karen to be confirmed in red shoes. Still, that is what happened.

Everyone looked at Karen's feet when she walked through the church to the choir door. Karen thought that even the old pictures on the tombs – those portraits of vicars and vicars' wives, with stiff collars and long black robes – stared at her red shoes. She could think only about those shoes – even when the vicar put his hand on her head and talked about the holy baptism, about the covenant with God, and how she was about to become a grown-up Christian. The organ played solemnly, the children's choir sounded beautiful, and the old cantor sang, but Karen could think of nothing but her red shoes.

By afternoon everyone had told the old lady that Karen's shoes were red. The old lady said that red shoes were altogether inappropriate and that Karen had done a horrible thing. From that time on, whenever she went to church, Karen was told to wear black shoes, no matter how worn they were.

The following Sunday Karen was supposed to go to communion. She looked at the black shoes, and then she looked at the red shoes. She looked at the red ones again and put them on.

It was a beautiful sunny day. Karen and the old lady walked through the field along the path, which was a little dusty.

An old soldier leaned on a crutch by the church door; he had a peculiar long beard that was more red than white because it *was* red. He bowed all the way to the ground and asked the old lady if he could wipe her shoes. Karen too stretched her little foot forward. 'Look at those beautiful dancing shoes,' the soldier said. 'May they stay on tight when you dance!' Then he slapped the soles of the shoes.

The old lady gave the soldier a tip and walked inside the church with Karen.

Everyone in the church looked at Karen's red shoes, and all the portraits looked at them. When Karen knelt at the altar and put the gold chalice to her lips, she thought only about the red shoes. It was almost as if they were floating in the chalice – she forgot to sing the hymn, and she forgot to read the Lord's Prayer.

Everyone left the church, and the old woman got into her carriage. As Karen lifted her foot to follow her, the soldier standing nearby said, 'Look at those beautiful dancing shoes,' and Karen could not help herself: she had to dance a few steps. When she started, her legs kept dancing; it was as if the shoes had taken over. She danced around the corner of the church – she couldn't help it; the coachman had to run after her and grab hold of her, and he lifted her into the carriage. But her feet kept dancing and gave the kind old lady some terrible kicks. Finally, they managed to get the shoes off and Karen's legs calmed down.

When they got home, the shoes were put away in a cupboard, but Karen could not stop looking at them.

The old lady was taken ill, and they said that she wouldn't live long. Somebody had to take care of her and nurse her, and no one was closer than Karen. But there was a ball in town, and Karen was invited. She looked at the old lady, who was not going to live long anyway, and then at the red shoes. She saw no harm in that. She put on the red shoes, and that was all right, but then she went to the ball and started to dance.

When she wanted to dance to the right, the shoes danced to the left. When she wanted to move one way on the floor, the shoes went the other way, down the stairs, through the street, and out of the city gate, and she danced – she had to dance – right into the dark forest.

Something bright shone above the trees, and she thought that it was the moon, because it was a face. But it was the old soldier with the red beard. He nodded and said, 'Look at those beautiful dancing shoes!'

She was terrified and wanted to kick off the red shoes, but they would not come off. She ripped off her stockings, but the shoes were stuck to her feet. So she danced – she had to dance – over the fields and meadows, in rain and shine, by night and by day. But it was worst at night.

She danced into the open churchyard, but the dead didn't dance – they had something much better to do than dancing. She wanted to sit on the grave of a humble person, where the bitter tansy weeds grew, but she found neither rest nor respite, and she danced towards the open door of the church. There she saw an angel in long white robes, with wings that reached from his shoulders all the way to the ground. His expression was serious and stern, and he held a shiny broadsword in his hand.

'You must dance!' he said. 'You must dance in your red shoes until you're pale and cold – until your skin shrivels like a skeleton's. You must dance from door to door, and wherever there are proud, vain children, you must knock on the door so that they hear you and fear you. You must dance – dance!'

'Have mercy!' Karen shouted. But she did not hear the angel's answer because her shoes carried her through the gate, into the field, across roads and trails – she had to keep dancing and dancing.

One morning she danced past a door that she recognized. She heard hymns inside, and they carried out a coffin covered with flowers. She knew then that the old lady had died, and she felt abandoned by everyone and cursed by God's angel.

So she danced – she had to dance – in the dark night. Her shoes carried her off, past whitethorns and over stubbled fields, which scratched her until she bled. She danced across the heath to a lonely house. She knew that the executioner lived there, and she tapped on the window with her finger and said:

'Come out! Come out! I can't come in because I'm dancing!'

The executioner said, 'You don't know who I am, do you? I cut off the heads of evil people, and I can feel my axe quivering.'

'Don't cut off my head!' Karen cried. 'Because then I won't be able to repent my sin. But chop off my feet with the red shoes.'

She confessed all her sins, and the executioner cut off her feet with the red shoes. But the red shoes, with her small feet in them, still danced, over the fields and into the deep forest.

The executioner made wooden legs and crutches for her and taught her a hymn, the one that sinners always sing. Then she kissed the hand that had swung the axe and went away over the heath.

'I've suffered enough for those red shoes,' Karen said. 'Now I want to go to church so everybody can see me.' She walked boldly to the church door, but when she got there, the red shoes danced in front of her. She was frightened and turned back.

All the next week she was miserable and kept crying heavy tears. But when Sunday came, she said, 'All right – I've suffered and struggled enough. I think I'm just as good as lots of those people who are sitting so smugly in church.' She walked ahead confidently, but she didn't get any farther than the gate – that was when she saw the red shoes dancing in front of her, and she was terrified. She turned back, and in her heart she repented her sins.

She went to the vicarage and asked whether they would take her as a servant. She promised to work hard and do whatever she could – it didn't matter what they paid her if only she had a roof over her head and lived among good people. The vicar's wife felt sorry for her and took her in. Karen was hardworking and pensive. She sat quietly and listened each evening when the vicar read aloud from the Bible. All their children were fond of her, but when they talked about dressing up in frills and finery – and talked about looking as beautiful as a queen – she shook her head.

They all went to church on the following Sunday, and they asked Karen whether she wanted to go with them. With tears in her eyes she looked sadly at her crutches. While they went to hear God's word, she went alone to her little room, which was only big enough for a bed and a chair. She sat down with her hymn-book and was reading it devoutly when the wind carried the sounds of the organ from the church. Tearfully, she lifted her head and said, 'Oh, God, help me!'

At that moment the sun shone brightly, and right in front of her, in white robes, stood God's angel, the one she had seen at night in the doorway to the church. But rather than his sharp sword, he carried a beautiful green branch covered with roses. He touched the ceiling with the branch, and the ceiling rose high in the air – a brilliant golden star appeared where he had touched it. Then he touched the walls, and they widened. Karen looked at the organ as it was playing, and she saw the old pictures of vicars and vicars' wives; the congregation sat in the ornate pews and sang from their hymn-books. The church itself had come to the poor girl in the little cramped room, or perhaps she had gone to the church. She sat in a pew with the other people from the vicarage, and when they had finished the hymn and looked up, they nodded and said, 'It was good that you came, Karen.'

'By the grace of God,' she replied.

Then the organ swelled, and the children's choir sounded sweet and beautiful. The bright warm sunshine streamed through the window into the pew where Karen sat. Her heart was so filled with sunshine – with peace and happiness – that it burst. Her soul flew up to God on the rays of the sun, and no one there asked about the red shoes.

The Little Match Girl

It was miserably cold. Snow was falling; it was already getting dark, for it was the last day of the year, New Year's Eve. A poor little girl, barefoot and with nothing on her head, walked along the street in the cold and dark. To be sure, she had been wearing slippers when she left home, but what good was that? The slippers were too big; her mother had been the last one to wear them – that's how big they were. The little girl lost them when she hurried across the street just as two carts rushed by at terrifying speed. One slipper was nowhere to be found, and a boy ran off with the other, saying that he could use it as a cradle when he had children of his own.

So the little girl walked along on bare feet, which had turned red and blue from cold. She carried a bunch of matches in an old apron and held a bundle in her hand. No one had bought anything all day; no one had given her a single penny. Hungry and frozen, she walked on, looking wretched – the poor thing! Snow fell on her long yellow hair, which curled very nicely at the back, but she certainly was not thinking about her pretty hair. Lights were shining from all the windows, and there was a

197

wonderful smell of roast goose in the street. It was, after all, New Year's Eve – and the little girl did think about that.

In a nook between two houses – one jutted out a little beyond the other – she sat down and curled up with her legs tucked under her. Still, she felt colder and colder, but she did not dare go home because she had not sold any matches and had not earned a penny. Her father would beat her, and, besides, it was cold at home; they had no more than a roof over their heads, and the wind whistled through it, although they had stuffed straw and rags in the biggest cracks. Her hands felt almost dead from cold. Oh! A lighted match would feel so good. If she only dared take one out of the bunch, strike it against the wall, and warm her fingers. She pulled out a match – *ritsch!* How it sputtered and burned.

When she cupped it with her hand, the match had a warm bright glow, like a tiny lamp. It was a strange kind of light: the little girl thought that she was sitting in front of a large iron stove with a brass belly and shiny brass knobs. The fire felt good, it was so nice and warm. It really was. The little girl stretched her feet to warm them and – the flame went out. The stove disappeared. The little girl was holding the end of a burned match in her hand.

She lit another match. It burned and shone, and where the light fell on the wall, it became transparent, like gauze. She looked right into a dining room, where the table was set with a bright white cloth and fine china, and where a roast goose, filled with prunes and apples, steamed wonderfully. And better still, the goose jumped off its dish, waddled along the floor with a fork and knife in its back, and came right up to the poor girl. Then the match went out, and all she could see was the thick cold wall.

She lit another match, and then she sat under the prettiest Christmas tree. It was even bigger and had more decorations than the one she had seen last Christmas through the rich merchant's glass door. A thousand candles burned on the green branches, and colourful pictures, of the sort that fill shop windows, looked down towards her. The little girl stretched her hands in the air – and the flame went out. All the Christmas lights rose higher and higher, and she saw that they were bright stars. One of them fell and made a long fiery streak across the sky.

'Someone has died,' the little girl said. Old Grandmother, the only person who had been nice to her, had told her that whenever a star falls, a soul goes up to God. But Grandmother was dead.

She struck another match against the wall. It cast a light around her, and in the glow she saw old Grandmother – vivid and radiant, gentle and loving.

'Grandma!' the little girl called out. 'Take me with you! I know you'll be gone when the match goes out – gone like the warm stove, the wonderful roast goose, and the big beautiful Christmas tree.' She quickly lit the rest of the matches in the bunch; she so wanted Grandmother to stay. The matches burned with such brilliance that they were brighter than the light of day. Grandmother had never been so beautiful or so tall; she lifted the little girl in her arms, and they flew higher and higher in light and joy. There was no more cold, no hunger, no fear – they were with God.

But in the cold dawn, the girl sat in the nook by the house. She had rosy cheeks and a smile on her lips: she was dead, frozen to death on the last night of the old year. New Year's morning brightened over her little body, sitting with her matches; most of the bunch had been burned. She had wanted to get warm, people said. No one knew the beauty she had seen or in what glory she had gone with her old grandmother into the joy of the New Year.

The Happy Family

The biggest green leaf in this country is definitely a burdock leaf. If you hold it in front of your stomach, it's like an apron, and if you put it on your head when it rains, it's almost as good as an umbrella – because it's just huge. A burdock leaf never grows all by itself. Where there's one, there are lots more. They're a beautiful sight, and all that beauty is snail food – big white snails, the kind that rich people turned into fricassee, ate, and declared, 'Umm – that's excellent!' because they thought it tasted wonderful. Snails like that lived off burdocks, which is why burdocks got planted in the first place.

There was an old estate where people no longer ate snails. The snails had died out, but the burdocks had not – they grew and grew, all over garden paths and flowerbeds. It was impossible to keep them down. They made a whole forest of burdock, and if it hadn't been for an apple tree or a plum tree here and there, no one would ever know that it was a garden. Everything was burdock, and among the burdocks lived the last two, extremely old, snails.

They had no idea how old they were, but they did remember

that there used to be a lot more of them, that their family came from a foreign country, and that the whole forest had been planted for their sake. They had never gone beyond the forest, but they nevertheless knew that there was something in this world called the Manor House and that up there you got boiled until you turned black, after which you were put on a silver platter. What happened after that, nobody knew. They could not actually imagine what it was like to be boiled and put on a platter, but it was supposed to be wonderful and exceedingly distinguished. When they asked the beetle, the toad, or the earthworm, no one could tell them anything about it. None of them had ever been boiled or put on a silver platter.

The old white snails were the most distinguished in the world, and they knew it. The forest existed for their sake, and the Manor House was there so that they could be boiled and arranged on a silver platter.

They lived happy and secluded lives, and because they did not have children, they adopted an ordinary snail and brought it up as their own. But the little snail wouldn't grow, because he was so ordinary. Still, the old parents, especially Mama – Snailmama – thought that she could see him getting bigger, and she told Papa, in case he couldn't see it, to examine the little shell and feel it. He felt the shell and found that Snailmama was right.

One day it rained heavily.

'Listen to the way it drums-tum-tums on the burdocks,' Snailpapa said.

'It's dripping too,' Snailmama said. 'It's running right down the stem! You'll see – it's going to get wet in here. I'm glad we have our own good houses and that the little one has his own house too. Obviously, more has been done for us than for any other creature in the world; it's easy to see that we're the privileged few. We've had a house from the time we were born, and the burdock forest was planted for our sake. I wonder how far it goes and what's on the other side.'

'There's nothing on the other side,' Snailpapa said. 'No place could be better than where we are, and there's nothing I want.'

'Well, yes,' Mama said. 'But I'd like to go to the Manor House, and be boiled and put on a silver platter. That's what all our ancestors did, and I know there's something special about it.'

'The Manor House might have fallen into ruin,' Snailpapa said. 'Or the burdock forest could have covered it so people couldn't get out. There's no rush. But you're always in such an awful hurry, and the little one is starting to be like that too. For three days he's been climbing up that stalk. I get a headache when I look at him up there.'

'You mustn't scold,' Snailmama said. 'He crawls very slowly. I'm sure he'll be a joy to us, and we old snails haven't anything else to live for. But have you thought about this: where do we find a wife for him? Don't you think there might be someone of our sort that far into the burdock forest?'

'I believe there might be black snails there,' the old snail said. 'Black snails without houses, but that's so vulgar and they're pretentious. We could hire the ants; they run back and forth as if they had something to do. They probably know where to find a wife for our little snail.'

'We know the loveliest of them all,' the ants said. 'But we're afraid it won't work, because she's a queen.'

'That doesn't matter,' the old snail said. 'Does she have a house?'

'She has a castle,' the ants replied, 'the most beautiful ant castle with seven hundred corridors.'

'Thanks all the same,' Snailmama said. 'Our son is not going to live in an anthill. If you haven't a better idea, we'll hire the white gnats. They fly all around in rain and shine, and they know the burdock forest inside and out.'

'We have a wife for him,' the gnats said. 'A hundred people-steps from here, there's a small snail with a house under a gooseberry bush. She's pretty lonely and old enough to get married. She's only a hundred people-steps away.'

'Well, let her come to him,' the old snail said. 'He has a burdock forest, and she only has a bush.'

They fetched the little snail maiden. It took her eight days to get there, but that's what was so nice about it: you could tell that she was the right sort.

Then they celebrated the wedding. Six glowworms glowed as best they could. Otherwise, it was a quiet affair, because the old snails couldn't stand drinking and carousing. Snailmama gave a beautiful speech; Papa couldn't do it because he was so moved. Then they bequeathed the couple the entire burdock forest and said what they had always said: that it was the best place in the world, and if they were honest and decent and multiplied, they and their children would one day make it to the Manor House, be boiled until they turned black, and be arranged on the silver platter.

After the speech the old snails crawled into their houses and never came out again; they slept. The young snail couple ruled the forest and had lots of heirs. But they were never boiled and never put on a silver platter, so they concluded that the Manor House had fallen into ruin and that all the people in the world had died out. Because no one contradicted them, it was true, of course. The rain drummed on the burdock leaves to make music just for them, and the sun brought colour to the burdock forest just for them. They were very happy, and the whole family was happy, just because it was.

The Shadow

In the hot countries the sun really burns. People get as brown as mahogany, and in the hottest countries they get burned black. It so happened that a learned man travelled from one of the cold countries to one of the hot countries. He thought that he could stroll around just as he did at home, but he dropped that idea pretty quickly. The learned man and all sensible people had to stay inside. During the day they kept their shutters and doors closed, and it looked as if everyone was asleep or no one was at home.

The learned man lived on a narrow street with tall houses; it was laid out so that it got sun from morning to night. It was really unbearable. To the scholar from the north – he was a young man, an intelligent man – it felt like being inside a fiery oven. It wore him out. He became quite gaunt – even his shadow shrank and became much smaller than it had been at home. The sun wore out his shadow too, and neither the man nor his shadow revived until evening, after sunset.

It was very amusing to watch the shadow: when the lamp was brought into the room, the shadow stretched all the way up the wall, even across the ceiling. It needed to stretch to recover its strength. The learned man also went out onto the balcony to stretch, and as stars appeared in the lovely clear sky, he felt that he too had come to life again. Up and down the street people stepped out onto their balconies (in the hot countries every window has a balcony) because you've got to have fresh air, even if you're used to being mahogany brown. It got very lively upstairs and down; cobblers and tailors – everyone – moved into the street. They carried tables and chairs outside and lighted candles – more than a thousand candles burned. One person talked, another sang, people strolled about, carriages drove by, donkeys with bells trotted along – *ðing-a-ling-a-ling!* Dead people were buried as people sang hymns, street children set off firecrackers, and church bells rang. There really was a lot of life in the street.

Only one house was quiet – the one right opposite the scholar. Yet someone lived there, because there were flowers on the balcony. They flourished in the hot sun, and they would not have without water. Someone must be watering them; people must be living there. During the evening the door over there was open. But it was dark inside, at least in the front room; from farther inside you could hear music. The learned stranger thought that it was quite wonderful, perhaps because he had persuaded himself that everything in the warm countries was wonderful – if it weren't for the sun. His landlord told him that he didn't know who had rented the house across the street. Nobody seemed to be there, and as for the music, the landlord thought that it was horribly boring: 'It sounds as if someone was practising a piece he couldn't master – always the same piece. "I'll get it right!" he's probably saying, but he can't do it, no matter how long he practises.'

One night the stranger woke up. He was sleeping with the balcony door open, a breeze lifted the curtain, and he thought he saw a strange shimmering from the neighbour's balcony. The flowers glowed like flames, with the most beautiful colours, and there was a slender graceful girl, who also seemed luminous, in the middle of the flowers. The sight of all this brightness hurt his eyes because he had just woken up and had opened them wide too suddenly. He jumped out of bed and crept softly over to the curtain, but the girl was gone and the radiance was gone. The flowers no longer glowed but looked fine, just as they always did. The door was ajar, and from far inside you could hear the music, so soft and soothing that you could easily lose yourself in pleasant thoughts. It was enchanting. But who lived there? Where was the real entrance? The whole ground floor was nothing but shops, and of course people could not always get in that way.

One evening the stranger was sitting on his balcony. The lamp burned in the room behind him, so it was quite natural for his shadow to appear on his neighbour's wall. Yes, there it was, right opposite him in the middle of the flowers on the balcony. When the stranger moved, the shadow moved. That's what shadows do.

'I think my shadow is the only living thing that you can see over there,' the learned man said. 'Look how nicely it sits there in the flowers. The door is ajar. Now, Shadow, be good enough to go inside, take a look around, come back, and tell me what you've seen. If you did that,' he went on, jokingly, 'it would be a real help. Please step inside. Well, are you going?' He nodded to the shadow, and the shadow nodded to him. 'Go on, then, but don't get lost.'

The stranger got up, and the shadow on the opposite balcony got up too. The stranger turned round, and the shadow turned round. If anyone had paid attention, they would have seen the shadow enter the half-open balcony door across the street at the very moment that the stranger went back into his room and let the long curtain drop behind him.

The next morning the learned man went out to drink coffee and read the newspapers. 'What's this?' he asked as he stepped into the sunlight. 'I haven't got a shadow! So it actually did leave me last night and didn't come back. That's really too bad.'

It annoyed him, not so much because his shadow was gone but because he knew the old tale about a man without a shadow – and everyone in the cold countries knew that story. If he came home and told his own story, people would say that he was an imitator, which was the last thing he needed to hear. So he was not going to talk about it at all, and that was very sensible of him.

In the evening he went out onto the balcony again. He put the lamp behind him, in just the right place, because he knew that a shadow always needs his master as a screen. But he could not entice it to come out. He made himself small, he made himself big, but he had no shadow – and none came. 'Hmm, hmm!' he said, but that didn't help either.

It was annoying. But in the hot countries everything grows rapidly, and after eight days, when the foreign visitor stepped into the sunlight, he noticed, to his great pleasure, that a new shadow was growing from his feet – its roots must have been left behind. After three weeks he had a decent enough shadow, and while he travelled again to the northern countries, the shadow grew longer and longer until in the end it was too long and too big by half.

The learned man came home. He wrote books about what was

true in the world and what was good and beautiful. Days passed, and years passed – many years went by.

One evening, while the learned man was sitting in his room, there was a soft knock on the door.

'Come in!' he said. No one came, and he opened the door. There, right in front of him, was an extraordinarily skinny person who had a strange effect on him. The caller, by the way, was very well dressed – no doubt he was a distinguished gentleman.

'With whom do I have the honour of speaking?' the scholar asked.

'Just what I thought,' the gentleman replied. 'You didn't recognize me! I've become so real that I'm actually flesh and blood and wear clothes. You probably never imagined that you'd see me so prosperous. Don't you recognize your old shadow? You probably didn't think I was going to show up again. I've done very well since the time we were together. I've grown rich in every way. I can buy my freedom now if I have to.' Then he rattled a cluster of expensive seals that were hanging from his watch, and he touched a thick gold chain around his neck – his fingers flashed with diamond rings. All the jewellery was real.

'I can't get over it,' the learned man said. 'What's all this about?'

'It's nothing ordinary,' the shadow said. 'But you're not an ordinary person, either. As you know, I've followed in your footsteps since I was a child. As soon as you thought I was mature enough to make my way in the world, I went my own way. I've done fabulously well. But I felt a sort of yearning to see you before you died – and you will die some day. I also wanted to see this country again – after all, everybody loves his homeland. I know you've got another shadow. Do I owe you – or it – anything? Please be good enough to tell me.'

'Is it really you?' the learned man said. 'This is very strange. I never thought that your own shadow could turn up again as a human being.'

'Tell me what I need to pay,' the shadow said, 'because I really don't want to owe you anything.'

'What are you saying?' the learned man said. 'What kind of debt are you talking about? You're as debt free as anyone. I'm absolutely delighted by your good luck. Sit down, old friend, and tell me a little about what happened and what you saw in the house across the street in the hot country.'

'I'll be happy to tell you,' the shadow said and sat down. 'But first you have to promise that when we meet in town, you won't tell anybody that I was your shadow. I'm planning to get engaged, and I'm rich enough to support more than one family.'

'Don't worry,' the scholar said. 'I won't tell anyone who you really are. Here's my hand on it – I'm a man of my word.'

'And I'm a shadow of mine,' the shadow said, because that's how he had to express it.

It was really quite strange how human the shadow was. He was dressed in black, and his clothes were made of the finest dark cloth. He wore patent leather boots and a collapsible hat that could be pressed flat, not to mention what we already know: the seals, a gold necklace, and diamond rings. Indeed, the shadow was beautifully dressed, which was precisely what made him just like a human being.

'Now I'll tell you what happened,' the shadow said, and with his patent leather boots he stepped as hard as he could on the sleeve of the learned man's new shadow, which lay by his feet like a poodle. He did this either out of arrogance or to make the scholar's new shadow stick to him. But it just lay there, still and calm, and listened. The new shadow wanted to know how it too could get away and earn enough to be its own master.

'Do you know who lived in the house across the street?' the shadow asked. 'The most beautiful of all: Poetry. I was there for three weeks, and it was like being there for three thousand years, reading everything that has ever been written. Believe me, I'm telling you the truth. I've seen everything and know everything.'

'Poetry!' the learned man shouted. 'Well, well. She sort of keeps to herself in the big cities. Poetry. I only saw her for a brief moment, but I was very sleepy then. She stood on the balcony and shimmered as the Northern Lights do. Tell me, tell me! You were on the balcony, you went through the door, and then – '

'Then I went to the front room,' the shadow continued. 'You always used to look into that room, and there was no light, just a kind of twilight. Door after door opened to a long row of rooms. They were all so brightly lit that the brightness would have killed me if I'd gone all the way to Poetry's room. But I was cool and collected. I took my time, and that's what you should do.'

'What did you see then?' the learned man asked.

'I saw everything, and I'll tell you about it. By the way – and I'm not saying this out of pride – but when you consider that I'm a free and educated man, not to mention my social position and my personal fortune, I'd really appreciate it if you would address me formally, as "sir" or "mister".'

'I'm sorry,' the scholar said. 'It's just an old habit. You're absolutely right – and I'll try to remember. But tell me everything you saw.'

'Everything,' the shadow said. 'Because I saw everything and I know everything.'

'What was it like in the room farthest inside?' the learned man asked. 'Was it like a fresh forest? Was it like a holy church? Was it like the clear starry sky when you stand on a tall mountain?'

'It was everything,' the shadow said. 'As you know, I didn't go all the way in; I stayed in the outer room, in the twilight, but I had a good view from there. I saw everything and I know everything. I've been in the antechamber of Poetry's court.'

'But what did you see? Did ancient gods walk through the great halls? Did heroes of the past fight there? Did sweet children play and tell you their dreams?'

'I'm telling you, I was there. As you can imagine, I saw all that there was to see. If you'd gone there, you wouldn't have become more human, but I did. I learned to understand my inner self – what I was born with, my connection to Poetry. Of course, when I was with you, I never thought about it. But as you know, every time the sun rose or set, I grew curiously large. In the moonlight I was almost more visible than you. I didn't understand it myself then, but in the neighbour's front room I suddenly realized that I'd become a man! By the time I left the house, I was an adult, and you weren't in the south any longer. As a man, I was ashamed to look as I did. I needed boots, clothes, and all the polish that makes us recognizable as people.

'I headed for – I'm telling *you* this because you're not going to put this in a book – I headed right to the woman who peddles cakes, and I hid under her skirt. The woman didn't realize what she was hiding. I didn't come out until evening, and then I ran around the street in the moonlight. I stretched myself against the wall – it tickled my back and felt so good. I ran up and I ran down. I peeped through the highest windows, at the ground floor and the top floor. I looked where no one else could look and I saw what no one else ought to see. The truth is, it's a nasty world.

'I wouldn't have wanted to be human if everyone didn't think it was something worthwhile. I saw the most unimaginable things going on between husbands and wives, and between parents and their precious children. I saw,' the shadow continued, 'what no one knows, but what everyone really wants to know about – scandalous behaviour next door. If I were to put out a news-paper, everyone would read it. But I wrote directly to the people involved, and there was an uproar everywhere I went. They were so afraid of me! They were terribly fond of me too. Professors made me a professor, tailors gave me new clothes – I'm well supplied. The master of the mint coined new money for me, women said I was very handsome, and I became the man that I am. Now I'll say goodbye. Here's my card. I live on the sunny side of the street, and I'm always home when it rains.' Then the shadow left.

'That was really strange,' the learned man said.

Years and days passed, and the shadow returned.

'How's it going?' the shadow asked.

'Ah, not well, sir,' the learned man said. 'I'm writing about truth and beauty and goodness, but nobody wants to hear about that sort of thing. I'm in despair, because it means so much to me.'

'It doesn't mean much to me,' the shadow said. 'I'm getting fat, and that's what we all should try to be. You don't understand the world – it makes you ill to try. You need to get away. I'm taking a trip this summer. Do you want to come along? I'd really like a travelling companion. Do you want to accompany me as my shadow? It would make me very happy to have you come along. I'll pay for the trip.'

'Now you're going too far, sir!' the learned man said.

'It depends on how you look at it,' the shadow replied. 'Travel would do you a lot of good. If you'll be my shadow, I'll pay for everything.'

'That's unfair,' the scholar said.

'But that's how the world is and always will be,' the shadow said, and it left.

Things went badly for the learned man. Grief and trouble pursued him, and what he said about truth, beauty, and goodness was as appealing to most people as roses would be to a cow. Eventually, he became quite ill.

'You really look like a shadow of yourself,' people told him, and the learned man shivered, because it made him think.

'You need to go to a spa,' the shadow, who came to visit, advised him. 'There's no choice. I'll go with you for old time's sake. I'll pay for the trip, and you can write it all down to keep me amused while we travel. I want to go to the spa too. My whiskers aren't growing as they ought to – that's also a kind of illness, because you have to have a beard. Now be reasonable and accept my offer. Of course, we'll travel as friends.'

And they left. The shadow was the master, and the master was the shadow. They rode together in carriages and on horseback; they walked side by side, in front of each other or behind, depending on where the sun was. The shadow always knew how to take the lead, and the learned man never gave this much thought. He was good-hearted, sweet tempered, and amiable, and one day he said to the shadow, 'Since we've become travelling companions, and since we've been together since childhood, shouldn't we stop being so formal? After all, it's friendlier not to keep saying "sir".'

'That's a thought,' said the shadow, who was now the real master. 'You're speaking frankly, and you mean well, so I'll be just as frank and well meaning. As a learned man, you know, I'm sure, how strange nature can be. Some people can't bear to touch grey paper – it makes them ill. Other people shiver when they hear a nail scrape against a pane of glass. I get just that kind of feeling when I think of you addressing me by my first name. It makes me feel small, as I used to feel in my position with you. It's just a feeling – it's not pride. I can't let you call me by my first name, but I'll be happy to use yours – then we're halfway there.'

Then the shadow called his former master by his first name.

'This really seems madness,' the learned man thought, 'that I have to say "sir" to him, and he uses my first name.' But he had to put up with it.

They arrived at the spa, where there were lots of strangers. Among them was a beautiful princess, who suffered from seeing things too clearly. That can be nerve-racking.

The princess saw straight away that the newcomer was quite unlike the others. 'He's here to get his whiskers to grow, people say, but I know the real reason: he can't cast a shadow.'

She became curious, and as soon as she went for a walk, she struck up a conversation with the strange person. Being a king's daughter, she could skip elaborate formalities, and she said, 'Your problem is that you can't cast a shadow.'

'Your royal highness must be much better,' the shadow said. 'I know what your illness is – that you see things far too clearly. But you're getting over it and you're cured. I just have a very unusual shadow. Don't you see that person who's always with me? Other people have an ordinary shadow, but I don't like what's ordinary. People often give their servants better cloth for their livery than they give themselves. In the same spirit, I've dressed my shadow up as a man. Indeed, as you can see, I've even given *him* a shadow. It's very expensive, but I like to have something that no one else has.'

'Really?' the princess thought. 'Am I really cured? This spa is the best there is – the waters have the most remarkable qualities these days. But I'm not leaving, because it's so much fun here. I really like the stranger. I hope his beard doesn't grow, because then he'll leave.'

That evening the princess danced with the shadow in the grand ballroom. She was light, but he was even lighter; she had never danced with a partner like that. She told him where she had come from, and he knew her country – he had been there. When she was not at home, he had peeped through all her windows from top to bottom and had seen both this and that. So he knew the answers to the princess's questions and could drop hints that amazed her. He must be the wisest man on earth! She was very impressed with what he knew, and when they danced again, she fell in love. The shadow sensed this, because it seemed as if she could look right through him.

They danced again, and she was just about to tell him, but she hesitated. She thought about her country and her kingdom and all the people she was going to rule over. 'He *is* a wise man,' she said to herself, 'and that's good. And he's a wonderful dancer, and that's good too. But I wonder if he's thoroughly educated – that's just as important. I must test him.' Then, little by little, she began to ask him the most difficult questions, which she couldn't have answered herself, and the shadow made a strange face.

'You can't answer that!' the princess said.

'That's child's play,' the shadow replied. 'I think that even my shadow over there by the door can answer that.'

'Your shadow!' the princess exclaimed. 'That would be *very* peculiar.'

'Yes, although I'm not certain,' the shadow said. 'But I think he can, because he's followed me around for so many years and paid attention. So I think he can. If your royal highness permits me, I'd like to explain: he's so proud of passing as a human being that if you want to put him in a good mood – and he needs to be in a good mood to answer properly – you have to treat him just like a real person.'

'I like that,' the princess said.

Then she walked over to the learned man by the door. She talked to him about everything under the sun and how people really are, inside and outside, and his answers were good and wise.

'What a man he must be to have such a wise shadow,' she thought. 'What a blessing it would be for my people and my kingdom if I chose him as my consort. I'm going to do it.'

They soon agreed, both the princess and the shadow, but no one was supposed to know anything about it until she returned to her kingdom.

'No one – not even my shadow,' the shadow said, and he had his reasons for saying this.

They arrived in the country where the princess ruled when she was at home.

'Listen, my good friend,' the shadow said to the learned man. 'Now that I'm as happy and powerful as anyone can be, I'd like to do something special for you. I want you to stay with me at the castle all the time, ride with me in my royal carriage, and have a hundred thousand *rix*-dollars a year. But in return you'll have to let everybody call you a shadow. You must not tell anyone that you've ever been a man. And once a year, when I'm sitting on the balcony in the sun – appearing before the people – you'll have to lie by my feet, as shadows do. I want you to know that I'm marrying the king's daughter, and the wedding is tonight.'

'That's just going too far,' the learned man said. 'I won't – I'm not going to do it. You'd be deceiving the whole country and the princess too. I'll tell them everything – that I'm the man, and you're the shadow, just dressed like a person.'

'No one will believe you,' the shadow said. 'Be reasonable, or else I'll call the guard.'

'I'm going straight to the princess,' the scholar said.

'But I'm going first,' the shadow said, 'and you're going to jail' – and he did go to jail, because the guards obeyed the one they knew was going to marry the princess.

'You're trembling,' the princess said when the shadow came to her chamber. 'Has something happened? You mustn't be ill on the night we're going to get married.'

'I've been through the worst thing anyone could go through,' the shadow told her. 'Just imagine – I should have known that a poor shadow's brain can't take very much. Just imagine – my shadow's gone mad. He thinks he's a person and that I – just imagine! – that I'm his shadow.'

'That's terrible,' the princess said. 'But he's been locked up, hasn't he?'

'He has, but I'm afraid he'll never get better.'

'Poor shadow,' the princess said. 'He's very unhappy. Truly, it would be a good deed to release him from the little bit of life that's left in him. When I actually think about it, I think that we need to get rid of him and do it very quietly.'

'That's very harsh,' the shadow said. 'He was a faithful servant.' He let out what sounded like a sigh.

'You're a noble character,' the princess said.

That evening the whole city was brightly illuminated, and cannon went off: *boom!* The soldiers presented arms. It was a real wedding! The princess and the shadow appeared on the balcony and received yet another round of hurrahs.

The learned man heard none of this because they had put him to death.

By the Outermost
Sea

A couple of big ships were sent all the way up to the North Pole
to find the boundaries between land and sea – to search for a
passage so that people could get through. The ships had already
sailed for days and years in fog and ice and had run into great
difficulties. Then winter began, and the sun disappeared; many
weeks turned into one long night. Everything around them was
solid ice, and every ship was stuck. The snow was deep, and it
was used to build houses that looked like beehives. Some were
big, like our Stone Age burial mounds; others were only large
enough to hold two to four men. It wasn't dark – the Northern
Lights shone red and blue, a grand, endless display of
fireworks – and the snow glimmered. The night was one long
blazing twilight.

When the day reached its brightest point, groups of natives
showed up, strange-looking in their hairy fur clothing. They
were on sledges made from pieces of ice. The sailors brought big
piles of fur and used them as warm rugs in their snow houses.
Furs were also turned into blankets and covers, which the sailors
made into beds under the snow domes. Outside, it froze so hard

that the air crackled. It was unlike anything we're used to, even in our most brutal winters.

Here at home it was still autumn. The sailors up north thought about that. They remembered home, and how the sun's rays shone on red-gold leaves hanging from the trees. Only their clocks told them that it was night and time to sleep, and two sailors lay down to rest in a snow house. The youngest sailor had brought from home his most valued possession, which his grandmother had given him before he left. It was the Bible, which he put beside his bed every night. Since childhood he had known what was in it, and he read a passage every day. As he lay there, he was often comforted by the holy words: *'If I took the wings of the morning, I would dwell by the outermost sea, and even there you would guide me, and your right hand would hold me fast.'*

With those words of truth and faith in mind, the sailor closed his eyes; sleep came, and dreams in which his spirit felt the presence of God. His body rested; only his soul was alive, and he sensed it like the melodies of favourite old songs. There was a mild breeze, warm like summer, and from his bed he saw brightness above him, as if something were shining through the dome from outside. He lifted his head and saw that the luminous whiteness did not come from the walls or ceiling but from great wings on an angel's shoulder.

He looked into the angel's gentle radiant face, and the angel rose from the pages of the Bible and spread its arms. The walls of the snow house vanished like an airy veil of mist: it was a beautiful, tranquil autumn day. The green fields and hills and reddish brown forests of home stretched out under the mild sunshine. The stork's nest was empty, but some apples still hung on the wild apple trees, although the leaves were gone. Red rose hips glowed, and a starling whistled in its little green cage above the window of the farmhouse – his home of homes. The starling whistled as it had been taught, and Grandmother hung chickweed on the cage, as her grandson always had. The blacksmith's daughter, who was young and very beautiful, stood beside the well and pulled up a bucket of water. She nodded to the sailor's grandmother, who waved, holding up a letter from far away. It had arrived that morning from the cold north, way up

by the pole itself, where her grandson was 'in God's hand'. They laughed and cried, and the sailor, covered by ice and snow up there in the world of the spirits, under the wings of the angel, saw and heard everything. He laughed with them and cried with them, as they read aloud the biblical words from the letter: *'By the outermost sea, even there you would guide me, and your right hand would hold me fast.'*

All around was the sound of a beautiful hymn, and the angel let its wings cover the sleeping sailor like a veil. The dream was over; it was dark in the snow house. The Bible lay under his head, and faith and hope filled his heart. God was with him, and so was home – *'by the outermost sea'.*

Hopeless Hans

(AN OLD TALE TOLD AGAIN)

Out in the country was an old manor where an old squire lived, and the squire had two sons who were too clever by half. They wanted to propose to the king's daughter, and they weren't afraid because the princess had let it be known that she would marry the man who really had something to say for himself.

The two brothers studied for eight days. That was all the time they had, but it was enough because they had already learned a thing or two, and that is always useful. One knew the entire Latin dictionary by heart as well as three years' worth of the local newspaper – not only forwards but backwards. The other brother had been through the by-laws of the guilds and what every alderman is expected to know. That's why he thought that he could say something about the state. He could also embroider suspenders, because he was refined and had nimble fingers.

'I'll win the king's daughter,' they both declared, and their father gave each of them a beautiful horse. The son who knew the dictionary and the newspapers got a horse as black as coal. The son who embroidered suspenders and was as clever as an alderman got one as white as milk. They rubbed the corners of

224

their mouths with cod-liver oil to make their lips more supple, and all their servants stood in the courtyard to watch them mount their horses. That was when the third brother turned up – for there were actually three. But no one really counted him as a brother, because he didn't have the learning of the others. They called him Hopeless Hans.

'Where are you going all dressed up?' he asked.

'To court – to win the king's daughter with our eloquence. Haven't you heard what the town criers announced to the whole country?' And they told him.

'All right! I'd better come along!' Hopeless Hans said, but his brothers laughed at him and rode off.

'Father, let me have a horse!' Hopeless Hans shouted. 'I really feel like getting married. If she'll have me, she'll take me. If she won't have me, I'll take her just the same.'

'That's just nonsense,' his father said. 'I'm not going to give you a horse. You don't know how to talk, but your brothers – they're splendid fellows.'

'If I can't have a horse,' Hopeless Hans said, 'I'll take the billy goat. He's mine, and he's strong enough to carry me.' He straddled the billy goat, jabbed its side with his heels, and tore down the road. Whew, he was off! 'Here I come!' Hopeless Hans cried, and he sang so shrilly that it echoed around him.

His two brothers rode ahead in silence. They didn't say a word, because they had to think about the great thoughts that they hoped to express. Everything they said was supposed to be so clever.

'Hey, hey!' Hopeless Hans shouted. 'Here I come. See what I found on the road.' He showed his brothers a dead crow he'd found.

'Hopeless,' they said. 'What are you going to do with that?'

'I'll give it to the king's daughter.'

'Yes, you do that,' they said, laughed, and rode off.

'Hey, hey! Here I come. See what I've found now. You don't find *that* every day on the road.'

The brothers turned around to see what it was. 'Hopeless!'

they said. 'It's an old wooden shoe without the leather top. Are you going to give that to the princess too?'

'I certainly am,' Hopeless Hans said, and the brothers laughed and rode off, getting far ahead.

'Hey, hey, here I come!' Hopeless Hans shouted. 'Oh, it's getting better and better – this is really something!'

'What have you found this time?' the brothers asked.

'Oh,' Hopeless Hans said. 'I can't begin to tell you how happy the princess will be.'

'Ugh,' the brothers said. 'That's just mud, straight from the ditch.'

'It certainly is,' Hopeless Hans said. 'And it's the very best kind – the kind you can't hold on to.' Then he filled his pockets with it.

The brothers rode on as fast as they could; they arrived a whole hour early and waited at the gates to the city. There, each suitor got a number as he arrived. They lined up, six in a row, and stood so close that they could not even move their arms. That was just as well; otherwise, they might have ripped each other apart just because someone was ahead of them in the line.

The rest of the inhabitants crowded around the castle, right up to the windows, just to watch the princess receive her suitors. As soon as one entered the hall, he was at a loss for words.

'No good,' the princess said. 'Goodbye!'

Then came the brother who knew the dictionary. But he had completely forgotten it while he stood in line. The floor squeaked, and the ceiling was all mirrors, so he saw himself upside-down. At every window three scriveners and an alderman wrote down everything that was said so it could be printed in the paper immediately and sold on the corner for two pennies. It was awful. And besides, they'd stoked the fire so that the stove was red hot.

'It's really hot in here,' the suitor said.

'That's because my father is roasting chickens today,' the princess said.

Duh! There he was – that was not the sort of conversation he had expected. He couldn't think of a single word to say, and he had wanted to say something witty. Duh!

'No good,' the princess said. 'Goodbye!' So he had to go.

Then it was the other brother's turn.

'It's awfully hot here,' he said.

'Yes, we're roasting chickens today,' the princess replied.

'Excuse me. Uh . . . what?' he said, and all the scriveners wrote, 'Excuse me-uh-what?'

'No good,' the princess said. 'Goodbye!'

Now it was Hopeless Hans's turn. He rode his billy goat right into the royal halls.

'It's boiling hot in here,' he said.

'That's because we're roasting chickens,' the princess told him.

'And a good thing too,' Hopeless Hans said. 'I suppose I can get a crow roasted then?'

'Of course you can,' the princess replied. 'But have you got something to cook it in? I haven't a pot or pan.'

'But I have,' Hopeless Hans said. 'Here's a pot with a tin handle.' He took out his old wooden shoe and put the crow inside it.

'That's enough for a whole meal,' the princess said. 'But where are we going to get the gravy?'

'It's in my pocket,' Hopeless Hans said. 'I've got so much that I have some to waste.' He poured a little mud out of his pocket.

'I like that,' the princess said. 'You know how to answer. You know what to say, and I want you as a husband. But do you know that every word we'll say and have said will be written down and published in the newspaper tomorrow? You see the three scriveners and an old alderman at every window? The alderman is the worst because he doesn't understand anything.' She said this just to scare him, and all the scriveners whinnied and spilled ink on the floor.

'I suppose they're the ones who count around here,' Hopeless Hans said. 'So the alderman deserves the best.' Then he turned his pockets inside out and threw mud right in the alderman's face.

'Well done!' the princess said. 'I couldn't have done that, but I'm sure I'll learn.'

Hopeless Hans became king. He got a crown and sat on a throne with a wife of his own. We got this straight from the alderman's newspaper – and you can't trust that.

Kids' Talk

At the merchant's house there was a big party for children – rich children and blue-blooded children. The merchant was well-to-do. He was educated too – he could have gone to the university. He had been pushed to study by his good-natured father, who had started out as a cattle dealer and was honest and hardworking. That trade had earned him money, which the merchant multiplied. The merchant had brains and heart too, but people talked less about that than about all his money.

Distinguished visitors would come and go – high-born people, as they say, cultivated people, as they say, as well as some who were both and some who were neither. And now there was that children's party; children were talking – and children say just what they mean. There was a lovely little girl, but she was terribly proud. The servants had kissed it into her, not her parents, who were far too sensible. Her father was a groom of the king's chamber, and that, the little girl knew, was really something.

'I'm a chamber child!' she said. She might as well have been a cellar child for all that anyone could do about it. She told the

230

other children that she was 'born', and she said that if you're not 'born', then you couldn't exist. It didn't help to study or to work hard; if you weren't born, you didn't exist.

'And those people whose names end with *sen,*' she said, 'they can never, ever become anything in the world! You should put your hands on your hips and keep those *sen! sen! sens!* far away from you.' Then, showing how to do it, she put her hands on her hips so that the elbows of those small pretty arms pointed out. Her small arms were very pretty – what a sweetheart!

But the merchant's little daughter got very angry. Her father's name was Madsen, and she knew that his name ended with *sen*. As proudly as she could, she said, 'My father can buy a hundred *rix*-dollars' worth of sweets and toss them to the crowd. Can your father do that?'

'Well,' a writer's little daughter said, '*my* father, he can put your father and your father and all fathers in the newspaper. Everybody's afraid of him, my mother says, because my father runs the paper.'

The little girl held her head high, as if she were a real princess who is supposed to hold her head high.

A poor boy stood outside the half-open door, and peeped in. The little boy couldn't even come into the room – that's how lowly he was. He had been turning the spit for the cook and had got permission to stand behind the door and look at the children in their fancy clothes who were having such a good time. It was almost too much for him.

'Oh, to be one of them!' he thought, and then he heard what they said. It was enough to put him in a bad mood. His parents did not have a penny saved and could not afford to get the newspaper, much less write for it. And then, worst of all, his father's name – and therefore his name too – ended, plain and simple, with *sen*. He would never amount to anything in this world. It was very sad. Yet he was born, he thought, really born. It could not be any other way.

Well, that was *that* evening!

Many years passed, and when that happens, children become grown-ups.

A grand house in the city was filled with beautiful things. Everyone wanted to see it; even people from the countryside came to see it. Who, of the children we have told you about, could call that house his own? Well, that's pretty obvious. No, perhaps not so obvious after all. That house belonged to the poor little boy. He became something even though his name ended in *sen* – *Thorvaldsen*.

And the three other children – the children of blood, money, and intellectual pride? Well, one is no better than the other; they're all equal. They all turned out just fine. At bottom they were good. Whatever they had once said and thought was only kids' talk.

Father's Always Right

Now I'll tell you a story that I heard when I was little. Every time I've thought about it since, it gets better, because stories are like lots of people – they get better and better as they get older, and that's awfully nice.

I'm sure you've been out in the country. You've seen a really old farmhouse, with a thatched roof, where moss and weeds grow all by themselves. There's a stork's nest on the roof (you've got to have a stork), the walls are crooked, the windows are low, and only one of them can be opened. The oven sticks out like a fat little stomach, and the elderberry bush leans across the fence, where there's a puddle of water with a duck or ducklings, right under the gnarled willow tree. There's also a dog on a chain, and it barks at anybody and everybody.

Out in the country in a farmhouse just like that lived a couple – a farmer and his wife. They didn't have much, but there was nevertheless one thing they could get along without, and that was a horse that grazed along the roadside ditch. Father rode it to town, the neighbours borrowed it, and he got something in return. But he thought that he could do better

by selling or trading it for something even more useful. What could that be?

'You know best, Father,' his wife said. 'It's market day in town. Why don't you go and sell the horse or make a good exchange? What you do is always right, so ride off to market.'

She tied his neckerchief because she knew how to do that better than he. She tied a double bow – it looked very dashing. She dusted his hat with her palm, kissed him on his warm mouth, and he rode off on the horse that he was supposed to sell or exchange. Yes, indeed – Father knew just how to do that.

The sun beat down. There were no clouds, and the road was dusty – a lot of people were going to market on horseback, in carriages, and on foot. It was sweltering, and there wasn't a bit of shade on the road.

Someone came along with a cow. It was as pretty as a cow could be. 'I'm sure it gives wonderful milk,' the farmer thought. 'Getting that cow could be quite a good exchange.'

'Hey, you with the cow,' he said. 'Let's have a little talk. Listen, I think a horse is worth more than a cow, but I don't care. A cow's more useful to me. Do you want to exchange?'

'Certainly!' the man with the cow said, and they exchanged.

That was that, and the farmer could have gone home; after all, he had done what he had set out to do. But because he had decided to go to the market, he would go to the market, if only to see it. So he walked on with his cow. He walked briskly, and the cow walked briskly, and soon they caught up with a man leading a sheep. It was a fine sheep – plump, with lots of wool.

'I'd like to own that sheep,' the farmer thought. 'It would always find enough grass by our ditch, and we could take it inside with us in the winter. Actually, wouldn't it make more sense to have a sheep than a cow?'

'Do you want to swap?' he asked.

Yes, indeed, the man who had the sheep was willing. They made the deal, and the farmer went down the road with his sheep. By the stile he saw a man with a big goose under his arm.

'That's a heavy one you've got there,' the farmer said. 'It's got feathers and it's got fat. It would look just right tied up by our puddle – just the thing for Mother to save scraps for. She's often said, "Oh, I wish we had a goose!" Now she can have one – and she *will* have one. Do you want to swap? I'll give you the sheep for the goose, and thanks too.'

The other man was willing enough, and they made the exchange. The farmer got the goose. He was close to town, and the crowd on the road got thicker with a crush of people and cattle. They walked on the road and along the ditch, right up to the toll keeper's potatoes, where he kept his hen tethered so that if it got frightened it wouldn't run off and get lost. It was a short-tailed hen that blinked with one eye and looked wonderful. 'Cluck, cluck!' it said. I can't tell you what the hen thought, but when the farmer saw her, he thought, 'She's the most beautiful hen that I've ever seen. She's prettier than the parson's brood hen. I'd really like to own her. A hen can always find a grain of corn – she can almost take care of herself. I think it would be a bargain if I can get her for the goose.'

'How about a swap?' the farmer asked.

'Not a bad idea,' the other said.

And they swapped. The toll keeper got the goose and the farmer got the hen.

He had accomplished quite a lot on his trip to town. It was hot, and he was tired. He needed a drink and a bite to eat, and he was just beside the tavern. Father wanted to go in, but the innkeeper's helper, who was carrying a sack chock full of something, wanted to go out, and they met in the doorway.

'What have you got there?' the farmer asked.

'Rotten apples,' the helper replied. 'A whole sackful for the pigs.'

'That's an awful lot. I wish Mother could see that. Last year we had only one apple on the old tree by the peat shed. We wanted to keep the apple, and it sat on the chest of drawers until it burst. That's always a sign of wealth, Mother says. This would really show some wealth. I wish she could see it.'

'Well, what will you give me?' the helper asked.

'Give? I'll give you my hen' – and he exchanged the hen for the apples, and went into the tavern, straight to the bar. He put his sack of apples up against the stove, where the fire was going, but he didn't pay attention to that. There were many foreigners in the room – horse traders, cattle dealers, and two Englishmen who were so rich that their pockets were bursting with gold coins. They were making bets, and here's what happened.

Hiss, hiss! What's that sound by the stove? The apples were beginning to roast.

'What's that?'

Soon they heard everything – the whole story about the horse that was exchanged for the cow right down to the rotten apples.

'Well, you're going to get it from Mother when you get home!' the Englishmen said. 'She'll really let you have it.'

'I'll get kisses, not punches,' the farmer replied. 'Mother will say, "Father's always right."'

'Will you bet on that?' they said. 'Gold coins by the barrel – a hundred pounds to a hundredweight!'

'A bushel is enough,' the farmer said. 'I can only come up with a bushel full of apples, and I'll throw in myself and Mother too. That way it'll be not only full but overflowing.'

'We'll take the bet,' they said, and the deal was done.

The innkeeper's wagon rolled out. The Englishmen got in, the farmer got in, the rotten apples got in, and then off they all went to the farmer's house.

'Good evening, Mother.'

'Good evening, Father.'

'I exchanged.'

'Yes, and you know how!' his wife said. She put her arms around his waist and forgot about the sack and the strangers.

'I've exchanged the horse for a cow.'

'Thank God for the milk,' his wife said. 'Now we can have milk, butter, and cheese on the table. That was a wonderful trade.'

'Yes, but then I exchanged the cow for a sheep.'

'Even better,' the farmer's wife said. 'You're always so thoughtful. We have plenty of grazing for a sheep. Now we can get sheep milk and sheep cheese and woollen stockings – even a woollen nightshirt. The cow can't give us that. She sheds her hair. You're such a thoughtful husband!'

'But I exchanged the sheep for a goose.'

'Are we really going to have goose for Michaelmas this year, little father? You always try to please me. It's such a lovely thought. The goose can be tied up and made even fatter for Michaelmas.'

'But I exchanged the goose for a hen,' the man said.

'A hen! That was a good move,' the wife said. 'The hen lays eggs, they'll hatch, and we'll have chickens. We'll have a chicken coop. That's what I've always really wanted.'

'But I exchanged the hen for a bag of rotten apples.'

'I've got to kiss you for that,' his wife said. 'Thank you, my dearest. I've got to tell you something: while you were away, I thought of making a really good meal for you – omelette with chives. I had the eggs but not the chives. So I went over to the schoolmaster's. I know they have chives there, but his wife is stingy, that nasty creature. I asked to borrow some – "Borrow?" she said. "Nothing grows in our garden, not even a rotten apple.

I can't even lend you that." Now I can lend her ten – a whole bagful even. Isn't that funny, Father?'

She kissed him smack in the middle of his mouth.

'I like that!' the Englishmen said. 'Always downhill, always carefree. That's certainly worth the money.' Then they gave a hundredweight of gold coins to the farmer, who got kisses and not punches.

Yes, indeed, it always pays when the wife realizes that Father is wisest and what he does is always right.

Well, that's that story. I heard it when I was little, and now you've heard it too and know that Father's always right.

The Gardener and
the Aristocrats

A few miles from the capital was an old manor house with thick walls, towers, and crenellated gables. That's where a rich and aristocratic family lived but only in the summer. The house was the best and prettiest of all the estates that they owned; on the outside it looked brand new, and inside it was cosy and comfortable. Carved in stone above the castle's gate was the family's coat of arms, and beautiful roses wound around the heraldic shield and balconies. The lawn spread out like a carpet of grass in front of the castle. There was red and white hawthorn in the garden, and rare flowers grew even outside the greenhouse.

Not surprisingly, the family had a talented gardener. The flowers, the orchards, and the vegetable gardens were wonderful to see, and next to them was a remnant of the estate's original old garden: a few boxwood hedges trimmed to look like crowns and pyramids. Behind them were two huge old trees; they had lost most of their leaves, and it was easy to imagine that a strong wind or a tornado had scattered big clumps of manure all over them. But every clump was a bird's nest.

For longer than anyone could remember, a commotion of screeching rooks and crows had made their nests in those trees. It was a whole city of birds. The birds were the masters, the propertied class, the estate's oldest family – the real lords of the castle. They couldn't have cared less about the people below. But they tolerated those earthbound creatures, even if they fired off their guns once in a while, which sent chills down the birds' spines and made them scatter in fear, crying 'Caw, caw!'

The gardener often talked to his employers about cutting down the old trees. The trees did not look healthy, and if they were gone, the screeching birds would probably disappear too and go elsewhere. But the family did not want to get rid of the trees or the flocks of birds; they were something that the estate could not lose – something from the old days that should not be wiped out.

'After all, my good Larsen, those trees are the birds' inheritance. Let them keep them.'

The gardener's name was Larsen, but that is neither here nor there.

'Don't you have enough to take care of, my good Larsen – what with the flower garden, the greenhouses, the orchard, and the vegetable garden?'

The gardener *did* have all that to take care of; he looked after the gardens – nursed and nurtured them – with enthusiasm and skill. The family realized that, but they also let him know that when they were guests in other people's houses, the fruit that they ate and the flowers that they saw were often superior to what grew in their own garden. It made the gardener unhappy, because he wanted to be the best and did the best that he could. He was a good-hearted man and a good gardener.

One day the master and the mistress of the estate summoned the gardener and told him in a gentle and gracious way that the day before, while visiting distinguished friends, they had eaten apples and pears that were so juicy, so tasty, that all the guests had expressed their admiration. The fruits were probably not from their own country but ought to be imported and grown at home if the climate permitted. They knew that the fruit had been bought in town from the finest fruit merchant. They told the gardener to see him and find out where the apples and pears had come from and then order some twigs for grafting.

The gardener knew the fruit merchant well. On behalf of his employers he had sold the surplus fruit from their gardens to that very merchant.

The gardener went to town and asked the merchant where he'd got those celebrated apples and pears.

'They're from your own garden,' the merchant said and showed him both the apples and the pears, which the gardener recognized.

That really made the gardener happy. He hurried home and told the family that the apples and pears had come from their own garden. The family could not believe it. 'That's not possible, Larsen! Can you get that in writing from the fruit merchant?'

He could, and he brought back a written statement.

'That's really odd,' the family said.

From then on, big bowls of those magnificent apples and pears from their own garden were on the dining table every day. They sent bushels and barrels of fruit to friends in town and outside town and even abroad. It was quite wonderful, but still you had to admit that the last two summers had been remarkably good for fruit trees. They had thrived all over the country.

Some time passed. The family had dinner at the royal court. The next day the master and his wife called for the gardener. At dinner they had had such juicy and tasty melons from their majesties' greenhouse.

'You must go to the royal gardener, my good Larsen, and get some seeds from those wonderful melons.'

'But the royal gardener got the seeds from us,' the gardener said, very pleased.

'In that case, their gardener was skilful enough to bring the fruit to another level,' his employers replied. 'Every melon was excellent.'

'Well, *I* can be proud then,' the gardener said. 'Actually, sir, the royal gardener hasn't had any luck with his melons this year. When he saw how splendid ours looked, and tasted them, he ordered three melons for the royal castle.'

'Larsen, don't try to tell us that those melons were from our garden.'

'I believe they were,' the gardener said. He went to the royal gardener and got a written testimonial that the melons on the king's table had come from their estate.

That was a real surprise for the family; the master and mistress did not keep the story secret and showed the testimonial to everyone. Then they sent the melon seeds far and wide, just as they had with the grafting twigs.

The family heard that the melon seeds took root and bore excellent fruit, which was named after the estate. Its name appeared in English, German, and French. They had never dreamed of such a thing.

'Let's hope that the gardener doesn't get too full of himself,' his master and mistress said.

But the gardener reacted in a different way. He worked hard to maintain his reputation as one of the country's best gardeners and to grow something superior every year in all the gardens. And that's what he did. Nevertheless, he was often told that the very first fruits he'd given them – the apples and pears – were actually the best and that what came after was far inferior. The melons were certainly very good, but that was a different matter entirely. You could say that the strawberries were first rate, but still they were not any better than what came from other estates. If the radishes did not do well one year, his employers talked only about the unfortunate radishes. They said nothing about the other good things that he had produced.

It was almost as if it were a relief for the family to declare, 'Things didn't work out for you this year, little Larsen.' They were quite happy to say, 'Things didn't work out.'

A couple of times a week the gardener brought fresh flowers into the drawing room. They were always arranged tastefully, and the combination seemed to make each colour brighter.

'You've got good taste, Larsen,' his employers said. 'But it's not something that you can take credit for – it's a gift from God.'

One day the gardener brought in a big crystal bowl with a water-lily leaf. On top of it was a radiant blue flower as big as a sunflower. Its thick stem reached into the water.

'A Hindustani lotus!' the family exclaimed.

They had never seen such a flower. During the day they put it in the sun and in the evening under a reflecting light. Everyone who saw it found it strangely beautiful and rare – even the most distinguished of all the country's young ladies agreed. She was a princess, wise and good-hearted.

The family saw it as an honour to present the princess with the flower, and it went with her to the castle.

Then the family went to the garden to pick the same kind of flower, if one could still be found. But they could not find it. So they called the gardener and asked where he had got the blue lotus.

'We've searched in vain,' they said. 'We've gone to the greenhouses and all around the flower garden.'

'No, it's definitely not there,' the gardener said. 'It's just a simple flower from the kitchen garden. But it *is* very beautiful, isn't it? It looks like a blue cactus, but it is only a blossom from an artichoke.'

'You should have told us that straight away,' his employers said. 'We couldn't help but think that it was a rare exotic flower. You've disgraced us in front of the young princess. She saw the flower here and thought it was beautiful. She didn't know what it was, and she knows quite a lot about botany. But that science has nothing to do with vegetables. Whatever gave you the idea, my good Larsen, of putting a flower like that in the drawing room? It makes us look ridiculous!'

The beautiful blue flower, which had been brought up from the kitchen garden, was expelled from the family's drawing room, where it did not belong. The family even apologized to the princess and told her that the flower was only a vegetable that the gardener had got it into his head to display. They'd given him a serious reprimand.

'That's a shame and it's not fair,' the princess said. 'I mean, really, he's opened our eyes to a beautiful flower that we've never noticed. He's shown us beauty where we never thought of looking for it. The royal gardener has been told to bring a flower to my room every day as long as the artichoke blooms.'

And that's what happened.

The master and mistress told the gardener that he could start bringing them fresh artichoke flowers again.

'It's actually beautiful,' they said. 'Highly peculiar.' They praised the gardener.

'Larsen likes to hear that,' they said. 'He's a spoiled child.'

That autumn there was a terrible storm. It got worse during the night – turning so violent that many big trees at the edge of the forest were pulled up by their roots. It was a great sorrow for the family – they actually referred to it as 'a sorrow' – but it was a joy for the gardener that the two big trees with all the birds' nests came down. In the storm you could hear the cries of rooks and crows; their wings banged against the windowpanes, the servants said.

'That makes *you* happy, Larsen,' the family said. 'The storm has knocked down the trees, the birds have taken to the woods. There's nothing left from the old days. Every sign, every trace, is gone – and it makes *us* sad.'

The gardener said nothing, but he thought about what he had long planned: use that splendid sunny spot that he had not been free to do anything with before. He wanted to turn it into the pride of the garden and the joy of the family.

The big toppled trees had crushed and flattened the ancient boxwood hedges with their topiary shapes. That was where the gardener cultivated a thicket of indigenous plants from the fields and woods. In the manor's garden he put in lots of plants that no other gardener had imagined, and he gave each as much shade or sun as it needed. He nursed the plants with love, and they responded with beauty.

A juniper tree from Jutland's heath grew there, in the shape and colour of an Italian cypress; the shiny, thorny holly, which stayed green during winter's cold and summer's sun, was beautiful to see. In front of those were ferns of every sort; some looked like the children of palm trees and others as if they were the parents of the lovely delicate fern that we call maidenhair. Here was the despised burdock, which is so beautiful when it is fresh that it looks good in a bouquet. Burdock grew in dry soil, but lower down, in moister ground, was broadleaf dock, also a scorned plant. Yet with its height and its magnificent leaves it had a painterly beauty. Mullein, transplanted from the field, stood six feet tall, flower by flower like a giant many-armed candelabra. Here were woodruff, primrose, lilies of the valley, wild calla, and delicate three-leaf sorrel. It was a beautiful sight.

Little pear trees from France, supported by steel wires, stood in front. They got lots of sun and care, and soon they were bearing big juicy fruit, just as they had in their own country.

Instead of the two old leafless trees, the gardener put up a tall flagpole flying the Danish flag. Another pole was nearby, and in the summer and autumn the hops wound their sweet-smelling flower clusters around it. In winter, following an old custom, the gardener hung a sheaf of oats so that the birds would have a meal during the joyous Christmas season.

'Our good Larsen is getting sentimental in his old age,' the family said, 'but he is faithful and devoted.'

As the new year began, one of the capital's illustrated journals published a picture of the old manor house. You could see the flagpole and the sheaf of oats for the birds at merry Christmastime. The journal made a special point of saying that it was a beautiful thought – that a custom so much a part of the old manor house had been preserved and honoured.

'People beat the drums for everything Larsen does,' the family said. 'He's a lucky man. I suppose we really ought to be proud of having him.'

But they weren't the least bit proud of having him. They knew that they were the employers and could sack Larsen. But they didn't do it, because they were good people, and there are lots of good people like them – which is a fortunate thing for every Larsen.

Well, that's the story of 'The Gardener and the Aristocrats'. Now you can think about it!

Auntie Toothache

Where did we get this story?

Do you want to know?

We got it from the rubbish bin – the one with old scraps of paper in it.

Lots of good rare books have gone to the general store and the grocer's – not to be read but as paper to wrap flour and coffee beans, salt herring, butter, and cheese. Literature, after all, has its uses.

Things are often tossed into the rubbish that shouldn't be tossed into the trash.

I know a grocer's boy, the son of a storekeeper, who rose from the basement to the street-level shop. He was someone who read a lot – a lot of wrapping paper, that is – both printed and handwritten. He had an interesting collection, which included several important documents from the rubbish bin of some far-too-busy, distracted bureaucrat; an intimate letter from one girlfriend to another; scandalous news that wasn't supposed to go any further and was not to be mentioned by anyone. The grocer-boy is a living rescue operation for a significant amount of literature.

He has a large domain. From his parents' and his boss's shops he has saved lots of books or pages from books that might have been worth a second look.

He's shown me his collection of printed and handwritten papers from the rubbish bin. The best of them came from the general store, and among these were a couple of pages from a large notebook. Their unusually beautiful and legible handwriting immediately caught my eye.

'The student wrote that,' he said. 'The student who lived just across the street from here and died a month ago. You learn that he suffered from terrible toothaches – it's sort of amusing to read. There's only a little bit left of what he wrote; it was a whole book and a bit more. My parents gave the student's landlady half a pound of green soap for it. Here's what I was able to save.'

I borrowed it, I read it, and now I'll tell you about it.

The title was:

Auntie Toothache

I

Auntie gave me sweets when I was little. My teeth could take it – they didn't go bad. Now I'm older and a university student. She still spoils me with sweets and says that I'm a poet.

I have the touch of a poet but not enough. Often when I walk around the streets of the city, it's as if I'm in a large library. The houses are bookcases – each floor a shelf of books. Here's an everyday story, there's a good old comedy, here are scientific works in every field; there's rubbish and good reading. I can fantasize and philosophize about all those books.

I have a touch of a poet in me but not enough. Many people have just as much as I have, yet they don't carry a sign or a collar around their necks with the word *poet*.

We've all been given a gift from God – a blessing big enough for one person but much too small to be divided with others; it comes like a ray of sunshine and fills your soul and thoughts. It comes like the fragrance of a flower, like a melody you know but don't remember from where.

The other evening I sat in my room. I wanted to read something but didn't have a book – not even a paper – when a leaf, fresh and green, fell down from a linden tree. The breeze carried it to me through the window.

I studied its branching veins. A little insect crawled across them, as if it wanted to study the leaf carefully. It made me think about human knowledge. We also crawl around on a leaf. The leaf is all that we know, but we immediately give lectures about the whole tree, the roots, the trunk, the crown – and the great tree: God, the world, and immortality – and out of all that, all we know is a little leaf.

As I sat there, I got a visit from Aunt Millie.

I showed her the leaf with the crawling insect, told her what I was thinking, and her eyes lit up.

'You're a poet!' she said. 'Perhaps the greatest we have. If I live to see it happen, I'll be happy to go to my grave. Ever since Brewer Rasmussen's funeral, you've always surprised me with your tremendous imagination.'

That's what Aunt Millie said, and then she kissed me.

Who was Aunt Millie and who was Brewer Rasmussen?

II

We children called my mother's aunt Auntie – we had no other name for her.

She gave us jam and sugar, even though it was very bad for our teeth. But she had a weakness for sweet children, she said. It was painful to deny them the sweets that they liked so much.

That's why we liked Auntie so much.

She was an old maid, and as far back as I can remember, she was always old. Her age never changed.

Earlier in her life she suffered a lot from toothaches and always talked about it. That's why her friend, Brewer Rasmussen, made a joke and called her Auntie Toothache.

He hadn't brewed for the last few years. He lived off the interest on his money, often visited Auntie, and was older than she was. He had no teeth at all – only a few black stumps.

When he was little, he ate too much sugar, he told us children, and that's how you get to look like that.

Auntie couldn't possibly have eaten sugar as a child – she had the prettiest white teeth.

She used them sparingly, she didn't sleep with them at night! Brewer Rasmussen said.

We children knew that he was being unkind, but Auntie said that he didn't mean anything by it.

One day at lunch she told us about a bad dream she'd had the night before; one of her teeth had fallen out.

'That means,' she said, 'that I'm going to lose a true friend.'

'Was it a false tooth?' the brewer said and chuckled. 'Then it would only mean that you're going to lose a false friend.'

'You're a rude old gentleman!' Auntie said, sounding angrier than I'd ever heard her before or since.

She later said that her old friend was only teasing, that he was the noblest person on earth, and that when he died he would become one of God's little angels in heaven.

I thought a lot about his transformation and whether I'd be able to recognize him in his new state.

When Auntie was young, and he was young too, he had proposed to her. She hesitated, dwelled on it, dwelled on it much too long. She remained an old maid but always a faithful friend.

Then Brewer Rasmussen died.

He was carried to his grave on the most expensive hearse, followed by a large crowd of mourners in uniforms with medals and ribbons.

Auntie, dressed in mourning, stood by the window with all us children, except for my little brother, whom the stork had brought only a week earlier.

The hearse and the mourners were gone, the street was empty; Auntie wanted to leave, but I didn't. I was waiting for the angel Brewer Rasmussen, for I knew that he was now a child of God with wings and had to appear.

'Auntie,' I said. 'Don't you think he's coming now? Or will the stork bring us Angel Rasmussen when he brings us a little brother?'

Auntie was completely overwhelmed by my imagination and said, 'That child is going to be a great poet.' She repeated it all through my school days – after my confirmation and now that I'm a university student.

She was, and still is, my most understanding friend, both when it comes to my torments as a poet and the torments of my teeth. I have attacks of both, you know.

'Just write down all your thoughts,' she said, 'and put them in the drawer in the table. That's what Jean Paul did, and he became a great poet, although I didn't really like him – he didn't excite me. You have to excite people – and you *will* excite people!'

The night after she'd said that, I lay awake in agony, longing to become the great poet that Auntie saw and sensed in me. I suffered a poet's ache, but there is a worse ache: toothache. It squashed and crushed me. I became a squirming worm with a hot poultice on my cheek.

'I know what that's like,' Auntie said.

She had a sad smile; her teeth shone so white.

But I have to begin a new chapter in the story about me and my aunt.

III

I had moved into new lodgings and had lived there for a month. I talked to Auntie about it.

'I'm living with a quiet family; they don't pay any attention to me, even if I ring three times. Actually, it's a very noisy house with a constant commotion of people and whatever blows through. I live just above the entryway. Every wagon, coming or going, makes the pictures on the wall rattle. The gate slams and shakes the whole house as if there were an earthquake. When I'm in bed, I feel the shocks through my whole body – but that's supposed to be good for the nerves. If the wind blows – and it always does in this country – the long window hooks outside swing back and forth and hit the wall. The bell to the neighbour's yard clangs with every gust of wind.

'The people who live in the house come dribbling in, late in the evening until the early hours. The lodger just above me, who gives trombone lessons during the day, is the last one to come home, and he doesn't go to bed until he's taken a short midnight stroll with heavy steps and hobnail boots.

'There are no storm windows, but, rather, a broken pane. The landlady has pasted paper over it, but the wind still blows through the crack, making a sound like a buzzing horsefly. It's music to sleep by. When I finally do fall asleep, I'm soon awakened by the rooster's crowing. The rooster and hen report from the basement chicken coop that it's soon morning. The little Norwegian ponies don't have stalls; they're tied up in the sandpit under the stairs and they kick the door and the wainscoting for exercise.

'It's dawn. The caretaker, who lives with his family in the attic, hurtles down the stairs. His wooden slippers clatter, the door slams, the house shakes, and when it's all over, the lodger above me does his exercises. With each hand he lifts a heavy iron ball that he can't hold on to and drops it again and again. At the same time the youth of the house, who are getting ready for school, rush by screaming. I go to the window and open it to get some air. It's refreshing when I can get it – if the woman at the back of the house isn't cleaning gloves with stain remover, which is how she makes a living. By the way, it's a nice house, and I'm living with a quiet family.'

That was the account of my lodgings that I gave Auntie. When I told her the story, it seemed livelier; the spoken word is more vivid than the written word.

'You're a poet!' Auntie exclaimed. 'Just write down your story, and you'll be just as good as Dickens. But you're much more interesting to me – you paint pictures when you talk. You describe your house so I can see it. It makes me shudder. Keep writing! Make your stories come alive with people – gracious people, preferably unhappy.'

I described the house as it is, with all its noises and annoyances. But I was the only one in the story; it had no plot. That would come later.

IV

It was during winter, late in the evening, after the theatre. Terrible weather – a snowstorm – you could hardly get around.

Auntie had gone to the theatre, and I was there to see her home. But it was difficult enough for one person to walk, let alone look after someone else. Cabs were all taken; Auntie lived on the outskirts of town, but my lodgings were close to the theatre. If it hadn't been for that, we would have had to take shelter for a while in a royal sentry box.

We staggered through the deep snow, with the swirling snowflakes rushing around us. I lifted her, I held her, I pushed her forward. We fell twice but landed gently.

We reached my front door where we shook ourselves; we shook ourselves on the stairs too, and we still carried in enough snow to cover the floor in the entrance hall.

We took off our overcoats and inner coats and all the clothes we could shed. The landlady lent Auntie dry stockings and a dressing gown – she simply had to change clothes, the landlady said. She added that Auntie couldn't possibly get home that night, which was true enough, and asked Auntie to make do with her living room. The landlady said that she'd prepare a bed on the sofa in front of the permanently locked door that led to my quarters.

That's what happened.

Fire burned in my wood stove, the samovar was on the table, and a cosy atmosphere spread through the little room – though not so cosy as it was at Auntie's, where in the winter thick curtains cover the doors, thick curtains cover the windows, and a double layer of rugs covers three layers of thick paper on the floor. You sit there as if you're in a tightly corked bottle full of warm air. Still, as I said, it was cosy at my place too; the wind whistled outside.

Auntie talked and told stories; old memories came back – her youth, the brewer.

She could remember when I got my first tooth and how thrilled the family was.

The first tooth! An innocent tooth, shining like a little white drop of milk – a milk tooth.

One came, more came, a whole row, side by side, above and below – the most beautiful baby teeth. Yet they were only the advance troops, not the real ones, which had to last a lifetime.

But they came too, and wisdom teeth as well, at the end of the row, born in pain and with great difficulty.

They leave again – every single one of them. They leave before their tour of duty is over; even the last tooth disappears, and that's not a festive day but a sad day.

Then you're old, even if your spirit is young.

That sort of talk and thought is not very pleasant;

nevertheless, we spoke about all of it. We came back again to her childhood – talked and talked. It was midnight before Auntie retired to the room nearby.

'Good night, my sweet child,' she called out. 'I'm going to sleep as if I were tucked away in my own chest of drawers.'

And she rested, but there was no rest in the house – inside or out. The storm shook the windows, banged the long dangling window hooks, clanged the neighbour's bell to the back yard. The lodger upstairs returned home. He went for another little night stroll, up and down the floor; he kicked off his boots, went to bed and to sleep, but he snored so that someone with a good ear could hear it through the ceiling.

I couldn't rest, I couldn't calm down. The weather didn't calm down, either – it became unusually lively. The wind whistled and sang in its own way, and my teeth also began to play up – they whistled and sang in their own way. It was the overture to a huge toothache.

There was a draught from the window. The moon shone onto the floor. Its brightness came and went as storm clouds came and went. Light and shadow shifted uneasily, but in the end the shadow on the floor looked like . . . something; I looked at this moving something and felt an icy cold blast.

A figure sat on the floor; it was thin and long, like those that a child draws with a pencil on a slate. It was supposed to look like a person: its body was a single thin line; another two lines made the arms; the legs were single lines too, and the head was all angles.

The figure soon became clearer. It wore a kind of dress – very thin, very fine – which showed that the figure belonged to the female sex.

I heard a humming. Was it her or was it the wind that buzzed like a horsefly in the crack of the windowpane?

No, it was Madame Toothache herself – Her Frightfulness, *Satania infernalis*, God save us from her visit.

'This is a nice place to live,' she hummed. 'It's a good neighbourhood – swampy, boggy ground. Mosquitoes used to buzz by here with poison in their sting. Now I'm the one with the stinger. It has to be sharpened on human teeth, and that fellow on the bed has such shiny white ones. They've held their own against sweet and sour, hot and cold, nutshells and plum pits. But I'm going to wiggle them, jiggle them, feed them with a draught, and chill them at their roots.'

That was a horrible story, a horrible guest.

'Well, you're a poet,' she said. 'All right, I'll teach you poetry in all the metres of pain. I'll put iron and steel in your body and wire in all your nerves.'

It was as if a red-hot awl went through my cheekbone; I writhed and twisted.

'An excellent set of teeth,' she said. 'A keyboard of pain. It's like playing a concert on a mouth organ – wonderful! – with kettledrums and trumpets, a piccolo, and a trombone in the wisdom tooth. Great poet, great music!'

And what music she made! She looked terrifying, even though you could see no more of her than her hand – that shadowy, grey, ice-cold hand with the long fingers, as thin as an awl. Each finger was an instrument of torture; the thumb and index finger were pincers and a screw. The middle finger ended in a needle-like tip. The ring finger was like a drill, and the little finger spurted mosquito venom.

'I'll teach you metre,' she said. 'Great poets must have great toothaches; small poets, small toothaches.'

'Oh, let me be small!' I pleaded. 'Let me not be at all! I'm not a poet – I only have attacks of writing poetry, the way I have attacks of toothache. Go away, go away!'

'Will you admit that I'm mightier than poetry, philosophy, mathematics, and all music?' she said. 'Mightier than all the feeling that went into paint and marble? I'm older than all of them. I was born close to the Garden of Eden but outside, where the wind blew and moist toadstools grew. I got Eve to wear clothes when it got cold and Adam too. I'm telling you, there was power in the first toothache!'

'I believe everything you say,' I cried. 'Go away, go away!'

'Well, then, if you'll stop writing poetry – never put a line down on paper, slate, or anything else you can write on – I'll leave you alone. But I'll be back if you write poetry.'

'I swear,' I said. 'As long as I never see you or feel you again.'

'You'll see me again,' she said, 'but I'll seem plumper and more lovable than I do now. I'll look like Aunt Millie, and I'll say, Write poetry, my sweet boy! You're a great poet – maybe the greatest we have. But if you believe me, and start to write, I'll set your words to music and play them on your mouth organ. You sweet child – remember me when you see Aunt Millie.'

Then she vanished.

As a farewell present I got what seemed to be a jab in the jaw with a red-hot awl. But the pain soon dulled, and it was as if I were floating on calm water; I saw white water lilies with their wide green leaves bend and sink beneath me. They withered and disintegrated; I sank along with them and slipped into peaceful rest.

'Die, melt away like the snow,' the water sang. 'Vanish into the clouds and drift away like the clouds.'

From down in the water I saw great luminous names, inscriptions on waving victory banners – claims of immortality written on the wings of a mayfly.

I slept, I slept without dreaming. I didn't hear the rushing wind, the banging door, the neighbour's clanging doorbell, or the lodger's weighty gymnastics.

Bliss!

Then there was a gust of wind, enough to make the locked door to Auntie's room spring open. Auntie jumped up, put on her shoes, put on her clothes, and came into my room.

I was sleeping like an angel, she told me, and she couldn't bear to wake me up.

I woke up by myself and opened my eyes; I'd completely forgotten that Auntie was in the house. But as soon as I remembered, I also remembered the spectre of my toothache. Dream and reality merged.

'I suppose you didn't write anything yesterday evening after we said goodnight?' she asked. 'I wish you had. You're my poet, and you always will be.'

It seemed to me that she smiled slyly. I didn't know whether it was the good-hearted Aunt Millie, who loved me, or Her Frightfulness to whom I'd given my promise the night before.

'Have you written any poetry, sweet child?'

'No, no!' I cried. 'You *are* Aunt Millie, aren't you?'

'Who else?' she said. And it was Aunt Millie.

She kissed me, got into a cab, and rode home.

I wrote down what's written here. It's not verse, and it will never be printed –

Here, the manuscript stopped.

My young friend, the prospective grocer's apprentice, couldn't find the missing pages. They'd gone into the world as wrapping paper for herring, butter, and green soap. They had fulfilled their destiny.

The brewer is dead, Auntie is dead, the student is dead – the one whose literary sparks went into the rubbish.

Everything goes into the rubbish.

That's the end of the story – the story of Auntie Toothache.

ACKNOWLEDGMENTS

This project began with the encouragement of David Remnick, editor of *The New Yorker*, who commissioned a biographical essay on Andersen's life for the magazine; our gratitude, and friendship, go to him and to Deborah Treisman, our editor at the magazine. We are grateful to Tina Bennett, our agent, for her intelligence, taste, energy, and decency; and to Eric Chinski, our editor at Houghton Mifflin, for his sensitivity, advice, and encouragement – all in the tradition of Horace Scudder, Andersen's editor at Hurd and Houghton. Thanks also to Anne Mette Lundtofte, who helped to fact-check the *New Yorker* essay.

In Denmark we owe a special debt to Det Kongelige Bibliotek – the Royal Library – and in particular to the *håndskriftsafdeling*, the department of handwritten documents, whose staff was not only helpful but showed enormous patience with our constant requests. It was a thrill actually to hold and read Andersen's letters and to trace his connections to the New World. Much good counsel came from Johan de Mylius, who more or less single-handedly runs the H. C. Andersen Center at Syddansk Universitet in Odense; from Viggo Hjørnager Pedersen, at the University of Copenhagen, who probably knows all there is to know about translating Andersen; and from Ejnar Askgaard, the Andersen curator at the Odense City Museums, who was generous with his time and knowledge. We are grateful to Philippa Geisler Crone for her research assistance, to Thomas Frank for valuable suggestions, and to Dr Allene M. Parker for giving us access to her thorough unpublished study '"Lady of Utopia": Rebecca Buffum Spring, 1811–1911'. Kaabers Antikvariat, one of Copenhagen's many amazing antiquarian bookshops, specializes in Anderseniana and somehow nearly always managed to have exactly what we were looking for.

NOTES

The Tinderbox

The first of four tales in Andersen's first collection, which was published in 1835, 'The Tinderbox' was different from the didactic and sentimental literature that was standard children's fare at the time. It is speedily told and suspenseful and takes place in a magic universe (although with recognizable Danish landmarks) that has no obvious moral cause and effect. The story introduces a familiar Andersen theme: a young man chosen by fate to succeed; it is his version of 'Aladdin', the *Arabian Nights* story.

page

34 *as big as the Round Tower:* The Round Tower is a Copenhagen landmark, about a hundred feet tall. It was commissioned by King Christian IV as an observatory and completed in 1642.

35 *the baker ladies' sugar pigs:* Cakes or sweets made in the shape of a pig were popular.

37 *The King's Gardens:* The King's Gardens, commissioned by King Christian IV, were completed in 1624 and opened to the public less than a century later. The King's Gardens today are a popular park in Copenhagen – filled with sunbathers in the summer.

38 *clever thing to do:* A similar confusion exists in 'Ali Baba and the Forty Thieves', from the *Arabian Nights,* a story Andersen's father read aloud to him.

39 *he could see people rushing:* Public hangings took place outside the city gates. When Andersen was a student in the Latin school, he witnessed a triple execution.

Little Claus and Big Claus

'Little Claus and Big Claus' (1835), based on a folktale, is uncharacteristically crude for Andersen – almost vulgar in comparison to his other tales and stories. In many ways it comes across like a modern cartoon. Like Bugs Bunny outwitting Elmer Fudd, Little Claus repeatedly fools a more powerful but less intelligent opponent. The world where these events take place is one where nothing is quite real and where appalling behaviour serves mostly to amuse.

43 *flat straw roof:* Thatched roofs, in Andersen's time, were the rule in the countryside. But the thatching is becoming rare because it is highly flammable and expensive to insure. (For the sake of the narrative, Andersen makes his roof flat, although in reality they were steeply pitched to let the rain run off.)

a real stork: The stork image appears in many Andersen stories, and the birds were once commonplace; in 1900 Denmark had an estimated ten thousand pairs of white storks. Today, because so many wetlands have been drained, storks have become exceedingly rare. The Royal Danish Embassy reports that 2001 was the first year since 1400 that no white storks were hatched in Denmark.

stopped off to say hello: Andersen softened suggestions of adultery to accommodate the tastes of his time.

46 *a deep river:* Andersen does not actually use the term *river*, because no streams in Denmark are big enough to qualify as rivers. The Danish term *aa* denotes a waterway sometimes navigable by a small flat-bottomed boat.

49 *grandmother ... she'd been ill-tempered:* Grandmothers are common in Andersen's stories, but a bad-tempered grandmother is a rarity. Andersen's own grandmother spoiled and encouraged him and made him believe that her background was distinguished and prosperous. He was fourteen the last time he saw her, when he left Odense for Copenhagen.

50 *the apothecary:* Before the nineteenth century, apothecaries took an active medical role – and bought and sold cadavers.

The Princess on the Pea

'The Princess on the Pea' (1835) is the shortest of Andersen's stories – 347 words in Danish – and Andersen probably regarded it as a trifle; he mentions it only twice in his journals, where he takes note of what he has been asked to read at fancy parties and gatherings.

what he has been asked to read: An Andersen diary entry of June 28, 1844, recorded a visit to Weimar, where he was a guest of the grand duke and read to real royalty: 'The Grand Duke chatted with me about Hamlet . . . Duchess Wolkonsky, a friend of the Empress of Russia, conversed with me for a long time in French. I was in a sweat. I gave the Grand Duchess my book "Only a Fiddler" bound in Moroccan leather (that was an expensive item) . . . Then we drove to Ettersburg where they . . . host occasional readings . . . The hereditary Grand Duke read a novella, probably by himself; I felt sick and was just about to throw up, it was a torment that had no end; I read the "Princess on the Pea", "The Emperor's New Clothes", and "Little Ida's Flowers" but was quite ill.' Yet, like other Andersen phrases and titles, it has become a shorthand way to describe any hypersensitive person, such as Andersen himself.

Thumbelisa

'Thumbelisa,' the tiny heroine of this tale from 1835, has many literary antecedents.

The tiny heroine: The figure of a tiny girl also appears in Andersen's prose fantasy, *Journey on Foot to Amager* . . . (1828). Andersen was familiar with *Gulliver's Travels* (1726), with its six-inch Lilliputians, and Voltaire's short story 'Micromégas' (1752), which also plays on the contrast between huge beings and tiny ones. Andersen gives it his own brand of weirdness, including the introduction of frogs and moles as suitors. And it has its comic moments – for instance, a beetle's view of beauty. It is also another instance where popular culture may have overrun the original: Danny Kaye singing the Frank Loesser song 'Thumbelina' is still familiar to children and their parents, more so than the story that inspired it.

57 *eager to have a little child:* According to the Andersen biographer Elias Bredsdorff, some nineteenth-century versions bowdlerized this passage – to prevent children from asking where children came from. Bredsdorff quotes Mary Howitt's version, which began: 'Once upon a time, a beggar woman went to the house of a poor peasant and asked for something to eat.'
   an old witch: Witches in Andersen's stories are not necessarily evil. Another benign witch appears in 'The Snow Queen'.
   in the middle of the flower: A similar image appears in E. T. A. Hoffmann's tale 'Prinzessin Brambilla' (1821).
   no taller than a thumb: Some Andersen students have suggested that the model for Thumbelisa is Andersen's close friend Henriette Wulff, who was very small, frail, and slightly hunchbacked. No written evidence supports that theory.

62 *warm and cosy:* Andersen had many friends in the comfortable bourgeoisie. From the end of his school days and for the rest of his life, he had dinner in friends' homes according to a fixed weekly routine. Early dinner hosts included the Collins and the Wulffs.

63 *the neighbour was a mole:* It is not hard to think of Simon Meisling, Andersen's headmaster at the school in Slagelse, who was a classical scholar and a minor poet. In a portrait from the time, he does look like a mole, and the description of Meisling by the Andersen biographer Cai M. Woel only reinforces the impression: 'below average height with a very round head . . . his mouth thin, his nose bulbous . . . His body was plump with a protruding stomach, big flat feet and short arms . . . Something about the man's appearance made you think about the underworld. His hands hardly ever touched water; they were so black that a quick glance would make you think he was wearing gloves. Only his finger tips were white; he licked them after every meal; or maybe it was because he pressed lemon into his punch every evening.' Meisling made life miserable for Andersen in many ways – above all, perhaps,

because he was blind to Andersen's talent. 'You're a stupid boy who'll never make it,' he told him.

'Beetle, Fly, Fly Away Home!' The songs that Thumbelisa sings are old-fashioned children's songs barely known today.

undoubtedly died from the cold: A book by F. C. Nielsen called *Natural History for Everyman* (1809), cited in volume 7 of the Dal, Nielsen, and Hovmann critical edition, informs the reader that certain species of birds, among them quail and storks but especially swallows, are thought to be able to hibernate in bogs and swamps. Nielsen is not convinced. Frozen swallows have been found, he admits, but he has no trustworthy evidence that they have been revived. Andersen himself had a real fear of being assumed dead and buried alive. Next to his bed he had a sign: 'I only appear to be dead.'

a piece of rotting wood: Certain fungi can make rotten wood phosphorescent.

the warm countries: During his first trip to Italy, Andersen felt that he had come to life; he called the date of his arrival in Rome, October 18, 1833, his Roman birthday. His first novel, *The Improvisatore*, is set in Italy.

The Little Mermaid

'The Little Mermaid', perhaps Andersen's most celebrated story, was published in 1837. In a letter to his friend the writer B. S. Ingemann, Andersen said that apart from a scene from his first novel, 'it's the only one of my works that moved me as I wrote it'. Andersen later said that the story was 'utterly his own invention', which is true enough, although a number of its themes – and mermaids in general – were popular subjects at the time. A statue of 'The Little Mermaid' in Copenhagen harbour has become as famous as the story itself.

74 *No one yearned to go:* After he saw his first theatrical performance at the age of seven, Andersen yearned to be part of another world. In 1825 he wrote to his benefactor Jonas Collin: 'From the day I saw my first play my entire soul was burning for this art. I still remember how I could sit for days completely alone in front of the mirror, with an apron over my shoulders instead of a knight's cloak, playing *Das Donauweibschen* and that in German, though I hardly knew five German words . . . I soon learned entire Danish plays by heart . . . and I also began to write plays (my good mother scolded me properly for it, for she was afraid that all these commotions might make me mad).' *Das Donauweibschen*, a comic opera by the Austrian composer Ferdinand Knauer, is about a water nymph.

the big city near the coast: When Andersen wrote 'The Little Mermaid', he was living on Nyhavn, a street in Copenhagen that starts at the harbour and runs along both sides of a canal where fishing vessels were moored.

75 *hills covered with grapevines:* Andersen loved Italy, which was the setting for

his first novel, *The Improvisatore*. Many of his stories reflect Italian landscape and architecture.

77 *fireworks:* In his diary and in a letter Andersen described the spectacular fireworks that he saw in Rome at Eastertime in 1834.

81 *wished that she could live among them:* In one traditional interpretation, 'The Little Mermaid' is about the sacrifices that Andersen made to be accepted by those of higher social rank – the Collin family, above all. A recent biographer, Jackie Wullschlager, believes that Andersen was a repressed homosexual and sees the longing and suffering in 'The Little Mermaid' as an expression of his painful, never satisfied, desires.

82 *They clapped for her:* Applause made Andersen very happy – at least for the moment. In his autobiography, *The Fairy Tale of My Life,* he described (and exaggerated) his pleasure at the success of an early play, *Love at St Nicholas's Tower:* 'I was overwhelmed with joy . . . I was bursting with happiness, rushed out of the theatre, into the street, into Collin's house, where only his wife was at home. Nearly fainting I threw myself into a chair, sobbing, crying hysterically. The sympathetic woman had no idea what it meant and so began to console me . . . I interrupted her, sobbing: "They applauded and shouted "Long Live!"'

85 *crocodile shedding tears:* A verse (freely translated) found in old primers:
> *When the crocodile pitifully cries,*
> *For humans it is probably goodbyes.*

88 *slave girls:* Denmark had serfs before Andersen's time but never slaves. Danes nevertheless participated in the African slave trade, which Denmark outlawed in 1803.

93 *little mermaid did not feel death:* In a letter to Ingemann on November 2, 1837, Andersen explained that 'I have not, like de la Motte Fouquet in *Undine,* let the mermaid's gaining an immortal soul depend on a stranger, on the love of another person. It is definitely the wrong thing to do. It would make it a matter of chance and I'm not going to accept *that* in this world. I have let my mermaid take a more natural, divine path.'
daughters of the air: To the modern reader the ending may seem a requirement of Victorian sensibilities, but it is fundamental to Andersen's idea. The working title for the story was 'The Daughters of the Air'.

The Emperor's New Clothes

In a preface to a later collection of his tales, Andersen explained that 'The Emperor's New Clothes', published in 1837, is 'of Spanish origin'. He went on to say, 'We owe the amusing idea to Prince Don Manuel,' who was born in the late thirteenth century. Andersen also pointed out that Cervantes used the idea in an 'entr'acte'. But if the idea of 'The Emperor's New Clothes' was centuries old, it did not become international shorthand for all sorts of conformist behaviour until Andersen wrote it his way. As he often did,

Andersen made the story personal – in this case, teasing the admirers of a celebrated contemporary, the poet F. Paludan-Muller, whose style was as classical as Andersen's was freewheeling. In a letter to Andersen of January 8, 1837, the writer J. C. Hauch gloated over a bad review for Paludan-Muller, writing that, unlike Andersen, he 'only possessed a beautiful poetic garment' and 'this time P. M. has put the garment away and stands there in his simple shirtsleeves . . . I believe the case is clear to anybody who has eyes.' Two months later Andersen made his final corrections to 'The Emperor's New Clothes'.

99   *But he hasn't got anything on:* Andersen had already sent the manuscript to the printers when he wrote to Edvard Collin, who proofread his work, asking him to change the ending. In doing so, he added the famous line 'which will give everything a more satirical appearance'. That line may have originated in a childhood memory. In 1872 Andersen told the painter William Bloch about standing with his mother in a crowd, waiting to see King Frederik VI. When the king stepped from his carriage, Andersen said, 'Oh, he's nothing more than a human being!' His mother, as Bloch recalled it in a memoir, tried to quiet him, and said, 'Have you gone mad, child?'

The Wild Swans

'The Wild Swans' was a retelling of a tale Andersen had come across in Mathias Winther's pioneering collection, *Danish Folktales*, published in 1823. In a letter to his friend B. S. Ingemann, he wrote, 'I read . . . the one about "the wild swans", and tell me if I've rewritten it well or badly.' The result, published in 1838, is one of Andersen's most suspenseful, well-plotted stories. It has a distinctly medieval flavour.

100   *Company's Coming:* Andersen's grown-up princess in 'The Swineherd' was also fond of this – a common children's game in Andersen's time.
    roses: Roses are images of truth and innocence and in the Middle Ages a symbol of the Virgin Mary.

103   *glowworms:* Glowworms, *Lampyris noctiluca*, are actually inch-long beetles that create light when two enzymes in their bodies mix with oxygen.

107   *wild horses:* Denmark had no wild horses and no plains. Andersen probably got the idea from Washington Irving's 'A Tour on the Prairies' (1835).

110   *mill wheels:* Andersen also uses mill wheels to describe the dog's eyes in 'The Tinderbox'.
    Fata Morgana: A special type of mirage – formed out of alternating warm and cold layers of air – which sometimes gives the impression of a castle half in the air and half in the sea.
    delicate green creepers: Andersen's autobiography describes a similar cave that he saw on his first trip to Italy: 'The walls were covered with a

tapestry of the most beautiful green Venus hair, a kind of fern which is infinitely delicate and beautiful and formed hanging curtains inside the cave.'

111 *stinging nettle:* Stinging nettles are, as most Danish children know, all too common. Touching the leaves can cause small blisters. Stinging nettles are rare in churchyards, which are kept weed free.

you must not speak: Requirements of silence were fairly commonplace in fairy tales of the eighteenth and nineteenth centuries; Andersen used this most effectively in 'The Little Mermaid'. Muteness seems to be a handicap suffered only by women.

115 *images of saints shook their heads:* Portraits that pass judgment is a device that Andersen used elsewhere, including 'The Red Shoes'.

116 *burn in the fiery flames:* From the early 1400s the Danes burned about a thousand women as witches; the last, a woman called Anne, was killed in 1693. Anne was beheaded before she was thrown on the flames.

118 *a wedding procession:* A wedding is a standard happy ending in fairy tales, but Elisa and the king make an odd couple. Elisa can endure the impossible but meekly submits to the king's will. The king is supposed to be a noble character, but he is a fool who listens to the nasty archbishop and betrays his beloved. To make everything more confusing, the king and Elisa seem to get married twice.

The Swineherd

'The Swineherd', which appeared in 1842, is another of the stories that Andersen heard when he was young. It uses a common folktale figure – the haughty maiden. (A variation of the character turns up in *The Taming of the Shrew.*) In Andersen's retelling 'for children', he alters the narrative from the bawdy version that he had certainly heard; his princess may be foolish, but she surrenders no more than kisses.

119 *marriage was what he wanted:* In 1837 Andersen wrote to his friend Henriette Hanck, 'I have a burning desire to get married.' He was thinking then of Sophie Ørsted, the daughter of the inventor of electromagnetism, H. C. Ørsted, in whose house Andersen was a regular guest. Sophie was sixteen – 'exactly half my age,' he wrote, 'and she treats me like an elderly gentleman whom she has known for many years.'

known far and wide: Andersen was by then becoming famous. The story of his life, by the French writer Xavier Marmier, had been published in 1837 in Paris.

120 *'Superbe! Charmant!':* At the time the upper classes attempted to speak French, a trend that had been satirized for years. It was said that refined Danes spoke French to each other, German to their servants, and Danish to their dogs.

121 *Ach, du lieber Augustin:* A German folk song that Danes sing in German.

Andersen uses Danish in the last line – thus the English in the translation.

The Nightingale

'The Nightingale', published in 1844, was no doubt inspired by Andersen's crush on Jenny Lind, who was about to become famous throughout Europe and the United States as the Swedish Nightingale. He had seen her that autumn, when she was performing in Copenhagen. Copenhagen's celebrated Tivoli Gardens opened that season, and its Asian fantasy motif was even more pronounced than it is today. Andersen had been a guest at the opening in August and returned for a second visit on October 11. In his diary that night he wrote: 'At Tivoli Gardens. Started the Chinese fairy tale.' He finished it in two days. 'The Nightingale' was included in the 1844 collection called *Nye Eventyr* (*New Fairy Tales*), along with 'Sweethearts' and 'The Ugly Duckling'. With this collection Andersen, who so often complained about critics, had every reason to be pleased. A typical review, cited by Dal, Nielsen, and Hovmann, appeared in the *Den Frisindede* (*The Open-minded*), saying that Andersen had now 'firmly established his greatest merit and honour as a Danish fairytale writer'.

127 *emperor is a Chinaman:* In Viggo Hjørnager Pedersen and Birgit Nedergaard-Larsen's *Om at Oversætte H. C. Andersen* (*On Translating H. C. Andersen,* pp. 67–79), the English novelist and translator William Glyn Jones contributed an essay that recalled his painful and sometimes amusing arguments with his publisher regarding this and other usages that may offend some modern sensibilities.

128 *poets – those who could write:* Andersen could not resist these asides, aimed at any number of people, many of them, no doubt, in the J. L. Heiberg literary circle.

only 'P!' The Danish text reads the same way – meant to suggest the same haughty dismissive sound.

129 *Tsing-pe!:* Probably nonsense, but Dal, Nielsen, and Hovmann say that it may be a variation of the Chinese *ch'in p'ei,* or 'as you please'.

130 *It's so plain:* In *The Fairy Tale of My Life* Andersen wrote about Jenny Lind: 'Her lovely young voice penetrated all hearts! Here was truth and nature; everything assumed significance and clarity.' Years later Andersen described Lind to his friend Nicolai Bøgh, who in 1915 published excerpts from a diary he had kept during an 1873 journey with Andersen: 'They say Jenny Lind was hideous to look at, and maybe she was. The first time she walked on stage, I said the same "She's hideous" . . . but then she sang and became divinely beautiful. "She was like an unlit lamp when she came in, and then, when you lit the lamp and she began to speak, it was as if her spirit cast a divine radiance on the stage and every seat in the theatre. You weren't in the theatre, you were in church.'

131 *the title of Real Kitchen Maid:* Andersen – not for the first time – is making fun of the order of rank, in particular a law from 1717 in which a judicial officer could be ranked higher with the addition of the word *real.*

  gold slipper: On September 18, 1843, Jenny Lind sang for the Danish king, Christian VIII, who rewarded her with diamonds.

137 *blood flowed faster and faster:* In a memoir Charlotte Bournonville, the daughter of the ballet master, told this story: 'One of my father's closest friends, a very musical young man, was very seriously ill, and his sadness at not being able to hear Jenny Lind sing did quite a lot to worsen his condition. When Jenny heard that, she shouted, "Sweet Mister Bournonville, just let me sing for the sick man!" Perhaps it was a dangerous experiment to expose a deadly ill person to such an emotional experience, but it was a success. After he had heard her lovely singing . . . he began to recover.' It is easy to imagine that Andersen had heard this story.

138 *songbird gets around:* Andersen believed that he never lost touch with ordinary people.

  something sacred about the crown: Andersen was immensely respectful of European royalty; he was brought up in the time of the absolute monarchy, when kings had divine rights.

  a little bird tells you everything: It would be nice to think that the phrase 'a little bird told me' came from this story.

The Sweethearts

'The Sweethearts', published in 1844, was written thirteen years after Andersen fell in love with Riborg Voight, the daughter of a wealthy merchant. 'I couldn't help looking at her,' Andersen wrote after she visited Copenhagen in the autumn of 1830. 'When I left, she gave me her hand to thank me for my reading. I pressed it to my lips, while my chest was about to burst. Now it became clear to me for the first time that I loved her!'

Nothing came of this, but Andersen apparently never got over her. A leather pouch that he always wore around his neck is said to have contained a letter from Riborg. Edvard Collin, his friend and executor, burned the letter upon Andersen's death without reading it; the pouch is on exhibition at the Hans Christian Andersen House in Odense.

139 *The Sweethearts:* Although 'The Sweethearts' is the correct translation of the Danish, the story is often called 'The Top and the Ball'.

  imagined herself to be a lady: In *Erindringer,* his memoir from 1832, Andersen wrote of Riborg Voight, 'She had a lovely, solemn face, which somehow seemed childlike; but her eyes were wise and intelligent, they were quite animated and brown . . . Her interest in my poems, even the fact that she seemed to have some sort of respect for me, tickled my vanity and instantly kindled some kind of interest in her.' She was twenty-four; he was twenty-five 'and had never fallen in love before'.

cork inside: Homemade balls were made bouncy by placing a cork in the centre.

never be whipped: Such tops were kept moving with a whip.

half engaged to a swallow: Voight was more than 'half engaged' to the son of a pharmacist, Poul Bøving, when Andersen met her. By the spring of 1831 she had married him. Andersen suffered like Goethe's Young Werther; a book of poems was one result of his misery. One of these poems, 'Two Brown Eyes', is still known in Denmark.

141 *no apple – it was the old ball:* Andersen did not see Riborg Voight again until July 1843, at a fair; by then she had obviously changed and so had he. 'Fair at Holstenshus', he wrote in his *Almanak*. 'Ran into Riborg her husband and children (it has been 13 years).'

142 *treated with honour and respect:* By 1843 Andersen was spending time with, among others, Alexandre Dumas, the painter Jacques-Louis David, and the poets Alfred-Victor de Vigny, Alphonse de Lamartine, and Heinrich Heine.

The Ugly Duckling

Andersen told the Danish critic Georg Brandes that 'The Ugly Duckling', published in 1844, was 'a reflection of my own life'. It is not only among his most famous stories – the title itself has become part of several languages – but the one that readers correctly identify most closely with its author. Andersen spent his summers with aristocratic friends, going from one castle to the next; in the summer of 1842, at Gisselfeldt Castle, south of Copenhagen, he had been in a bad mood because a new play had done poorly. But he went for a walk, a diary entry notes, and 'got the idea for a story about a duck. Improved my mood.' In late July – he was now a guest at the castle of Bregentved – he says, 'Began the young swan yesterday' – a hint that the idea had not quite worked itself out.

146 *bitten, pushed, and teased:* As a boy in Odense, Andersen was teased so much that he did not play with other children.

147 *large swamp:* Andersen called himself a swamp plant, believing that he had grown up in a social swamp.

two wild ganders: Andersen did not have much of a wild youth, but two of his close friends did. Fritz Petit, who would later translate Andersen into German, and the writer Carl Bagger, to whom the volume containing 'The Ugly Duckling' is dedicated, were bohemians who drank and pursued women and encouraged Andersen (unsuccessfully) to do the same.

149 *a horribly big dog:* Andersen was terrified of dogs.

150 *getting ideas:* When Andersen was a boy in Odense, several people suggested that he should learn a trade. Later, as a young man, he was told to forget about writing and think about becoming a solid citizen.

teach you something: All of Andersen's benefactors – the Wulff and Collin families in particular – felt that they had the right to educate him, even when he was a grown man. Their good intentions drove Andersen to distraction. On September 26, 1834, when he was twenty-nine, he wrote to his close friend Henriette Wulff, whose mother frequently corrected him, saying that 'if once in a while a didactic preacher turns up, one of those who used to be so eager to educate me, then first I listen to find out if it is nonsense, and if I find that it is, then I snub him . . . Nobody treats me like a boy any more.'

151 *it got smaller and smaller:* In 1822 in Copenhagen the teenage Andersen was running out of choices. He had failed in the theatre and as a dancer, singer, and writer.

152 *rushed into the milk pan:* The chaos brings to mind the home of Simon Meisling, Andersen's headmaster in Slagelse. Andersen was a lodger in this extremely untidy household, which also enlisted him to play with the children.

153 *swan's egg:* The story could have ended here – and to modern readers should have. The critic Georg Brandes considered the ending unworthy of the duckling/swan. 'Let it die, if necessary,' Brandes wrote in 1869. 'That is tragic and grand. Let it lift its wings and fly soaring through the air, jubilant at its own beauty and strength.'

The Snow Queen

'The Snow Queen', with its famous and much-quoted prologue – complete with non sequiturs – goes in many directions. It even includes a rumination on the Indian custom of suttee, and Andersen seems to have had a splendid time getting it all down. The story, published in 1845, also promotes Andersen's recurring revolt against formalism; as the modern Danish critic Villy Sørensen has observed, Andersen saw the snow queen's icy world as the proper home for someone whose heart has been replaced by chilly reason – a category in which Andersen certainly placed many of his contemporaries.

155 *an evil troll:* Trolls – those evil creatures of Norse mythology – found a place in Christianity as allies of the devil. In 'The Snow Queen', the devil and his trolls are sometimes interchangeable.

he had made a mirror: The mirror idea is not an Andersen original. It appeared in his friend B. S. Ingemann's poem 'Visions of an Artist'.

157 *a large wooden box:* Andersen notes in *The Fairy Tale of My Life* that the little garden on the roof comes straight from his own childhood: 'In the rain gutter between our house and the neighbour's was a box of earth with chives and parsley, my mother's entire garden. In my fairy tale the "Snow Queen" it still blooms.'

158 *Gerda:* The little girl was probably named after Edvard and Henriette Collin's daughter Gerda, who died at the age of four in 1845. In a June 9, 1853, letter to Henriette Collin, Andersen wrote: 'Yesterday when I left Kalundborg on the steamship 'Gerda', I thought about Kai and

Gerda, and about her whom the fairy tale's Gerda was named after.'

they freeze over very strangely: When his father died, Andersen says in *The Fairy Tale of My Life,* he was reminded that when 'our windows were frozen over, my father had shown us on the windowpane what looked like a young woman who stretched out her arms. 'I think she wants me!' he said jokingly. Now that he was dead [it] occupied my mind.'

159 *In the valley:* These are stanzas from a well-known and still popular hymn (especially around Christmas) by H. A. Brorson, 'The Loveliest Rose' (1732). In the hymn the rose is the newborn Christ child, and for Andersen it was a symbol of innocence.

163 *the gate of the city:* The medieval walls around Copenhagen still existed at Andersen's time, and the keys to the gate were delivered to the king every night. But most of the walls were levelled before Andersen's death in 1875. Several Copenhagen place names reflect their historic presence, and a small section has been preserved.

165 *combed Gerda's hair:* In fairy tales, such as the Grimm brothers' 'Snow White', hair combing induces sleep and tends to cause forgetfulness.

167 *dreamed their own fables:* The flower stories are somewhat mind-boggling and barely connected to the main narrative, but Andersen apparently was brimming over with ideas. On November 20, 1843, he wrote to Ingemann: 'I have a lot of material, for me it is often as if every wooden fence, every little flower said, "Look at me for a little while and you'll know what my story is," and if I do, then I have the story.' The *Berlingske Tidende* reviewer worried that Andersen's imagination had run so wild that children would not understand the flower stories – an understatement.

Flames leap around her: Obviously, a reference to the Hindu custom of suttee, the burning of widows, but why he included this reference is not clear.

sweet little girls: The scene is like a Fragonard painting, but Andersen may well have observed it in real life at one of the many manor houses he visited in the summer.

168 *tells us they're dead:* In Greek mythology Apollo accidentally killed his favourite companion, Hyakinthos, from whose blood the flower grew. A hyacinth is not a widely known symbol of death, but the flower has a very strong, sweetish smell, which evidently made Andersen think about death.

171 *a husband who knew what to say:* This theme of knowing what to say reappears as the main theme of the 1855 tale 'Hopeless Hans'.

172 *newspaper had a border of hearts:* Death notices in newspapers sometimes have a black border, so Andersen gives his marriage announcement a border of hearts.

174 *something rushed by her like shadows:* This makes no more sense than a dream.

180 *Spitsbergen:* Spitsbergen (or Svalbard, as the Norwegians call it) is an

archipelago in northern Norway. It is so far north that the sun does not rise for four months in the winter. The area was described by a tenth-century Viking poet in the saga that bears his name, 'The Saga of Egill Skallagrimsson'.

181 *an old Lapp woman:* Andersen was familiar with a book by B. M. Keilhau: *Journey in East- and West-Finnmark as Well as Beeren-Eiland and Spitsbergen in the Years 1827 and 1828,* published in 1831. He probably got his information on the lifestyle of the Lapps from it.

182 *dried codfish:* Codfish was (and still is) dried as a way of preserving it. The fish is split, and the flat sides become stiff and easy to write on. In modern times as a joke, people sometimes put a stamp on a side of dry codfish and send it as a card.

hide was covered with strange letters: The old Viking letters, runes, fell into disuse but were considered useful for magic.

183 *fearsome, ice-cold Finnmark:* Temperatures there reach a high of about 60 degrees Fahrenheit and a low of about - 40.

185 *Chinese puzzles:* A game consisting of diamond-shaped pieces of wood that are put together in geometric patterns.

ice puzzle of the mind: Erik Dal says that Andersen borrowed this image from Novalis's fragmentary novel, *Heinrich von Ofterdingen.*

The Red Shoes

'The Red Shoes', published in 1845, is considerably more gothic, more Grimm-like, than most Andersen stories. It is one of his most popular tales and was made into a film with Moira Shearer. When the story came out, the critic P. L. Møller connected it to an incident in Andersen's autobiography, where Andersen described how proud he had been of the boots that he wore at his confirmation. 'My feeling about the boots . . . was not consciously on my mind when I wrote "The Red Shoes", but no matter,' he replied to Møller on June 23, 1845. Yet in his preface to an 1863 story collection, Andersen conceded the point and went on: 'This memory gave rise to "The Red Shoes", which in Holland and America seems to have gained its greatest audience.'

190 *Karen:* Andersen's older half-sister, born in 1777, was called Karen Marie; she was born out of wedlock, and Andersen always referred to her as 'my mother's daughter'. Karen became a washerwoman like her mother and lived with a labourer in Copenhagen. Andersen tried to avoid her all his life, but in February of 1842 Karen contacted him, and when she came to his lodgings later that year, he gave her a small amount of money.

lowly straw coffin: Indigents were buried in cheap coffins made of straw.

191 *let people admire her:* Andersen too dressed to be admired. On April 3, 1839, he wrote to his friend Henriette Hanck: 'I'll arrive in silk stockings, white satin vest, my French hat . . . Indeed, I'll be a lovely sight.'

sewn them for a nobleman's daughter: In his autobiography Andersen tells of silk slippers that his father made for a countess. The assignment, he thought, was going to lead to a job at the manor and even a little house. Unfortunately, his shoes were as crude as Old Mother Shoemaker's; the countess rejected his work, and Andersen's father returned to his life of poverty in Odense.

192 *thought only about the red shoes:* In his 1863 preface Andersen repeats the story about his confirmation and his new boots: 'They squeaked when I walked across the church floor, and it thrilled me to the core that the congregation could hear that the boots were new, but I was distracted in my devotion; I knew it, and at the same time I suffered terrible pangs of conscience because my thoughts were as much on my boots as on the good God.'

The Little Match Girl

'The Little Match Girl', published just before Christmas 1845, had a curious origin. That autumn Andersen had received three drawings by post, with a request that he write a story about one of them. Andersen chose the illustration by the popular Danish artist J. Th. Lundbye that showed a girl selling matches. The drawing was not new; it had already appeared in an 1843 calendar, accompanied by a charitable plea, 'Do good when you give.' It is believed to be the only Andersen story inspired by a picture, and he completed it with great speed – probably in less than a week. Andersen wrote about this sad example of abject poverty while staying with the Duke of Augustenborg at Graasten Castle, in Jutland.

197 *carried a bunch of matches:* Poor people often made and sold matches; the practice was essentially a cover for begging, which was illegal.

198 *did not dare go home:* In *The Fairy Tale of My Life* Andersen wrote about his mother: 'As a young girl, her parents chased her out to beg, and when she had no luck, she spent a whole day crying under a bridge by Odense's river. As a child, I imagined all this so clearly and I cried about it.' Late in life Andersen told his friend Nicolai Bøgh what his mother had said about that time (cited by Dal, Nielsen, and Hovmann in the notes to *Eventyr*): 'I have never been able to ask anybody for anything. When I sat there under the bridge I was so hungry. I dipped my finger in the water and put a few drops on my tongue because I thought it would help. Finally, I fell asleep and slept till evening. Then I went home, and when my mother heard that I hadn't brought anything home, she scolded me a lot and said I was a lazy girl.'

199 *Old Grandmother, the only person who had been nice:* In his autobiography Andersen wrote, 'Grandmother came every day to my parents' house, if only for a few minutes – above all to see her grandson, little Hans Christian. I was her joy and happiness. She was a quiet, much loved old woman; she had gentle blue eyes and a delicate appearance.'

200 *they were with God:* Andersen believed in God and in the immortality of the

soul; he felt certain that God rewarded good people after death. This belief appeared to help him reconcile the social and material inequities that he witnessed in nineteenth-century Europe.

she was dead: Elias Bredsdorff notes in his Andersen biography that one translator found this to be so distressing that an 'adaptation', published in the United States in 1944, ends it differently. Its dust jacket announces: 'The little match girl on that long ago Christmas Eve [*sic*] does not perish from the bitter cold, but finds warmth and cheer and a lovely home where she lives happily ever after.'

The Happy Family

'The Happy Family', a somewhat morbid tale, was first published in 1847, in an English collection called *A Christmas Greeting to My English Friends* (the one that Andersen dedicated to Dickens). It came out a year later in Denmark. In his notes to an 1862–63 edition of his stories Andersen recalled that some material for the story came from the time he had spent at Glorup Castle on Fyn, where the garden was 'partly overgrown . . . with huge burdocks that had been planted to feed the large white snails, which were a delicacy'.

201 *a burdock leaf:* According to tradition, monks introduced the burdock plant to Denmark in the Middle Ages. It was believed to have useful medicinal qualities.

big white snails: Some people believe that edible snails, *Helix pomatia*, were brought to Denmark in 1808 by Spanish soldiers, who were briefly stationed in Fyn around the time of the Napoleonic Wars.

202 *never gone beyond the forest:* Andersen may have thought of the Collins when writing this and would have heard them express similar sentiments. Jonas Collin's oldest daughter, Ingeborg, with whom Andersen got on well, wrote to him in Rome, on February 25, 1841, saying, 'Heaven knows why you do not stay at home and see the many lovely things we have here! What is the pleasure of being cold in Rome? It would be better to be cold in Copenhagen.'

203 *black snails:* Black snails, *Arion ater*, resemble the white ones, but they have no shell.

The Shadow

Perhaps no story in the Andersen canon is as bitter, and personal, as 'The Shadow' (1847), for it was born of deep enduring hurt: Edvard Collin, Andersen's closest friend – the son of Jonas Collin, his most important benefactor – rejected Andersen's suggestion that they address one another with the familiar 'thou' form. Their exchange of letters in 1831 (when Andersen was twenty-six) did not close the subject for Andersen. After 'The Shadow' was published sixteen years later, the now-famous Andersen wrote to Edvard, 'You can see in [an English] newspaper, along with my picture that

I'm "one of the most remarkable and interesting man [*sic*] of his day!" Yet you're still too good to say "thou" to me.' Andersen wrote 'The Shadow' in Naples in the summer of 1846 – thus the focus on the city's heat. When 'The Shadow' was published in 1847, the critic for *Berlingske Tidende* pointed out that there was little reason to review Andersen; after all, the public knew what to expect and liked his tales.

206   *the sun really burns:* Naples, where Andersen wrote much of 'The Shadow,' is 120 miles southeast of Rome. On June 8, 1846, he made this entry in his diary: 'The heat is pouring down. I hardly dare go outside.' On June 9 he wrote, 'In the evening began writing the story of my shadow.'

209   *that he was an imitator:* Andersen knew that his readers were familiar with the Adelbert von Chamisso story 'Peter Schlemihls wundersame Geschichte' ('Peter Schlemihl's Wondrous Story'), in which Schlemihl sells his shadow to the Devil. And Andersen himself, in an early work, had a character barter away a shadow.

210   *a cluster of expensive seals:* A sign of importance: an engraved seal, pushed into wax or some sort of soft substance, was used (and in some cases still is) to seal envelopes and authenticate documents.

everybody loves his homeland: Andersen tended to love Denmark (and to feel sentimental about it) when he was away and to hate the way he was treated when he was at home. On April 29, 1843, he wrote to his soulmate, Jette Wulff: 'Here in this large foreign town [Paris] I'm surrounded by the most noble and famous among Europe's intellects, they treat me like a kinsman; and at home, the boys spit on the dearest creation of my heart . . . The Danes can be evil, cold, and satanic – a people well suited for their wet mouldy-green islands.'

212   *address me formally:* On May 28, 1831, Edvard Collin wrote to Andersen, using very similar language: 'There is something inside me which I cannot explain . . . But when I have known for a long time someone whom I respect and like and he invites me to say '*Du*' [thou], then this unpleasant and inexplicable feeling arises in me.' More than fifty years later, in his memoir, *H. C. Andersen og det Collinske Hus*, Edvard defended himself, explaining that he had told Andersen of his difficulty 'openly and honestly, and in the most loving tone'. What he did not tell his friend was that Andersen's personality had always been too dreamy for him – that Andersen's idea of friendship seemed to come from novels. Furthermore, Edvard claimed that he wanted to be on a *du* basis only with people he had known since childhood.

ancient gods: Probably a reference to classical literature. Fighting heroes were popular during the golden age of Danish literature, which revived many tales from Norse mythology and Danish history; Adam Oehlenschläger's *Nordic Poems* (1807) was one major influence;

Andersen's friend B. S. Ingemann wrote popular novels on themes from Danish history.

213 *ashamed to look as I did:* In October 1839 Andersen wrote to Henriette Hanck: 'The thing that interests me most these days is a Mackintosch [*sic*] I've bought, and an elegant winter coat. This is the first winter in which I've appeared like a human being; I've become stuffed and polished, so I'm really very attractive. I'm a dandy.'

214 *Do you want to come along?* The shadow, who is already planning his revenge, is an unusual character for Andersen. People in his stories may be evil and behave badly, but they are rarely so calculating and vengeful.

truth, beauty, and goodness: One of the people Andersen admired and whose taste he trusted was the scientist H. C. Ørsted. In 1846 Andersen wrote to him from Italy, telling him about the wonders of the railroad and adding, 'Reason produces one flower after the other, and after all, these do belong to poetry, for truth is part of its triad. By saying so I am thinking of what you wrote in my album: "Reason in reason is truth; reason in will is goodness; reason in imagination is beauty."'

travel as friends: Later in life Andersen often travelled with younger people as helpers, especially members of the Collin family. He always paid their travel expenses and was more often than not dissatisfied with their company.

215 *can't bear to touch grey paper:* In Collin's 1831 letter he used the same language: 'I once knew a woman who felt such a dislike towards wrapping paper that she was ill whenever she saw it.'

219 *they had put him to death:* Originally, Andersen had the learned man beheaded, but friends advised him to tone it down.

By the Outermost Sea

In 1855, when Andersen brought out 'By the Outermost Sea,' he was aware of the voyages of John Ross, a British arctic explorer. Ross, whose memoirs were translated into Danish, had made a particularly harrowing expedition in 1829 in search of the Northwest Passage. 'By the Outermost Sea' is a short, strange story, unlike any other that Andersen wrote, and was certainly not meant for children. Among its early readers was John Brown, the radical abolitionist. Andersen learned that Brown was given a translation of the story (the title comes from Psalm 139) in the days before he was hanged.

220 *search for a passage:* In a diary entry in June 1851, Andersen wrote, 'Reading Captain Ross's second voyage of discovery to the northern Polar region,' and ten days later added, 'finished Ross's voyage to Polar region, when he and his crew got to their ship again and were rescued, it brought tears to my eyes'.

every ship was stuck: Although the story begins with two ships, Andersen evidently thought there were others.

221 *hold me fast:* We translated these lines of Psalm 139 from Danish to

English to give readers a better sense of the original. In the King James Version the psalm reads, 'If I take the wings of the morning,/And dwell in the uttermost parts of the sea;/Even there shall Thy hand lead me,/And Thy right hand shall hold me.'

presence of God: The passage in Danish is unclear but translated literally refers to 'God's manifestation in the spirit.'

222 *his home of homes*: The phrase that Andersen always used to describe the house of the Collin family, his closest friends and benefactors. Their house was as close as he got to having a home.

Hopeless Hans

'Hopeless Hans', published in 1855, was very different in tone and plot from the other, bleaker, and more original stories that Andersen wrote in roughly the same period. It is almost as if Andersen, who was then about fifty, wanted to return to the spirit of his first stories, such as 'The Tinderbox' – also retellings – which had brought him such rapid, wide popularity.

224 *Hopeless Hans*: The Danish title is 'Klods-Hans', which also suggests stupidity and clumsiness. In English the story has been given many names: 'Jack the Dullard', 'Simple Simon', and 'Clod Hans'.

alderman: An alderman was the head of a guild.

225 *cod-liver oil*: According to *The Fairy Tale of My Life*, Andersen's mother feared for his sanity when, as a ten-year-old, he acted out an entire ballet. She threatened to make him an apprentice to an Italian tightrope walker who was visiting Odense and warned the boy that he had to eat cod-liver oil to make his limbs supple.

don't know how to talk: Andersen was never accused of an inability to talk, but he was often told that he did not know how to write (his style was too informal to please some critics).

228 *tin handle*: The leather top on a wooden shoe is sometimes reinforced with a strip of metal.

threw mud: Andersen spent a lot of time with royalty. He often made fun of courtiers – although rarely in a way that seems calculated to make a child laugh.

Kids' Talk

'Kids' Talk', published in 1859, is a distinctly unsentimental view of upper-class children. It was undoubtedly inspired by what Andersen had observed in the wealthy and aristocratic homes where he was a regular guest; in an afterword to an 1874 collection that included the story, Andersen called it *'selvoplevede eventyr'* – one of those he had personally experienced. Although he got on well with the children of several friends and even corresponded with a few of them, he also understood what it felt like to be poor and not expected to amount to much.

230 *gone to the university:* This implies that the merchant has finished 'Latin school,' which required Greek and Latin. A successful final examination by a student at a Latin school, like the one that Andersen attended in Slagelse, guaranteed admission to the university.

groom of the king's chamber: A somewhat ridiculous but real title; it denoted a high-ranking courtier.

231 *whose names end with* sen: The Danish telephone book is full of Larsens, Hansens, and Andersens – names ending in the suffix that meant 'son of'. Originally, a person's last name was his father's first name with a *sen* added. Then, in 1828, Denmark's 'name reform' went into effect. Under the new law one's name for the previous ten years became the permanent family name. Because the aristocracy already had family names, *sen* implied a common origin.

sen! sen! sens!: This obviously bothered Andersen, and sometime between 1854 and 'Kids' Talk' he made a list of accomplished Danes whose names ended in *sen*. Andersen includes himself and many other recognized artists.

232 *Thorvaldsen:* Bertel Thorvaldsen (1770–1844) was, like Andersen, poor and talented; his neoclassical sculptures made him one of Europe's most celebrated sculptors. The two met in Rome, where Thorvaldsen lived for more than forty years, and became friends. Thorvaldsen returned to Denmark in 1838 at the height of his fame and died six years later. He is buried in the courtyard of the Copenhagen museum that houses his art and is named for him.

Father's Always Right

Andersen was more famous than ever; when his health was good, he simply enjoyed being the celebrated Hans Christian Andersen. In his later tales Andersen could still show flashes of charm, vigour, and youthful wit. 'Father's Always Right', published in 1861, has all that along with an undertone of affection for the somewhat stock character (as in 'Little Claus and Big Claus') of the sly Danish peasant.

233 *a stork:* One of Andersen's favourite birds (it shows up in many stories) and a common symbol of good luck.

235 *the stile:* A step, or steps, that people use to cross over a fence – designed so that animals cannot do so.

A hen can always find a grain: A variation of the Danish saying, 'A blind hen also finds a grain.'

236 *Soon they heard everything:* Erik Dal believes that the impetus for the story was Andersen's complaint (noted in his diary) about having to switch currencies as he travelled, and losing with each exchange.

237 *goose for Michaelmas:* Michaelmas, the feast of St Michael, is celebrated on September 29; the traditional meal is goose. In Denmark the celebration has lost virtually all its religious connotations.

The Gardener and the Aristocrats

'The Gardener and the Aristocrats', published in 1872 and set in the Denmark of Andersen's time, can be read in many ways: an indictment of the class system? Bitterness at the way the nobility treated servants? There appear, in any case, to be parallels between the way this very talented gardener was handled by his employers and the way that Andersen believed that his fellow Danes had treated him. On August 28, 1872, at about the time this tale was published, three years before his death, Andersen wrote this intriguing note in his diary: 'Got the idea for [a story about] the foundation of life: lineage, money, and genius but didn't have the strength to shape it.' Perhaps in 'The Gardener and the Aristocrats' he did.

240 *screeching rooks and crows:* On May 28, 1871, in a letter to his friend Dorothea Melchior, Andersen wrote from an estate called Basnæs, 'If you turn right, you reach a tall, old tree-lined promenade . . . Here's a whole world of birds: rooks, crows, and blackbirds circle the tall trees. They are covered by nests that look as if manure had been dropped on the branches.'

the masters, the propertied class: Andersen had witnessed the bloodless abolition of the ancien régime in Denmark. King Christian VIII died in January 1848; his successor, King Frederik VII, considered odd by his contemporaries, was living with a commoner who was given the title of Countess Danner. In March 1848 – a year of revolution in Europe – Frederik received a petition for a change of government, and two days later he declared himself a 'constitutional monarch', although Denmark did not yet have a constitution. 'Now I can sleep as late as I want,' the king said. On June 5, 1849, Denmark adopted a democratic constitution. In 1871, just before Andersen wrote 'The Gardener and the Aristocrats', the last French emperor, Napoleon III, was driven out of France and the short-lived commune of Paris was established. Andersen's own feelings about democracy were as complicated as his life story.

probably not from their own country: It infuriated Andersen that his work was often praised abroad before it was recognized in Denmark. On July 6, 1847, he wrote to Edvard Collin: 'At this moment, probably, I'm at the pinnacle of my success . . . more recognition than I have received here in this metropolis [London] I cannot hope for . . . I am a famous man . . . but to Denmark, to Copenhagen, I'm nothing.'

243 *what came after was far inferior:* In 1872 Andersen was almost certainly hearing much the same thing about his own work. Most of his best-known stories were written before 1850.

arranged tastefully: Andersen was an artist with flowers too. Even in winter he made inventive arrangements with plants that he found in fields and ditches of the estates that he visited.

Hindustani lotus: The name, invented by Andersen, gives the flower an exotic flavour. In his diary, in an entry from July 30, 1868, he noted that he had found an artichoke in Copenhagen: 'I put it in water and it blooms beautifully.'

a princess, wise and good-hearted: Andersen's feelings towards royalty were generally positive. When he arrived in Copenhagen in 1818, Crown Princess Caroline invited him to sing for her; she also gave him money and sweets. The last absolute monarch in Denmark, Christian VIII, supported the arts, and Andersen told a royal German friend that the king was 'so good, so cultured, so intellectual that one must love him'.

244 *Whatever gave you the idea:* Because the flower grew up in the wrong section of the garden, it was not considered worthy. Andersen heard much the same thing about himself from Jonas Collin's brother-in-law, who once told Andersen not to go to a royal ball because of his origins. Andersen replied with fury, 'My father was an artisan, and by God's and my own help I have made myself into what I am now, and I thought you would respect that.'

245 *Jutland's heath:* In Andersen's childhood much of Jutland was poor and covered by heath; towards the end of his life the heath had begun to yield to aggressive cultivation to compensate for the loss of Schleswig and Holstein to Germany in the 1864 war. Today only a small piece of Jutland's heath is preserved.

woodruff, primrose: All the flowers listed here grow wild in Denmark; some consider them to be weeds.

246 *Danish flag:* The Danish flag is a white cross on a red background. Patriotism was in high gear after the loss to Germany in 1864. Denmark had to cede almost a third of its domain.

sheaf of oats: Hanging a sheaf of oats for the sparrows remains a Christmas custom in Denmark today.

Auntie Toothache

'Auntie Toothache,' the last story in Andersen's last collection, was published in 1872. It took two years to write – an unusually long time for him. What makes the story startling is that the narrator is not disguised as a duck or a ball or some other imaginary creature but seems to be Andersen himself – a modern voice, speaking to his readers with self-deprecating humour in the first-person singular. It is obvious too that Andersen plundered his diaries – sometimes almost word for word – on the subject of toothaches; he made more than a hundred entries on the subject. 'I have to make something of the torments that are inflicted on me,' he wrote to Henriette Collin in June 1870. When 'Auntie Toothache' was published, the journal *Near and Far* remarked on Andersen's 'unabated imagination', which was 'particularly prominent [here] with its painterly personification of the toothache and her roomful of instruments of torture'. The story does not read like the work of the old man whose health was failing, or even the man who, on February 29, 1864, plagued by new false teeth, wrote in his diary, 'Better to be dead and buried. I'm falling apart piece by piece.' In the very next line of his diary he wrote, 'Inside I'm still sixteen.'

247 *the rubbish bin:* Andersen knew all about the rubbish bin. When he was a teenager in Copenhagen and desperate to get ahead, he wrote a book under a pseudonym, William Christian Walter. (The names came from the writers who meant most to him: Shakespeare, his own middle name, and Walter Scott.) He tried to sell it by subscription and persuaded a handful of friends to buy it; the rest were eventually sold as waste paper. The impermanence of life and fame is a recurrent theme in Andersen's stories.

paper to wrap: Just as newspaper was used to wrap fish and chips in Britain, pages from books, journals, newspapers, and the like were used as wrapping for grocery items in Denmark.

250 *a poet ... Perhaps the greatest:* To be 'a great poet' – a *digter* – was Andersen's lifelong wish. On January 4, 1837, he wrote to his friend Madam Iversen: 'A great poet in this world and an even greater one in the next, that's what I dream of being.'

252 *Jean Paul:* The reference is to the German romantic poet Johann Paul Friedrich Richter (1763–1825), who wrote under the name Jean Paul. Jean Paul tried to write down every thought – he hated to let any idea perish – and they showed up in such works as his novels *Hesperus* and *Der Komet.* Jean Paul is known to the English-speaking world primarily through the writings of Thomas Carlyle and Emerson, who quoted Richter in his essay 'Love'. Andersen had been a Jean Paul fan during his last year in the Latin school.

253 *living with a quiet family:* On September 19, 1870, Andersen moved to a new apartment in Copenhagen. He duly noted its drawbacks in his diary: innumerable entries about the doors slamming, people running noisily downstairs, and the wind 'making a sound like a buzzing horsefly'. All this made its appearance in the story.

window hooks: Windows in many Danish houses are casement style. When the windows are open, they are secured by hooks to keep them from swinging in the wind.

254 *spoken word is more vivid:* In all his tales Andersen tried to write as people speak.

just as good as Dickens: This mention of Dickens may carry a touch of bitterness because the great writer dropped Andersen after his disastrous 1857 visit to England. Andersen never understood why.

snowstorm: The winter of 1870–71 was very severe in Denmark.

255 *in a tightly corked bottle:* Around 1830, when Andersen was twenty-five, he drew a picture of himself inside a corked bottle – a self-portrait of youthful desperation. Forty years later the image remained intact, but good-natured humour had replaced the desperation.

260 *Everything goes into the rubbish:* Andersen later removed this bleak line, and it doesn't appear in most modern editions. The Dal-Nielsen-Hovmann critical edition, however, includes it.

BIBLIOGRAPHY

Among the following primary and secondary sources, several were indispensable: Erik Dal, Erling Nielsen, and Flemming Hovmann's *Eventyr,* the complete annotated edition of Andersen's stories and tales, which we used as our Danish text and which provided many valuable notes; *H. C. Andersens Dagbøger, 1825–1875,* volumes 1–12, Andersen's diaries, with an index searchable by name, place, and theme, and his *Almanakker,* a spare, often daily, notebook; *H. C. Andersen og Henriette Wulff: En Brevveksling,* volumes 1–3, the sometimes heartbreaking correspondence between Andersen and his close friend Henriette Wulff; *H. C. Andersen og Horace E. Scudder: En Brevveksling,* the exchange of letters between Andersen and his American editor; and the collections of letters to and from Andersen, published by C. S. A. Bille and Nicolai Bøgh in 1877–78. All are remarkable for their scrupulosity and scholarship.

For Andersen's early career, and especially his relationship with England, we often relied on Elias Bredsdorff; three of his books are included here. Of special importance to our introduction were letters that we found at Det Kongelige Bibliotek (the Royal Library) – in the *håndskriftsafdeling,* the library's department of handwritten documents. The Andersen letter to Longfellow that we cite is there; so are letters from admirers in the New World and his correspondence with the editors of the *New-York Tribune* and *Philadelphia Evening Bulletin.* Andersen's friendship with Marcus and Rebecca Spring is mentioned in the Andersen-Wulff letters and elsewhere, but written evidence of this bond exists mainly in these unpublished letters between Andersen and a remarkable American couple.

H. C. Andersen's Works and Papers

Eventyr. Edited by Erik Dal, Erling Nielsen, and Flemming Hovmann. 7 vols. Copenhagen: Hans Reitzels Forlag and C. A. Reitzels Forlag, 1963–90. The critical edition. Dal edited vols. 1–5, the tales and stories; Dal, Nielsen, and Hovmann edited vols. 6 and 7, critical reception to the stories, along with notes, commentary, and index.

H. C. Andersens Eventyr. Edited by Hans Brix and Anker Jensen. 5 vols. Copenhagen, Gyldendalske Boghandel, 1919. An early critical edition with notes and commentary.

Hans Christian Andersen: 80 Fairy Tales. Translated by R. P. Keigwin. Odense, Denmark: Hans Reitzel, 1976.

The Complete Andersen. Translated and edited by Jean Hersholt and illustrated by Fritz Kredel. New York: Heritage Press, 1942. Tales and stories.

Hans Christian Andersen: Complete Fairy Tales and Stories. Translated by Erik Christian Haugaard. Foreword by Virginia Haviland. New York: Doubleday, 1974.

H. C. Andersens Almanakker, 1833–1873. Edited by Helga Vang Lauridsen and Kirsten Weber. Copenhagen: G. E. C. Gad, 1990. Andersen's almanac, notes about his daily activities, published as a supplement to the diaries.

H. C. Andersen Dagbøger, 1825–1875. Edited by H. Topsøe-Jensen and Kåre Olsen. 12 vols. Copenhagen: G. E. C. Gad, 1971–76. Andersen's diaries.

Erindringer (Memoirs). Edited by Jens Jørgensen. Copenhagen: Hovedland, 1994. This memoir from 1832, sometimes called *Levnedsbogen* (The Book of His Life), was first discovered in 1926.

Kun En Spillemand (Only a Fiddler). Copenhagen: Gyldendal, 1908. Andersen's second novel, first published in 1837.

Mit Livs Eventyr (The Fairy Tale of My Life) and *Mit Livs Eventyr, Fortsættelse (1855– 1867)* (The Fairy Tale of My Life, Continued). Copenhagen and Kristiana: Gyldendalske Boghandel, 1908. Andersen's autobiography.

Letters

Breve fra H. C. Andersen (Letters from H. C. Andersen). Edited by C. S. A. Bille and Nicolai Bøgh. 2 vols. Copenhagen: C. A. Reitzel, 1878. A collection of Andersen's letters to many of his contemporaries. The reference to John Brown appears in this collection.

Breve til H. C. Andersen (Letters to H. C. Andersen). Edited by Bille and Bøgh. Copenhagen: C. A. Reitzel, 1877. A collection of letters to Andersen from a range of correspondents.

Deres broderlig hengivne: Et udvalg af breve fra H. C. Andersen (With Brotherly Greetings: A Selection of Letters from H. C. Andersen). Edited by Niels Birger Wamberg. Copenhagen: Gyldendal, 1975.

H. C. Andersen: Brevveksling med Jonas Collin den Ældre og andre Medlemmer af det Collinske Hus (H. C. Andersen's Correspondence with Jonas Collin the Elder and Other Members of the Collin Family). Edited by H. Topsøe-Jensen, Kaj Bom, and Knud Bøgh. 3 vols. Andersen's correspondence with the Collins. Copenhagen: Munksgaard, 1945.

H. C. Andersen og Henriette Wulff: En Brevveksling (H. C. Andersen and Henriette Wulff: A Correspondence). Edited by H. Topsøe-Jensen. 3 vols. Odense, Denmark: Flensteds Forlag, 1959–60. The letters between Andersen and Wulff are sad and illuminating; the accompanying notes can be a revelation.

H. C. Andersen og Horace E. Scudder: En Brevveksling (H. C. Andersen and Horace E. Scudder: A Correspondence). Edited by Jean Hersholt, with notes by Waldemar Westergaard and a postscript by H. Topsøe-Jensen.

Copenhagen: Gyldendal, 1948. Editor to author to editor, in Danish and English, complete with literary gossip from the late nineteenth century.

H. C. Andersen og Jonas Collin den yngre: En Brevveksling, 1855–1875 (H. C. Andersen and Jonas Collin the Younger: A Correspondence). Edited and introduced by Kirsten Dreyer. Copenhagen: Museum Tusculanums, 2001. Andersen's correspondence with the grandson of his benefactor.

H. C. Andersens Brevveksling med Edvard og Henriette Collin (H. C. Andersen's Correspondence with Edvard and Henriette Collin). Edited by H. Topsøe-Jensen. 6 vols. Copenhagen: Levin and Munksgaard, 1933–37. Of particular interest are the letters in which Edvard rejects Andersen's attempt to use the 'thou' form, but this traces a troubled lifelong friendship.

H. C. Andersens Brevveksling med Henriette Hanck, 1830–46 (H. C. Andersen's Correspondence with Henriette Hanck). *Anderseniana*, vols. 9–13. Copenhagen: Munksgaard. Translated by Elias Bredsdorff and cited in his *Hans Christian Andersen*, p. 135, this is Andersen's correspondence with Henriette Hanck.

Secondary Sources

Bain, R. Nisbet. *Hans Christian Andersen: A Biography.* New York: Dodd, Mead, 1895. The first serious biography in English.

Bloch, William. *På Rejse med H. C. Andersen, Dagbogs Optegnelser* (Travels with H. C. Andersen, Diary Entries). Copenhagen: n.p., 1942. Cited by Johan de Mylius in *H. C. Andersen, Liv og Værk*, pp. 195–96.

Böök, Fredrik. *H. C. Andersen.* Copenhagen: Fremad, 1967. A biography that traces many of Andersen's literary influences.

Bournonville, Charlotte. *Erindringer fra hjemmet og fra scenen* (Memories from Home and Stage). Copenhagen: Gyldendal, 1903. Cited by Dal, Nielsen, and Hovmann in vol. 7 of *Eventyr.*

Boyesen, Hjalmar H. 'An Acquaintance with Hans Christian Andersen'. *Century Magazine,* March 1892, pp. 785–89.

Brandes, Georg. *Fem danske digtere* (Five Danish Writers). Copenhagen: Gyldendal, 1902. Brandes's famous essay on Andersen, including his criticism of 'The Ugly Duckling', pp.183–241.

Bredsdorff, Elias. *Hans Christian Andersen.* New York: Charles Scribner's, 1975. A valuable biography.

———. *H.C. Andersen og Charles Dickens: Et Venskab og dets Opløsning* (H. C. Andersen and Charles Dickens: A Friendship and Its Breakup). Copenhagen: Rosenkilde og Bagger, 1951.

———. *H. C. Andersen og England* (H. C. Andersen and England). Copenhagen: Rosenkilde og Bagger, 1954. A comprehensive study of Andersen's connections to England.

Bremer, Fredrika. *Den nye Verden, en Dagbog i Breve* (The New World: A Diary in Letters). 2 vols. Copenhagen: n.p., 1854. A Danish translation from the Swedish and a fascinating look at pre-Civil War America.

Brix, Hans. *H. C. Andersen og hans Eventyr* (H. C. Andersen and His Tales).

Copenhagen: Det Schubotheske Forlag, 1907. An early critical study of Andersen's tales.

Brovst, Bjarne Nielsen. *H. C. Andersen.* 4 vols. Copenhagen: Centrum, 1993–98. A more recent biography, without a complete index or bibliography.

Bøgh, Nicolai. *Uddrag af en Dagbog paa en Rejse sammen with H. C. Andersen, 1873* (Excerpts from a Diary of a Journey with H. C. Andersen). (*In Julebogen*, an annual Christmas publication.) Copenhagen, 1915. Cited by Woel in *H. C. Andersens Liv og Digtning*.

Collin, Edvard. *H. C. Andersen og det Collinske Hus* (H. C. Andersen and the Collin Household). Copenhagen: C. A. Reitzel, 1882. A work that was somewhat shocking when it was published, seven years after Andersen's death, for its less than flattering picture of Andersen. Collin defends himself against accusations of snobbery and insensitivity towards his friend.

Dal, Estrid, and Erik Dal. *Fra H. C. Andersens boghylde* (From H. C. Andersen's Bookshelf). Copenhagen: Rosenkilde og Bagger, 1961. A study of the writer's private library, which included books by some of his favourite European and English-speaking authors.

Dean, Bradley P. *Thoreau Research Newsletter* 1, no. 2 (April 1990).

Dreslov, Aksel. *H. C. Andersen og 'denne Albert Hansen'* (H. C. Andersen and 'This Albert Hansen'). Copenhagen: Samleren, 1977. Albert Hansen was the pseudonym of a Dane who in 1901 wrote about Andersen's alleged homosexuality for a German publication.

Frémont, Jessie Benton. *Souvenirs of My Time.* Boston: D. Lothrop, 1887. Frémont visited Copenhagen and met Andersen towards the end of his life.

Garff, Joakim. *'Den Søvnløse': Kierkegaard læst æstetisk/biografisk* (The Sleepless: Reading Kierkegaard Aesthetically and Biographically). Copenhagen: C. A. Reitzel, 1995. Contains some material about the philosopher's relationship with Andersen.

———. *SAK: Søren Aabye Kierkegaard. En Biografi.* Copenhagen: G. E. C. Gad, 2000. A Kierkegaard biography.

Gosse, Edmund. *Northern Studies.* London: Walter Scott, 1890. A still fascinating description of the older Andersen.

———. *Sir Edmund Gosse's Correspondence with Scandinavian Writers.* Edited, with notes and comment, by Elias Bredsdorff. Copenhagen: Gyldendal, 1960.

———. *Two Visits to Denmark.* London: Smith, Elder, 1911. More on Denmark and Andersen.

Griffin, G. W. *My Danish Days.* Philadelphia: Claxton, Remsen, and Haffelfinger, 1875. Griffin's descriptions of the dying Andersen are interesting, but Griffin's pomposity is infuriating.

Heltoft, Kjeld. *H. C. Andersens Billedkunst* (H. C. Andersen's Visual Art). Albertslund, Denmark: Fællesforeningen for Danmarks Brugsforeninger, 1978.

Helweg, Hjalmar. *H. C. Andersen, et psykiatrisk Studie* (H. C. Andersen: A

Psychiatric Study). Copenhagen: Hagerup, 1927. Helweg argues against the possibility that Andersen was homosexual.

Hilen, Andrew. *Longfellow and Scandinavia*. Yale Studies in English, vol. 107. New Haven, Conn.: Yale University Press, 1947. Cited in the Andersen–Wulff letters.

Hude, Elisabeth. *Fredrika Bremer og hendes venskab med H. C. Andersen og andre danske* (Fredrika Bremer and Her Friendship with H. C. Andersen and Other Danes). Copenhagen: G. E. C. Gad, 1972.

————. *Henriette Hanck og H. C. Andersen: Skribentinden og Digteren* (Andersen's Friendship with Henriette Hanck). Odense, Denmark: Flensteds Forlag, undated.

Høybye, Poul. *H. C. Andersens franske ven, Xavier Marmier* (H. C. Andersen's French Friend, Xavier Marmier). Copenhagen: Branner og Korch, 1950.

Jacobsen, Fritse. *H. C. Andersens ordspil i original og engelsk oversættelse* (Andersen's Puns, in the Original and in English Translation). No. 9 in a series of Danish papers on translating Andersen, edited by Viggo Hjørnager Pedersen. Copenhagen: København Universitet, 2000.

Jacobsen, Hans Henrik. *H. C. Andersen på Fyn, 1819–75* (H. C. Andersen in Fyn). Odense, Denmark: Skandinavisk Bogtrykkeri, 1968.

James, Henry. *William Wetmore Story and His Friends*. 2 vols. Boston: Houghton Mifflin, 1903. James's description of Andersen and the Brownings is found here.

Jørgensen, Jens. *H. C. Andersen: En sand myte* (H. C. Andersen: A True Myth). Copenhagen: Hovedland, 1989. Jørgensen tries to make the case for Andersen's having royal blood.

Kierkegaard, Søren. *Af en endnu Levendes Papirer* (From the Papers of One Still Living). Vol. 1. Copenhagen: Gyldendal, 1962. Kierkegaard's debut book, which attacks Andersen, in particular his novel *Only a Fiddler.*

————. *Papirer* (Papers). Vols. 1–4, 14. Copenhagen: Gyldendal, 1968. The philosopher's notebooks, which contain many contemporaneous references to Andersen.

Kofoed, Niels. *H. C. Andersen og B. S. Ingemann: Et livsvarigt venskab* (Andersen and Ingemann: A Lifelong Friendship). Copenhagen: C. A. Reitzel, 1992.

Larsen, Svend, ed. *H. C. Andersens moder: En brevsamling* (H. C. Andersen's Mother: Letters). Odense, Denmark: Rasmus Hansens Boghandel, 1947. None of the letters is from Andersen.

Library of Congress. *Catalog of the Jean Hersholt Collection of Hans Christian Andersen.* Washington, D.C.: Library of Congress, 1954.

Mylius, Johan de. *H. C. Andersen – Liv og Værk: En Tidstavle, 1805–75* (H. C. Andersen – His Life and Work: A Timetable). Copenhagen: Aschehoug, 1993. De Mylius runs the Hans Christian Andersen Center in Odense, and the book documents important events in every year of the author's life. For the entire timetable, see the center's Web site at www.andersen.sdu.dk/liv/tidstavle; it is searchable in English and Danish by name and place.

Møller, P. L. *Kritiske Skizzer fra Aarene, 1840–47* (Critical Sketches). Copenhagen: Gyldendals Trane-Klassikere, 1971. A selection of Møller's critical essays.

Olrik, H. G. *Hans Christian Andersen.* Copenhagen: H. Hagerup, 1945.

Parker, Allene M. "'Lady of Utopia": Rebecca Buffum Spring, 1811–1911'. Unpublished paper.

Pedersen, Viggo Hjørnager, and Birgit Nedergaard-Larsen, eds. *Om at Oversætte H. C. Andersen* (On Translating H. C. Andersen). No. 4 in a series of Danish papers on the problems of translation. Copenhagen: København Universitet, 1993. See, especially, William Glyn Jones on political correctness.

Petersen, Carl S., and Vilhelm Andersen. *Illustreret Dansk Litteraturhistorie* (Illustrated Danish Literary History). Vol. 3. Copenhagen: Gyldendal, 1924.

Reumert, Elith. *H. C. Andersen og det Melchiorske Hjem* (H. C. Andersen and the Melchior Family). Copenhagen: H. Hagerups Forlag, 1924.

Salitan, Lucille, and Eve Lewis Perera, eds. *Virtuous Lives: Four Quaker Sisters Remember Family Life, Abolitionism, and Women's Suffrage.* New York: Continuum, 1994. For Rebecca Spring's account of her visit to John Brown, see pp. 117–24.

Spring, Rebecca. See Salitan and Perera, *Virtuous Lives.*

Sørensen, Villy. *Digtere og dæmoner: Fortolkninger og vurderinger* (Poets and Demons: Interpretations and Evaluations). Copenhagen: Gyldendal, 1959.

Thoreau, Henry David. See Dean, *Thoreau Research Newsletter.*

Topsøe-Jensen, H. 'H. C. Andersen og U.S.A.' (H. C. Andersen and the U.S.A.) *Anderseniana.* Edited by Svend Larsen and Topsøe-Jensen. Copenhagen: Munksgaard, 1948.

Wamberg, Niels Birger. *H. C. Andersen og Heiberg* (H. C. Andersen and Heiberg). Copenhagen: Politikens Forlag, 1971.

Westergaard, Erik Koed. *Omkring H. C. Andersens første eventyr* (Around H. C. Andersen's First Tales). Odense, Denmark: Flensteds, Hans Reitzel, 1985. Westergaard takes into account the early critical reception to the writer.

Woel, Cai M. *H. C. Andersens Liv og Digtning* (H. C. Andersen's Life and Work). 4 vols. Copenhagen: Uhlmanske Forlag, 1953.

Wullschlager, Jackie. *Hans Christian Andersen: The Life of a Storyteller.* London: Penguin, 2000. A very useful recent biography.